Fedor Il'ich Dan
Two Years of Wandering

Fedor Il'ich Dan

Two Years of Wandering

A Menshevik leader in Lenin's Russia

Translated and edited,
with an introduction, by Francis King

Lawrence & Wishart
London 2016

Lawrence and Wishart Limited
Central Books Building
Heath Park Industrial Estate
Freshwater Road
Chadwell Heath
RM8 1RX

Typesetting: e-type
Cover design: Andrew Corbett

© Francis King 2016

The author has asserted his rights under the Copyright, Design and Patents Act, 1998 to be identified as the author of this work.

All rights reserved. Apart from fair dealing for the purpose of private study, research, criticism or review, no part of this publication may be reproduced, stored in a retrieval system, or transmitted, in any form or by any means, electronic, electrical, chemical, mechanical, optical, photocopying, recording or otherwise, without the prior permission of the copyright owner.

British Library Cataloguing in Publication Data.
A catalogue record for this book is available from the British Library

ISBN 9781910448724

Contents

Abbreviations and Acronyms	vi
Introduction: Fedor Dan, his party and his two years of wandering, Francis King	1
1 An 'official' exile	46
2 In Ekaterinburg	57
3 To the front!	78
4 At the Congress of Soviets	91
5 Petrograd	99
6 In Peter-Paul Fortress	113
7 In the remand prison	127
8 The Petrograd and All-Russia Chekas	149
9 In Butyrki	160
10 Hunger strike and leaving the country	173

Appendices

I Socialist-Revolutionary leader Viktor Chernov's speech to the mass meeting in Moscow in honour of the British Labour delegation, May 1920	193
II Letter from the Russian Social-Democratic Workers' Party central committee to members of the British Labour delegation	198
III Menshevik leaflets and appeals from the time of the Kronstadt revolt, February-March 1921	201
IV Cheka documents on Dan's case	211
V Review of *Two Years of Wandering* by A. K. Voronsky	219
VI Further reading	224
Index	226

Abbreviations and acronyms

CC	Central Committee
CEC	All-Russia Soviet Central Executive Committee
DRG	Democratic Republic of Georgia (1918-1921)
GPU	State Political Administration of the People's Commissariat of Internal Affairs. Official title of the Soviet political police between February 1922 and November 1923
ILP	Independent Labour Party
Komsomol	Communist Youth League
NEP	New Economic Policy
RKP	Russian Communist Party. This was the official title of the Bolshevik party between 1918 and 1925.
RSDRP	Russian Social-Democratic Workers' Party
SPD	Social Democratic Party of Germany (Sozialdemokratische Partei Deutschlands)
SR	Socialist-Revolutionary

INTRODUCTION:

Fedor Dan, his party and his two years of wandering

Francis King

'Dan is a man whose whole life is organically fused with the revolutionary movement, moreover with the *working-class, social-democratic movement* ...'[1]

Nikolay Sukhanov, chronicler of the Russian revolution.

This is the first translation into any language of Fedor (Theodore) Dan's *Dva goda skitaniy* [Two Years of Wandering], written in early 1922, and published in Russian in Berlin later that year. It is a remarkable portrayal of Soviet Russia during and after the civil war, as seen by one of the most senior social-democratic Menshevik leaders in Russia at that time.

Dan's memoir is not the account of a politically disinterested witness. He had been active in the Russian revolutionary movement since 1894, and had been a consistent critic of Lenin and his supporters in Russian Marxist politics for almost two decades. It was written not for posterity, but first and foremost as a political intervention. But this does not detract from its value as a source on this period of early Soviet history, for several reasons. First, it is very immediate. Shortly after his expulsion from Russia at the end of January 1922, Dan started writing the memoir, and by June of that year he was already correcting the proofs. Second, although it seems to have been written without notes, it is generally very accurate. Where it has been possible to check Dan's recollections against other accounts or archival documents, they tally, despite occasional minor errors of detail. Third – a related point – it seems to be a generally honest memoir. It contains little obvious exaggeration or hyperbole, and Dan usually clearly delineates what he actually witnessed from what he may have heard at second or third hand. Fourth, its style is mostly very measured and calm, with a certain wry humour. It avoids the demagogy, pathos and vituperation characteristic of much Bolshevik writing at that time, typified here in the Bolshevik litterateur A. K. Voronsky's review of Dan's book, which is included as an appendix. Fifth, Dan is a very well-informed and well-connected witness. He knew most of Soviet Russia's top leaders personally, many from the days when Russian social democracy functioned as one party, others from his time as one of the leaders of the Petrograd Soviet and the All-Russia Soviet Central Executive Committee (CEC) in 1917. He was a shrewd observer who could keep his ear to the ground. Finally, Dan's story itself is compelling, as he moves around the country meeting and talking to people, from the capitals to the provinces and the civil war fronts, from soviet congresses to workers' risings and jails in Petrograd and Moscow, before his eventual deportation to Germany. In many respects, it captures the ordinary day-to-day reality of extraordinary times.

Fedor Dan was not the only erstwhile leader of the soviet majority in 1917 who produced a memoir within months of leaving Lenin's Russia. Most notably, Viktor Chernov, the veteran leader of the Socialist-Revolutionary (SR) Party who managed to escape from Russia in early 1921, wrote an account of his experiences which by the end of that year had appeared in French, German and Swedish editions.[2] It is interesting to compare these two memoirs. They reflect two very different experiences of civil war Russia, and intersect at only one point – the episode in May 1920 with which Dan begins his story, when Chernov emerged briefly from clandestinity in Moscow to address a workers' meeting attended by a British Labour delegation, before promptly disappearing back underground.

Chernov had been sought by Lenin's political police, the Cheka, since at least the middle of 1918. In June that year, he had been involved with the 'white' *Komuch* (Committee of Members of the Constituent Assembly) government formed in Samara, after Soviet power had been overthrown on the Volga by the Czechoslovak Legion. Following Admiral Kolchak's right-wing coup in the white-held territory in November 1918, Chernov had been in hiding, liable to instant arrest on both sides of the frontline. His memoir is a story of life underground, of near escapes, attempts at entrapment, and enormous personal risk for himself and those who helped him. The Bolshevik regime, the 'regime of the Cheka',[3] appears solely as a malevolent external force in Chernov's story.

Dan's perspective is very different. He was never in hiding from the Soviet authorities. Between 1918 and 1923 his party was struggling, against ever-greater odds, to operate openly and legally on Soviet territory, in accordance with the laws ostensibly in force at that time. For much of this time he was both within the state apparatus, as an employee of the Commissariat of Health and as an occasional delegate to Soviet congresses, and outside it, as one of the leaders of a party subject to periodic repression. Even after his arrest and imprisonment in early 1921, Dan was sometimes able to request, and get, meetings with senior Cheka officials like Iosif Unshlikht concerning his case. The ambiguities of his status, and of Bolshevik attitudes to the Mensheviks at this time, are among the factors that make Dan's story so remarkable and revealing.

FEDOR DAN

A Russian social democrat

Fedor Il'ich Gurvich (he adopted 'Dan' as his main party name in 1901) was born in 1871 into a middle-class assimilated Jewish family in St Petersburg, where his father owned a pharmacy. He was educated away from home at a *gimnaziya* (grammar school), and then studied medicine at university in Dorpat (now Tartu, Estonia). While a student he also studied Marxism, and when he joined the underground social-democratic movement in 1894 he was already well versed in Marxist theory. Returning to St Petersburg in 1895 after graduation, he joined the group now known as the League of Struggle for the Emancipation of the Working Class, one of the most important forerunners of the Russian Social-Democratic Workers' Party (RSDRP), formally founded in 1898. The League of Struggle counted among its members Vladimir Ul'yanov (Lenin) and Yuliy Tsederbaum (Martov), later to become prominent leaders within Bolshevism and Menshevism respectively. In a much-quoted passage in his memoirs, Martov, whose own personal and political life would be intimately intertwined with that of Dan for the next three decades, described their first encounter that year:

> Soon after I arrived in Petersburg […] I met the doctor F I Gurvich, who had only just finished at Dorpat University. Although he had not yet taken part in practical revolutionary work, and had come

to social democracy purely through theory, the confidence with which he talked about the tasks of the party convinced me from our very first meetings that he would be a leading revolutionary force in the future. He immediately got involved in our efforts, with the help of our youngsters, to set up a serious technical apparatus, with hectographs, mimeographs, Remington typewriters and apartments where we could store all this equipment and carry out our work.[4]

This talent for practical and organisational work remained one of Dan's main strengths throughout his political career.

Following the arrests in late 1895 and early 1896 of Lenin and Martov, Dan became one of the main leaders and organisers of social-democratic activity in St Petersburg during which time, in May-June 1896, there was a large-scale strike of the capital's workers.[5] Dan was arrested for the first time in August 1896. He was on remand and in prison for a year and a half, before being exiled to the small, remote town of Orlov in Vyatka gubernia, north east of Moscow. He chose not to seek employment as a doctor there, and instead worked as a statistician and published a study on the conditions of the Vyatka peasants. He shared his exile with his first wife, Vera Kozhevnikova, the widow of another revolutionary and herself involved in revolutionary politics. The couple had two sons.[6] Aleksandr Potresov, a more experienced social democrat, had also been exiled to Orlov at this time, and acted as a kind of mentor to the relative neophyte Dan.[7]

On completing his term of exile in 1901, Dan moved to Berlin, where he was involved with the social-democratic paper *Iskra*, writing for it and arranging for it to be smuggled into Russia. At this time, Dan, Martov, Lenin and others around *Iskra* worked together as one faction within the RSDRP. It was Dan who arranged the transport of Lenin's *What is to be Done?* (1902) into Russia, even though it would seem that he was very critical of its contents.[8] Besides his purely RSDRP activities in Berlin, Dan also worked there with Karl Kautsky and the SPD in preparing the first published edition of Marx's *Theories of Surplus Value*.[9] From this time onwards, Dan and Kautsky maintained friendly personal relations, despite episodes of serious political disagreement, right up to Kautsky's death in 1938.[10]

In 1902, Dan was again in Russia for underground party work, but was betrayed by a police provocateur and arrested in Moscow. He spent another year and a half in prison, before being sent into exile in

Eastern Siberia – from where he promptly escaped abroad again. He missed the second congress of the RSDRP, which had taken place in London in the summer of 1903. Divisions at that congress had led to the emergence of the Bolshevik and Menshevik factions, and the leaders of both were keen to have Dan in their ranks. Lenin, according to Boris Dvinov's subsequent account, attempted to show Dan a 'secret dossier' containing compromising material about the Mensheviks. This had the opposite effect from the one Lenin intended: repelled at this tactic, Dan chose Menshevism, and never wavered from that factional allegiance.[11] This was further reinforced by personal ties – Dan's marriage to Vera Kozhevnikova had come to an end, and in 1905 he married Martov's sister Lidiya, with whom he remained for the rest of his life.

1905 and after

An amnesty at the end of 1905, at the height of the revolution of that year, allowed Dan and other revolutionaries to return to Russia. On 9 November he wrote to Kautsky from Petersburg that 'we are reeling here, the revolutionary air acts like wine'.[12] The political optimism and the very changed circumstances led to a serious attempt to reunite the RSDRP leadership. Dan was one of the key figures in the 'Unification Congress' held in Stockholm in April-May 1906, was elected to the party Central Committee (CC) and the editorial board of its journal. He opposed the calls to boycott elections to the Duma (the largely consultative 'parliament' conceded by the Tsar after 1905), and provided political leadership to the social-democratic deputies in the first and second Dumas in 1906-1907. This marked the beginning of Dan's close working relationship with Iraklii Tsereteli, a young and very capable social democrat elected to the second Duma from Georgia.

In 1907, following Prime Minister Petr Stolypin's 'coup' of 3 June against the left, Dan was obliged to leave Russia again. In the atmosphere of growing political reaction, the attempt to reunify the RSDRP was breaking down in ongoing factional quarrelling, and within Russia, much of the RSDRP organisation itself was breaking down in the face of state persecution. On 6 December 1907, Dan lamented to the veteran Russian Marxist Pavel Aksel'rod in a letter from Helsinki that 'Menshevism simply no longer exists organisationally in Russia, and it is impossible to bring it back together again mechanically'.[13] He contrasted this with the position of the Bolsheviks, 'who have kept the top of their organisation'.[14] In the same letter, he complained of Menshevik intellectuals opting to concentrate on the new, albeit limited, possibilities for legal political work in broader organisations and abandon the (illegal) party and faction.

Dan joined Martov in Geneva and then Paris, and alongside Aksel'rod, Aleksandr Martynov and (until 1909) Georgii Plekhanov, edited the émigré Menshevik journal *Golos sotsial-demokrata*. In an article in that journal in March 1908, Dan criticised the Bolshevik notion that the revolution in Russia could result in a dictatorship of the proletariat, with or without the poor peasantry. The bourgeoisie, he affirmed, would be obliged to return to the struggle against the remnants of the pre-capitalist order, and would be obliged to seek the support of the proletariat in that struggle. In the meantime, Dan saw hope in the fact that events had obliged the working class 'to pass through the rich school of open political and economic struggle, open political, trade union, co-operative, educational and other organisations'.[15] He anticipated that this would transform the workers' movement in Russia 'from a spontaneous movement of the working masses, led by radical intellectuals in socialist garb, into a movement of the working *class*, subordinating to itself those intellectual forces gravitating towards it'.[16]

All Mensheviks were keen to use whatever legal opportunities existed for working-class political organisation, but they were divided both on whether it was necessary to retain the illegal party structures, and on whether there was any point in trying to coexist in the same party as Lenin and his supporters. Dan, Martov and other émigré leaders generally favoured trying to maintain both common RSDRP structures with the Bolsheviks, and some kind of underground apparatus. Others, most notably Potresov, along with most of the Mensheviks inside Russia, thought both endeavours futile.[17] Lenin and his followers, in their turn, denounced this abdication from illegal party work as 'liquidationism' – a term they used liberally, extending it to Dan, Martov and others who sought to elevate the importance of legal work without abolishing the underground organisation.

The Menshevik émigrés continued to take part in all-RSDRP structures until 1911. Along with Pavel Aksel'rod and Noy Ramishvili, Dan attended the RSDRP Fifth All-Russia Conference in Paris, at the end of December 1908, where they were outvoted on their proposals that the social-democratic group of deputies in the third Duma be a party committee of equal status to the Central Committee, that the CC's (Bolshevik-controlled) Foreign Bureau be abolished, and that the party CC be based in Russia.[18] At the RSDRP Central Committee plenum in Paris in January 1910, Dan and Martov became the Menshevik representatives on the central party journal *Sotsial-Demokrat*, controlled by Lenin. This arrangement, always fraught with tension, finally broke down in June 1911.[19] Thereafter, although the RSDRP label continued to be used by a variety of factions, blocs and committees, which periodically attempted to regroup, there was no longer any single centre which could claim authority over all of them.

Mass political work was at a low ebb in this period – Dan's frequent letters to Aksel'rod mainly discuss inner-party trivia. His main activity, apart from trying to make ends meet, was contributing articles to a projected six-volume collection on social movements around the 1905 revolution.[20] He was able to return to Russia at the beginning of 1913, taking advantage of an amnesty to mark the 300th anniversary of the Romanov dynasty. Once back, he wrote articles for the legal press, and directed the political work of the eight-strong Menshevik faction in the fourth Duma, which had been elected in 1912.

The outbreak of war in 1914 put an end to the Russian government's limited toleration of revolutionary socialists, and the Dans were arrested almost immediately and sent into administrative exile in Eastern Siberia. The next year, Dan was mobilised for war service as a doctor and posted first to Irkutsk, and then to Khodzhent in Turkestan, where he remained until the fall of the Romanov dynasty in February 1917.

The question of the war had split the socialist movements of most European countries, including Russia. The Mensheviks in particular were divided. Some, like Potresov, had supported Russia's war effort from the outset, pointing to the aggressive nature of German militarism, and had acquired the label 'defencists'. However many, including Dan, Martov and Aksel'rod, had opposed the war from a socialist, 'internationalist', standpoint. Aksel'rod had attended the anti-war socialist conferences organised by Swiss socialists in Zimmerwald (1915), and had been joined by Martov at Kiental (1916). In Russia, Dan had joined the diverse group of internationalist internal exiles who identified with the Zimmerwald movement, the so-called 'Siberian Zimmerwaldists', in which Iraklii Tsereteli was a leading figure. Agreement on opposition to the war did not necessarily mean agreement on other questions; Tsereteli recalled frequent arguments with Dan on whether the 'Progressive Bloc' of Duma politicians formed in 1915 on a reformist programme could be a useful ally in the proletariat's fight against the autocracy. At this stage, Dan did not see any such potential, given these politicians' wholehearted devotion to 'war to a victorious conclusion'.[21] Internationalist sentiment among Russian socialists overall was undoubtedly strengthened by the fact that, unlike the socialists in many other belligerent countries, in Russia they had no stake in the existing political order, and could expect few benefits from any military victory for tsarism.

1917

The February 1917 revolution changed all that. Political freedoms, the formation of soviets in Petrograd and across Russia, meant that Russia's revolutionaries suddenly found they had a stake in, and a certain responsibility for, a country at war – a war that was not going well. In this new situation, many former internationalists, including Dan, shifted their position, and the main body of Mensheviks adopted a standpoint which became known as 'revolutionary defencism'. This line was reflected in the Petrograd Soviet appeal of 14 March, moved by the Menshevik Nikolay Chkheidze, which called on the German workers in particular to 'throw off the yoke of your semi-autocratic rule' in order to end the war, while declaring that 'we will firmly defend our own liberty against all reactionary attempts both from within and from without'.[22]

It was not too hard to square this new line with the Zimmerwald demand for 'peace without annexations or war indemnities'[23] – a formulation incompatible with the annexationist war aims of the old tsarist government, but also with any idea of a separate peace with Wilhelm's Germany, which would have been a capitulation to German imperialism unworthy of a great revolution. A lasting, just peace could only brought about by the combined efforts of the working class of all countries. In the meantime, the war effort had to be supported to defend revolutionary Russia against its external enemies. There was also another important consideration which buttressed revolutionary defencism. The generals who had pressed Tsar Nicholas to abdicate, the liberal politicians who had taken power in March and formed the first Provisional Government, and much of propertied Russia, had wanted Nicholas removed in order to see the war prosecuted more successfully. In the initial period after February, many socialists feared these still-powerful groups might revert to support for autocracy, threatening Russia's newly-won and long-awaited freedom, if the revolution took a sharp anti-war turn.[24]

It is hard to overstate Dan's role in the events of 1917. Nikolay Sukhanov, the chronicler of the revolution and a factional opponent and fierce left-wing critic of Dan in 1917, described him as 'one of the most major figures in the Russian revolution, one of the most outstanding actors in both the Russian workers' movement and the events of 1917'.[25] Dan arrived in Petrograd at the end of March, and, together with Tsereteli, who arrived at much the same time, immediately became involved with the leadership of the Petrograd Soviet. At the head of an informal alliance of Mensheviks and mainstream SRs, they continued with the soviet's policy of conditional support for the Provisional Government, including its prosecution of the war.

The official Menshevik perspective on war and peace was expressed in a resolution moved by Dan at the all-Russia RSDRP conference in May 1917. In essence, it differed little from the Soviet resolution of 14 March. It called on the peoples of the world to wage a decisive struggle against their imperialist governments, but 'the goal cannot be a separate peace', which would merely strengthen one bloc and help it defeat the other, but rather 'a general peace won through the united efforts of the international proletariat'.[26] From these premises the conclusions followed:

> ... until the war has been ended by the efforts of the international proletariat, all the revolutionary democracy is obliged to help strengthen in every way the fighting ability of the army, for the all-round defence of the country from the external dangers which threaten it ... while helping defend the country against the danger of military rout, it is essential to develop the widest and most energetic campaign for a general peace.[27]

The minority of Mensheviks who continued after February to refuse to support the war effort grouped around Martov, who for much of 1917 headed a semi-independent faction within his party. This period, between March and November 1917, was the only time when Dan and Martov were not political allies. They had major differences not only over the war, but also over their assessments of the Provisional Government and, after April 1917, whether Mensheviks should take part in it. Personal relations between them seem to have remained good, however – for much of 1917 Martov lived in Fedor and Lidiya Dan's apartment in Petrograd, along with several other Mensheviks of various political complexions.[28]

Dan and Tsereteli, representing the Menshevik mainstream, maintained their close working relationship throughout the whole period of the Provisional Government. In May 1917, Tsereteli took the portfolio of Minister of Posts and Telegraphs after the Mensheviks had abandoned their refusal on principle to take a direct part in government. Around the same time, Dan became the chief editor of the soviet's paper *Izvestiya*, a post he held until the Bolsheviks took power in October. Following the First All-Russia Congress of Soviets in June 1917, Dan was also on the Presidium of the CEC of Soviets.

Sukhanov took a very sour view of the partnership between Dan and Tsereteli: 'I know for sure that if Dan had not gone along with him – or behind him – Tsereteli would have been deprived of his hands.'[29] Sukhanov's presentation of this political relationship was clearly strongly coloured by personal feelings, rivalries and a sense of missed opportunity. He had been present at the foundation of the Petrograd Soviet, but by the end of March he had been largely eclipsed by Tsereteli – whom Sukhanov regarded as 'the leader of the peasant-philistine, helplessly-capitulationist soviet majority'.[30] As a supporter of Martov and Menshevik Internationalism in 1917, Sukhanov believed that Dan, by putting his political, organisational, publicist and theoretical skills at the disposal of Tsereteli and the Soviet majority, had played a 'fatal' role in the Petrograd Soviet and the revolution.

> If Dan had gone against Tsereteli, and had not gone against Martov, who only arrived [in Petrograd] a month later when the fate of the revolution had already been determined; if Dan had taken Martov's place at first, and then worked with him, he could have achieved an extraordinary amount and significantly altered the balance of forces within the Soviet.[31]

That may have been so, but it was not out of character for Dan to be attracted to what he saw as the responsible exercise of power. The Bolshevik David Ryazanov sarcastically remarked in July 1917 that Dan had displayed a 'state sense' since the time of the second Duma, which Dan took as a compliment.[32] Sukhanov, too, saw Dan as 'the most state-minded person' in the leading Soviet nucleus.[33]

Unfortunately, this willingness to shoulder their responsibilities did not mean that the leaders of the Menshevik/SR bloc, which dominated the soviets between February and October 1917, were at all effective in dealing with the dilemmas they faced. The war question was the most intractable. Neither revolutionary defencists nor internationalists in 1917 imagined that a just peace could be reached with Wilhelm's Germany; both put all their hopes in the international working class movement. The main difference between them was that defencists tried to address the question of what to do in the meantime, pending a German workers' rising, while the internationalists generally tried to avoid the question. The problem with the revolutionary defencists' answer was that it committed Russia to continue fighting, but not in order to 'win'. Such a stance (as Dan ruefully admitted at the end of 1918)[34] might have made sense if an end to the war had been more or less imminent, but in mid-1917 all the other belligerent powers were still looking to defeat their enemies. As time went on, the untenability of the policy became increasingly evident. On 14 June 1917 Dan addressed the First Congress of Soviets:

> ... Russia cannot end this war on its own. The old regime locked us into a bloody circle, and Russian democracy on its own cannot break out it. The war can only be ended by the joint efforts of international democracy. On Friday [16 June], a delegation of the All-Russia Congress [of Soviets] will be going abroad, and will propagandise the idea of peace in all countries. And if the democracy of Petrograd and all Russia shows its strength, unity and will to peace on the demonstration of 18 June, this will put the task of the delegation on a firm foundation ...[35]

The demonstration of 18 June had been agreed six days previously at the Soviet congress. The soviet leaders hoped that the marchers would show support for the Provisional Government and the Russian army, and scheduled the event to coincide with a military offensive by

Russian troops. In the event, the demonstration was a political fiasco for the soviet majority, and an indication of what was to come: the largest contingents marched under Bolshevik slogans calling for an end to the war and denouncing the 'ten capitalist ministers' in the Provisional Government.[36]

Sukhanov's indictment of Dan's record in 1917 includes the charge that he stuck to the line of support for a coalition Provisional Government, of continuing the war effort, and of postponing fundamental changes (such as land reform) until a Constituent Assembly had been elected, 'right to the end'.[37] This is largely true, although in the wake of General Kornilov's counterrevolutionary military revolt at the end of August, Dan sought to redefine 'coalition' to mean an alliance of soviet parties not with the liberal Constitutional Democrats (Kadets), but with other 'democratic' forces instead. He proposed first in the Menshevik CC, and then at the Soviet CEC on 27/28 August that a 'Democratic Conference' be convened – a 'parliament of democracy' which could oversee a reconstituted Provisional Government.[38] The Democratic Conference took place in Petrograd in mid-September, but failed to reach consensus on Dan's preferred option of an 'all-democratic' government without 'capitalist ministers'.[39] Late on 24 October, Dan, together with the SR leaders Abram Gots and Nikolay Avksent'ev (the chair of the 'Council of the Republic' which emerged from the Democratic Conference) went to see Kerensky at the Winter Palace to urge a radical change of government policy. They sought at the very last minute to cut the ground from under the Bolsheviks and avert a rising by persuading the government to promise immediate peace talks, transfer all landlord-owned land to the land committees, and speed up the convocation of the Constituent Assembly.[40]

It was already much too late for that. The 'end' to Dan's career in the soviet leadership came dramatically, late in the evening of 25 October 1917. As a member of the Presidium of the Soviet CEC elected at the First Congress in June, it fell to Dan to open the Second Congress of Soviets from the chair. This time round, he faced a very different set of delegates. In June there had been 248 Mensheviks, plus 32 Menshevik Internationalists, to 105 Bolsheviks. But from the summer of 1917 the Mensheviks' erstwhile urban supporters, as well as many party members, had been deserting to the Bolsheviks in droves.[41] In October, just 65 Mensheviks, of whom 30 were Internationalists, were ranged against 252 Bolsheviks. A clear majority of delegates supported the overthrow of the Provisional Government, the members of which were still besieged in the Winter Palace as Dan declared the soviet congress open. The first item of business was the selection of a new Presidium. The Menshevik factions and mainstream Socialist-Revolutionaries refused to nominate members, and shortly thereafter left the congress.[42]

The Bolshevik seizure of power rapidly led to a shift in Dan's own position, and a political realignment within Menshevism more generally. It revealed starkly the failure of the policies followed between February and October. Revolutionary defencism, and the attempt at all costs to keep representatives of Russia's liberals and propertied elements in the government, had become increasingly discredited. Although all shades of Menshevik opinion condemned the Bolshevik seizure of power in Petrograd, the party was divided on how to respond. Immediately on leaving the Soviet congress, Menshevik and SR delegates met and formed an anti-Bolshevik 'Committee to Save the Motherland and Revolution', in which Dan participated on behalf of the Menshevik CC. On 29 October, the SR leadership of that committee launched an ill-fated rising of military cadets in Petrograd. Sensing the spectre of military counterrevolution, Dan and the centre ground in Menshevism recoiled from the prospect of an armed overthrow of Lenin's Council of People's Commissars (Sovnarkom).

That same evening, the railway workers' union executive (*Vikzhel*) convened negotiations to try to avert a crisis and settle the question of power. Dan represented the Menshevik CC, while Martov represented the Menshevik Internationalists. Dan's speech at the first session of the *Vikzhel* talks reflected his party's dilemma in trying to find a solution to the crisis: first he rejected Bolshevik participation in any reconstituted government because it 'would repel the masses' given their 'responsibility for the events of the last few days'. Yet a few sentences later he observed that 'we would all prefer to have the Bolsheviks inside the government rather than outside it'.[43] Outside the talks, Martov was working hard on convincing Dan of the need for a new tactical line.[44] On 30 October, the Menshevik CC called for the immediate creation of an 'All-Russia committee of united democracy, including representatives of all socialist parties and democratic organisations',[45] which would create a 'homogeneous democratic government, which could be recognised by the whole country, and behind which would stand the proletarian and democratic masses'.[46]

Both Dan and Martov supported this attempt to reach some kind of compromise settlement with the Bolsheviks, against the furious opposition of the right wing 'Menshevik-defencists', including Dan's former colleagues in the Petrograd Soviet, Mark Liber, Kuz'ma Gvozdev and Matvey Skobelev. Even though the *Vikzhel* talks ended in failure, the realignment which brought Dan and Martov closer together endured. Neither had experienced a miraculous conversion to the other's point of view, but the changed circumstances meant that the questions which had previously divided them, such as coalition with non-socialists, or revolutionary defencism, were losing their importance. At the Mensheviks' Extraordinary Congress in November-December 1917, a new CC was elected, on which Martov and Dan were the leading figures. The semi-detached status of Martov's 'internationalists' within the party largely came to an end, while the most irreconcilable defencists on the right created their own, separate 'Provisional Bureau'.[47]

The congress took place at a time when the Mensheviks were at their lowest ebb. Dan tried to defend the party's record since February. His report on peace pointed to the failure of Bolshevik peace policy, the collapse of the remnants of the army, and the likelihood of a separate peace on German terms.

> ... Now we can judge, who was right. However many mistakes we made, our line was correct. True, it suffered a defeat, but that was a defeat of the revolution itself ... The only means by which something can be salvaged is the Constituent Assembly. It can organise a government that will be recognised by the country. The Allies could respond to a call from this government and join negotiations on a general peace ... [48]

In fact, the elections to the All-Russia Constituent Assembly, held at the same time, showed just how far the Mensheviks' support had sunk by the end of 1917. They won little more than three per cent of the total poll, and almost half of that vote was concentrated in their Georgian stronghold.[49]

1918 and after

In the spring and summer of 1918, Menshevik fortunes seemed to be reviving. The party saw a significant rise in its popularity as workers and others, disillusioned by the Bolsheviks' inability to prevent the further collapse of Russia's economy and their living standards, began more frequently to support Menshevik and SR candidates and resolutions in the soviets. In response, the Bolsheviks increasingly resorted to arrests and harassment of non-Bolshevik activists, and the dissolution of soviets where elections had been won by the wrong parties. The Menshevik press, which was unrelenting in its criticism of Lenin's administration, became a particular target. Different approaches were tried: in April 1918 Stalin attempted to sue Martov for 'slander' over an article in the central Menshevik paper of that time, *Vpered*, which mentioned Stalin's role in bank robberies in the Caucasus ten years previously. When this did not work out as planned, the entire editorial board of *Vpered*, including Dan, was arrested on charges of 'libellous agitation against the Soviet power', for articles which alleged, among other things, that the Bolshevik authorities had shot workers.[50] At this stage, the Bolshevik authorities still tried these cases in public, and Dan did his best to act as his accusers' accuser. He demanded to call witnesses to the incidents where workers had been shot, so that their evidence could go on public record. He challenged the Bolshevik prosecutor, Nikolay Krylenko: 'Admit that you are trying us for political views!'[51] The case was abandoned inconclusively, but the Bolsheviks' campaign was not. Abandoning inefficient quasi-legal procedures, from May 1918, the Cheka was increasingly used to close inconvenient publications and prevent them from reappearing in any other guise.

A further step towards neutralising any opposition was taken on 14 June 1918, when the All-Russia Soviet CEC resolved to 'exclude the representatives of the Socialist-Revolutionary (right and centre) and Menshevik parties, and to propose that all soviets of workers', soldiers', peasant and Cossack deputies remove representatives of these fractions from their midst'.[52] On this basis, Dan was removed from the Soviet CEC. From this time onwards, he and his party comrades could only participate in the higher-level soviet representative bodies by special dispensation of Lenin's government.

The scope for Dan and other Mensheviks to engage in politics continued to narrow in the second half of 1918. Armed rebellions and civil war were spreading across Russia. Following assassination attempts against Bolshevik leaders that summer, the Bolsheviks unleashed a 'red terror' against 'counterrevolutionaries', which, in the febrile atmosphere of the time, meant that any opponent of Lenin's party was at risk. As Russian politics became increasingly polarised between 'red' and 'white', the official Menshevik view was that counterrevolution represented the greater danger. A motion Dan presented to an all-Russia Menshevik conference in the last days of 1918 firmly rejected all ideas of overthrowing Soviet power by force, arguing that this:

> in the present historical circumstances would inevitably amount either to igniting a civil war within the labouring classes, or to direct collaboration with the forces of landowner-capitalist and imperialist reaction. In either case, this would lead to the victory of the blackest reaction and would be a betrayal of the cause of the international proletariat.[53]

At the same time, Dan sought to position the Mensheviks as an opposition party within the Soviet system. His motion called for the democratisation of the Soviet apparatus, free elections to the soviets, the restoration of civil liberties, an end to judicial and extra-judicial executions, and the renunciation of state terror. It opposed the Bolsheviks' project to socialise the entire economy. While it reaffirmed the Mensheviks' support for a united Russian state, it opposed any attempts to suppress by force 'those currently separate parts of Russia where there are democratic governments in power' – meaning in the first instance, presumably, social-democratic Georgia.[54]

Menshevism's contest with Bolshevism during this period was unequal not only because the Bolsheviks controlled the state machine, the means of repression, almost all the press and most mass organisations. Perhaps no less importantly, the Bolsheviks *wanted* political power, and believed they could *use* it to build a socialist society. The Mensheviks, as led by Martov and Dan, did not. As Dan put it in October 1919, when the tide in the civil war was beginning to turn against the white forces:

> We are not struggling with the Bolsheviks for power. We are not struggling with them in order to tear from their hands and seize for ourselves the means of exerting state coercion and force over the masses. We are struggling with Bolshevism above all for ideological domination of the spirit, intelligence and will of the working class.[55]

This stance, although it flowed logically from the political assumptions of Menshevism, suffered the same fatal flaw as the 'revolutionary defencism' of two years previously, in that it obliged the Mensheviks to fight, but not in order to 'win'.

Dan's life between 1920 and his expulsion from Soviet Russia in early 1922 from his own perspective is exhaustively described in the present volume. As a conscripted employee of the People's Commissariat of Health during this phase of the civil war, he could in theory be sent wherever the Bolshevik authorities chose. In practice, as his memoir shows, his 'wanderings' were the outcome of an ongoing process of negotiation between him, the health commissariat, and the political leadership of the Bolshevik party. Following his arrest and imprisonment around the time of the Kronstadt rising in March 1921 (in which neither Dan nor the Petrograd Menshevik group had played any part), his fate continued to be the subject of negotiation, and was discussed at the highest levels of the Bolshevik leadership, in particular the Political Bureau (Politburo). The minutes of the Bolshevik Politburo occasionally provide laconic confirmation of episodes in Dan's account. The most striking of these concern the question of what should be done with him and the other leading Mensheviks who had been held in prison since the clampdown on all opposition forces that accompanied the suppression of the Kronstadt rising in March 1921. The minutes for 1 December 1921 contain the following item:

22. On freeing Dan and other Mensheviks.	22. Authorise the Cheka to examine and bring a proposal to the Politburo on the permissibility of freeing Dan, Ezhov and other prominent Mensheviks, sending them to some distant non-proletarian region to perform some kind of work in line with their qualifications.[56]

A week later, the Bolshevik Politburo returned to this question. Its resolution is revealing, not only about the Bolsheviks' indecision even at this stage about what to do with those Mensheviks who would not abandon political activity, but also about their concern that on no account should Dan or other Menshevik leaders have any contact with the working classes. Even as they hounded the last remnants of their rival party out of existence, the Bolshevik leaders were clearly terrified of it.

> Politburo resolution on point 15 [a report by Unshlikht on the Mensheviks]
> a) No political activity by them can be allowed. Particular attention must be paid to uprooting their political influence in industrial centres.
> b) When making members of the Menshevik party answerable before the law, the charge against them should not be simple membership of the RSDRP, but activity, directly or indirectly aimed against Soviet power.
> c) The most active of them should be expelled administratively to non-proletarian centres, deprived of the right to take up any elected position or any position involving contact with the broad masses.
> d) Authorise a commission of comrades Unshlikht, Shmidt and Kursky ... to consider the question of removing Mensheviks and SRs from trade union, Commissariat of Labour, co-operative and economic bodies.
>
> 2. Authorise comrade Samsonov to work out in detail regulations on the places of administrative exile where Mensheviks will be sent.
>
> 3. Raise no objections to the CC's proposals concerning the administrative exile of Ezhov and Dan.[57]

During the year Dan spent in prison, he was not isolated from the life of what remained of his party in Russia. Visits from his wife Lidiya allowed him to send and receive notes, theses and resolutions. Boris Dvinov, the most senior Menshevik not incarcerated in the 1921-1922 period, recalled that 'F. I. Dan, and other members of the CC in prison, proved to be more "left" than those of us at liberty', on the question of whether to demand democratic rights for all or just for the working people.[58] 'Left' in this context meant that Dan was cautioning against pushing too hard and too fast for the full democratisation of the Soviet system as the New Economic Policy (NEP) developed, for fear of opening the door to capitalist, and therefore counterrevolutionary, forces. Dan expressed much the same views in a deposition he made for his Cheka interrogators in April 1921:

For the present moment I consider it essential for the interests of the working people and particularly the proletariat in Russia that the Soviet system be preserved. However that system should be, in accordance with its theory and its constitution, a genuinely free form of workers' self-government, rather than a cover for party dictatorship. I believe this system's further evolution towards fully democratic forms to be indispensable for the socialist reorganisation of society. But the tempo and nature of this evolution will depend so much, from the point of view of working class interests, on a series of currently unforeseeable international and domestic factors ... the slogan of the Constituent Assembly, as an immediate practical political goal, I consider to be damaging, given the mood of the broad mass of peasants, largely as a result of the Bolshevik government's policies.[59]

The view that the Soviet system was reformable, that reform was necessary for its successful development towards socialism, and that attempts at overthrowing it would merely open the door to counter-revolution was one that Dan held for the rest of his life. The fact that Martov had largely shared this perspective gave it – and Dan – an enduring authority among the Mensheviks for the next two decades.

Dan in emigration

Although he was loath to leave Russia and abandon the struggle and his remaining comrades, faced with the alternative of internal exile in the remotest parts of Russia, with much of the countryside in the grip of famine, Dan pressed to be allowed to go abroad instead. This was almost certainly a fortunate choice; his brother-in-law S. O. Ezhov, whose case was considered at the same time and who opted to remain in Soviet Russia, spent the 1920s and 1930s in and out of prison before being shot in February 1939.[60]

On arrival in Berlin in the winter of 1922, Dan immediately involved himself in the work of the Menshevik Delegation Abroad (*Zagranichnaya delegatsiya*), which was based there. Martov was already mortally ill with tuberculosis, and when he died in April 1923, Dan became the editor of the Mensheviks' journal *Sotsialisticheskiy vestnik* (Socialist Herald), and party chairman. He was assiduous in his defence of what became known as the 'Martov line', which combined the sharpest criticism of the Bolshevik regime for its brutality, incompetence and dictatorial nature with strong opposition to any attempts at overthrowing it by force. This was reinforced by Dan's continuing belief that the Soviet regime contained socialist elements, had conserved some of the achievements of 1917, and retained a degree of working-class support.[61] In 1928, for example, as the NEP period was about to come to a violent end, Dan was proposing theses calling for working class unity in the USSR to 'save the basic gains of the revolution, defend the class interests of the proletariat, avert the Bonapartist danger and struggle for the democratic liquidation of the terrorist dictatorship'.[62]

Up to that point, the 'gains of the revolution' could be equated broadly with 'what had been won in 1917'. From 1929 onwards, rapid industrialisation and the forcible collectivisation of agriculture in the USSR made matters more complicated. Dan, and some of his comrades on the Menshevik left, were inclined to see aspects of these later changes – particularly the further socialisation of the Soviet economy – also as potential 'gains' worthy of being defended. Another key figure in the Delegation, Rafail Abramovich, rejected this view, on the grounds that if progress towards socialism could be made by a terrorist dictatorship like that of Stalin, this called both the Mensheviks' version of Marxism and the very raison d'être of their party into question.[63]

The Nazi seizure of power in early 1933 obliged the Berlin Menshevik colony, all 73 of them, to decamp to Paris on visas Dan had secured through the French socialist leader Léon Blum.[64] Hitler's victory also suggested an altogether more concrete form that 'the counterrevolution' in the USSR might take, and Dan's political allies on the left in the Labour and Socialist International – particularly Otto Bauer, the Austrian socialist leader – were keen to encourage labour movement unity against fascism. In the increasingly polarised atmosphere of the 1930s, impressed with the apparent successes of Soviet industrialisation and collectivisation, and fearful at the rise of fascism, Dan's view of the USSR became more supportive. A memorandum published in August 1935 by Dan, Bauer, and two French socialists referred to the Soviet Union living 'under a terrorist dictatorship', but argued that the regime 'can, and must, evolve successively towards a type of socialist democracy',[65] if only fascism is stopped and Soviet living standards continue to rise. In the event of war between Nazi Germany and the USSR, Dan and his colleagues called on the socialist parties to undertake a 'revolutionary defence of the USSR' and, for the war's duration, to 'subordinate all their demands to the need for victory, a need dictated by the interests of the world proletariat'.[66]

Mensheviks on the centre and right of the Delegation Abroad were more inclined to see Stalin's 'terrorist dictatorship' not as a passing phase but as the very essence of the Soviet system itself. Despite these divisions, there was a rare outbreak of unanimity over the Soviet invasion of Poland in mid-September 1939 following the Molotov-Ribbentrop pact – all currents in the Delegation, including Dan's, approved a resolution denouncing 'Stalin's despotism', which 'has revealed itself as the rule of a degenerate national-imperialist clique which has fallen to the level of Hitlerism'.[67] Dan's critics in the Delegation pressed their advantage; at the end of 1939, Grigoriy Aronson pointed out that such resolutions 'represent a final break' with a line which envisaged the democratisation of the USSR and sought accommodation with the communists, and argued that the Nazi-Soviet pact 'has revealed the complete ideological bankruptcy of left Menshevism'.[68] In early 1940, just before the Menshevik emigration was obliged to decamp again, this time to New York, Dan lost his position as editor of *Sotisialisticheskiy vestnik*. In his last seven years, estranged from the main body of the Menshevik emigration, he ran his own journal, first *Novyy mir* (New World) in Paris and then *Novyy put'* (New Path) in New York, with a small group of supporters.[69] He also wrote a long historical work, *The Origins of Bolshevism*, first published in Russian in New York in 1946. In his epilogue to the book, he expressed his continuing expectation that the 'socialist reconstruction of Europe', would allow for 'the further evolution of the Soviet regime and for its political democratisation', which he remained confident 'will become politically more and more necessary'.[70] Already very ill with lung cancer, Dan died on 22 January 1947, before the development of the cold war could shake his optimistic prognosis for Soviet post-war development.

Lidiya Dan survived her husband by more than sixteen years. Although in her youth she had been a very active social democrat in her own right, her political role after her marriage to Fedor Dan was largely one of facilitating the activities of her husband, her brother Yuliy Martov and other leading figures in Russian social democracy.

In March 1917, still in Siberia, she submitted her resignation from the RSDRP. The circumstances of this remain unclear, and rather mysterious, given that following her return to Petrograd the Dans' apartment would be one of the centres of Menshevik activity in 1917.[71] Lidiya accompanied Fedor Dan into exile in Germany, where in February 1924 the RSDRP Delegation Abroad resolved to readmit her to the party.[72] She represented the RSDRP for a time on the International Socialist Women's Committee. With Fedor Dan and the rest of the Menshevik Delegation Abroad she moved to Paris in 1933, and eventually to New York in 1940. Between 1937 and 1940, Lidiya Dan worked for the Jewish charity OSE, sending Jewish children from Lithuania to children's homes in France. She only narrowly avoided being stranded in Lithuania when Soviet troops annexed the country in mid-June 1940.[73]

Although Lidiya generally shared Fedor Dan's political views, she did not fall out with the rest of the Menshevik emigration after 1940, and rebuilt her connections with them after Fedor's death. Her reminiscences are valuable sources on the early history of Russian social democracy.

MENSHEVIKS AND MENSHEVISM IN 1917 AND AFTER

'Menshevism' defined itself against 'Bolshevism'; 'Bolshevism' defined itself against 'Menshevism', and after 1917 the leaderships of both parties were keener to amplify the differences rather than the commonalities. Bolsheviks would stress their firm revolutionary resolve, in contrast to the vacillating Mensheviks. Mensheviks would stress their commitment to democratic freedoms and rejection of Bolshevik terroristic methods.

The initial split within the RSDRP in 1903 on the question of who should be considered a party member widened to embrace a whole range of shifting positions and perspectives, particularly after the 1905 revolution. Neither faction was remotely monolithic, but certain approaches to politics became characteristic of each faction between 1905 and 1917. In their revolutionary strategies, Mensheviks tended to envisage an alliance with urban liberals against the autocracy, convinced that the next stage for Russia had to be a 'bourgeois' revolution, while Bolsheviks tended to envisage an alliance with the poorer peasants, and were more open to the idea that the revolution could go beyond a mere 'bourgeois' one.⁷⁴ Fewer Mensheviks than Bolsheviks were willing to question Plekhanov's version of Marxist philosophy and try to combine empiriocriticism or Nietzscheanism with Marxism. More Mensheviks were inclined to abandon conspiratorial activity in favour of using opportunities for legal work after 1905, while Bolsheviks denounced this as 'liquidationism', and continued to stress the importance of underground revolutionary organisation. But none of these differences were hard and fast, and both factions embraced a range of opinions and approaches to politics. Within the wider RSDRP, moreover, individual members could and often did move from one faction to the other, or to none. George Denike, a Bolshevik around 1905 and a Menshevik in 1917, suggested towards the end of his life that 'in most cases ... it was a matter of temperament' which determined individual social democrats' factional allegiances at a given time.⁷⁵ Certainly by the late summer of 1917 the temperamental differences between the Bolshevik and Menshevik leaderships were not hard to discern. Nonetheless, in the spring of that year, the reconstitution of a united party was seriously canvassed.

Social democratic unity?

Russian socialism emerged from illegality in March 1917 in a very fluid state. The war had shaken everything up, shattered many old alignments, and created many new issues on which socialists needed to define their positions. On practical matters, social democrats and SRs had been working amicably together across Russia, and not infrequently found they had more in common with one another than with other members of their respective parties. In some parts of Russia, especially where social democrats were thin on the ground, united non-factional RSDRP organisations had continued to exist. There were many other divisions within the party – including between defencists and internationalists – which cut across the Bolshevik-Menshevik divide. There were also numerous social democrats – Trotsky is perhaps the best known – who refused for a long time to side with either faction. Others sought to work with both factions, or formed local groups of their own. There were many supporters of the party who had not been in a position to undertake activity during the post-1905 years of reaction who wanted to resume political work – and there were many new members who wished to get involved.

This was the context in which social democrats sought to reconstruct and build their party. Various Menshevik-oriented groups in Petrograd were rapidly brought together by the Organising Committee of the RSDRP, hastily reconvened on 28 February 1917. There was, however, considerable initial enthusiasm for making another attempt at overcoming the old factional divide. It was Lenin, newly returned from exile, who decisively scotched these efforts. On 4 April, Iosif Gol'denberg and his initiative group for uniting Russian social democracy convened a large meeting in Petrograd of all social-democratic currents, including Bolsheviks and Mensheviks. Gol'denberg was himself a prime example of social-democratic fluidity – a Bolshevik from 1903 until 1914, during the war he had become a defencist and joined Plekhanov's pro-war-effort group *Edinstvo*. After Lenin had spoken, Gol'denberg admitted defeat: 'This is pure insurrectionism, which will lead us into the swamp of anarchy. The social democrats need to unite, but not with communists who call us a "rotting corpse".'[76]

Even if Russian social democracy could not be united across the entire spectrum, there were still serious initiatives to realign the party along different lines of fracture. Later in April 1917, Maksim Gorky founded *Novaya zhizn'* (New Life) – a 'non-factional' internationalist social-democratic newspaper, staffed largely by erstwhile Bolshevik intellectuals (including Gol'denberg). Its overall political stance was very close to that of Martov, who wrote for it. Its aim was to bring about a realignment in the RSDRP, uniting in one party the internationalist Mensheviks and those Bolsheviks unhappy with Lenin's radical course. To this end, in June the *Novaya zhizn'* group helped initiate an RSDRP unity conference, but their hopes were dashed when the conference took place in August: the Bolsheviks just ignored it, and it served instead to help patch up the differences between the defencist and internationalist Mensheviks.[77]

Developments later that year precluded any further attempts to reunify the RSDRP. The main issue on which there could be no compromise was the question of 'soviet power'. Lenin's party, and the group around Trotsky which united with it in August, believed that the soviets could and should substitute themselves for the whole of the old Russian state apparatus. All the Mensheviks, even those like Martov who were calling in late 1917 for a government *answerable* to the soviets, did not think the soviets could or should try to *become* the state machine, and looked to the forthcoming Constituent Assembly to create a parliamentary republic. The soviets, Mensheviks believed, were class organisations of struggle which should exist alongside, but not displace, a democratised state apparatus.[78]

Living with 'soviet power'

Following the dispersal of the Constituent Assembly by Lenin's government in January 1918, the Mensheviks faced a quandary: as a working-class party, they needed to participate in the organisations of that class, including the soviets. But they fundamentally rejected the whole notion of 'soviet power', which they thought was neither desirable in principle nor workable in practice. Moreover, as noted above, if the Mensheviks alone or with the Socialist-Revolutionaries won a majority in any local soviet from the spring of 1918 onwards, the Bolshevik authorities were likely to dissolve it, replace it with a military-revolutionary committee of their own choosing, declare the elections null and void or arrest its inconvenient members.[79] In the late spring some Mensheviks in Russia's industrial heartland, mainly on the right of the party spectrum, attempted to bypass the gerrymandered soviets by organising their own movement of workers' plenipotentiaries (*upolnomochennye*). Despite its initial success, this movement was also suppressed at the end of June 1918.[80]

However, Bolshevik power was far from firmly embedded across much of Russia. It was particularly weak on the periphery of the empire, especially those areas where ethnic Russians constituted settler communities, largely detached from the non-Russian hinterland. With the economic situation deteriorating rapidly, and with few remaining legal outlets for expressing popular discontent, by the summer of 1918 rebellions were breaking out across the empire. In this early phase of the civil war, many of the rebellions were planned and led by the Socialist-Revolutionaries, often with the participation of army officers. 'Soviet' (effectively Bolshevik) power was overthrown locally and administrations were formed from local non-Bolshevik political forces. Local Mensheviks, particularly those on the right wing of the party, often took part in these risings and sometimes joined the 'governments' which resulted from them. For example, on 6 July 1918 a rising overthrew Bolshevik power in Yaroslavl' gubernia, less than 200 miles from Moscow, in which the prominent Yaroslavl' Mensheviks I. T. Savinov and Kh. I. Ioffe were closely involved.[81] In early June 1918, following the overthrow of Bolshevik rule in the Volga region by the Czechoslovak Legion, a group of largely SR deputies formed a short-lived government in Samara which claimed a democratic mandate for its authority over all Russia. Ivan Maisky, subsequently Soviet ambassador in London but at that time a member of the Menshevik CC, served as its Minister of Labour.

The Menshevik CC in Moscow, with its centre-left majority headed by Martov and Dan, tried as best it could to put a stop to this sort of thing. It was committed to trying to work legally and openly within Soviet Russia, and could not afford to allow the party to be associated with any 'white' adventures. Consequently, a resolution on the Yaroslavl' events on 16 July reminded party members that 'on no account should they get involved in risings of this type or be a tool in the hands of the groups which lead them. The task of the party in such events is to organise the workers into an independent third force ...'.[82] A further resolution on 2 August warned party organisations and members against taking part in 'such adventures',[83] and in mid-September 1918 the CC disavowed the actions of Maisky, expelled him from the CC and subsequently from the party as well.[84] Figures on the party's right wing were unimpressed with this attempt to stand aside from the anti-Bolshevik struggle. A proclamation in late August 1918 by a self-styled 'Group of Struggle for Independence and a Democratic System for Russia', criticised the CC's 'mistaken passive tactics' which had turned a once influential party into a 'doctrinaire sectarian circle of leaders without an army'.[85] In the summer of 1918, the logic of political struggle in places as diverse as Votkinsk in Udmurtia and Ashkhabad in Turkmenistan impelled individual Mensheviks to disregard the policy of their party's CC and take part in local anti-Bolshevik risings and administrations, usually as junior partners of the SRs.[86]

The Mensheviks in the civil war

This phase of 'democratic counterrevolution' did not outlast the summer of 1918, as the initiative in the anti-Bolshevik struggle passed from the SRs to the overtly counterrevolutionary white armies. As the civil war intensified in 1919, the idea of trying to be an 'independent third force' lost all credibility. The Menshevik CC concluded that the white forces, which were advancing rapidly that summer, represented the greater danger to the gains of the revolution. On 12 July 1919, it addressed an appeal to all workers in which it stressed the need to 'smash all the counterrevolutionary hordes who have risen up against Soviet Russia'.[87] Arguing that only a thoroughgoing democratisation and abandoning reliance on coercion in economic policy could secure that victory, the Menshevik CC called for all socialist parties to cooperate in defence of the revolution. This attempt to find some kind of accommodation with the Soviet authorities characterised official Menshevik policy in 1919 and 1920.

There was, as ever, no unanimity in the Menshevik ranks on how to understand, or relate to, the Bolsheviks. Some on the right of the party not only dissented from the CC line, but even advocated support for the white forces. They contended that according to Marx progress consists in the development of the forces of production, and that therefore Bolshevik rule, which had resulted in unprecedented economic collapse, was reactionary.[88] Others tried to discern the hidden class essence behind surface phenomena: David Dalin, for example, argued in May 1919 that Soviet Russia was on the verge of a bourgeois counterrevolution in Soviet garb, and suggested the ongoing civil war between reds and whites was objectively between 'the new bourgeoisie, and the old nobility and old bourgeoisie'.[89] The official line, represented by Dan, saw the Mensheviks competing with Bolshevism 'for ideological domination of the spirit, intelligence and will of the working class'.[90]

Ambiguity and inconsistency also characterised Bolshevik attitudes towards the Mensheviks. At the same time as Bolshevik journalists were depicting them as the worst kind of perfidious counterrevolutionaries, others from the ruling party were seeking their collaboration in running the state apparatus. In June 1919 L. B. Kamenev apparently asked the Menshevik CC (through an intermediary, P. L. Lapinsky) for a list of names of Mensheviks suitable for responsible state employment. Martov rebuffed the approach, pointing, among other things, to recent mass arrests of Menshevik party members in state employment.[91] This sort of inconsistency on the part of the Soviet state towards its own Menshevik employees is one of the themes running throughout Dan's memoir.

Going underground

The period following the expulsion of Dan and other leading Mensheviks from Soviet Russia in early 1922 was characterised by greater economic liberalisation but ever-intensifying political repression. The dwindling band of Mensheviks remaining at large in Soviet Russia continued to try to conduct open and legal work, although some of their most important activities – corresponding with the Delegation Abroad, receiving and distributing *Sotsialisticheskiy vestnik* – had to be conducted in a clandestine fashion. Their unwilling descent into the political underground was charted in a memoir written in 1924 by Boris Dvinov, Dan's successor as de facto Menshevik leader in Russia until his own enforced emigration in January 1923. As Dvinov observed, after July 1922 a mass operation by the GPU (formerly the Cheka) made it clear that 'the question of legal and underground work had been decided for us by the Bolsheviks'.[92]

The Mensheviks' dilemma within Russia – to go underground and abandon legality, or to continue to fight for their legal rights and be arrested – was compounded by an international dilemma. In April 1922, representatives from the Communist International, the reorganised Second International, and the International Working Union of Socialist Parties (the 'Vienna Union'), to which the Mensheviks were affiliated, met in Berlin to discuss a 'united front' of all socialist forces. The aim was to try to restore the shattered unity of the international labour movement, and the Menshevik party strongly supported the idea. However, raising the question of the persecution of socialists within Russia could scupper the whole initiative, which meant that the Mensheviks, as Dvinov put it, 'had to fight actively for the united front conference at the cost of giving up our sacred duty to accuse and expose the Bolsheviks in front of the international workers' movement'.[93]

Georgia

Georgia, as always, was a different story. Here the Menshevik wing of Russian social democracy had long been the most influential political force, with mass support not only among the tiny Georgian working class, but also among the peasants. It had dominated political institutions at all levels since March 1917. Following the Bolsheviks' seizure of power in Petrograd, the Georgian social democrats acted decisively to secure their own position. They disarmed Bolshevik-inclined Russian soldiers in Tiflis, and expelled them from Georgia.

Facing an immediate military threat from Turkey, the Georgians organised their own forces to resist both Russian and Turkish incursions.[94] From May 1918 to February 1921, the social democrats under Noe Zhordania – by then organisationally separate from the Russian party – ran the 'Democratic Republic of Georgia' (DRG) as an ostensibly independent state, at first under German, then for a while under British protection. The Bolshevik party in Georgia, which sought the country's reincorporation into Soviet Russia by any means necessary, had been banned in early 1918. It remained underground until May 1920, when it was re-legalised as a condition of Moscow's (temporary and tactical) recognition of the DRG.[95] Even after the Bolsheviks' re-legalisation in Georgia, their earlier suppression in the DRG was much used by Soviet publicists to parry social-democratic criticism of repression in Soviet Russia.[96]

Menshevism suppressed

This complex history sets part of the scene for the difficult and ambiguous relationship between Dan's and Lenin's parties reflected in this memoir. In particular, it helps account for the Bolsheviks' success in securing a 'monopoly of revolutionary discourse', and gaining general acceptance for a presentation of the unfolding civil war in which their socialist critics could, whenever necessary, be depicted as belonging to the 'counterrevolutionary' camp.[97] Bolshevik publicists, always as ready to magnify injustices against their side as to dismiss their own injustices against their opponents, used this civil war discourse unsparingly at the time and afterwards to justify their repression and eventual complete suppression of the Menshevik organisation. Voronsky's review of Dan's memoir (Appendix V) provides a vivid example of this.

As Dan's narrative shows, following the Kronstadt rising in March 1921, the Soviet authorities systematically sought to eliminate any possibility of political organisation by opposition parties. By 1922 the Menshevik party as an organised political party was all but destroyed in Soviet Russia, and most of its prominent leaders, like Dan, had been expelled from the country. For another decade tiny, scattered groups existed in conditions of deep clandestinity in the USSR, but few were able to avoid the attention of the political police for long. But this was not the end of the story. Menshevik ideas in various guises continued to play a significant intellectual and political role for several more decades.

Menshevism exiled

The RSDRP Delegation Abroad was the public face of the Mensheviks as a party. When it was initially created towards the end of 1920 in Berlin, it was envisaged as merely an agency abroad of a party based in Russia, and most of the delegation's members hoped to be able to return to Russia before long. With the foundation of *Sotsialisticheskiy vestnik* in Berlin in February 1921, and the greatly intensified clampdown on the party in Soviet Russia after Kronstadt, the Delegation Abroad increased in significance as the party itself diminished. The journal in particular was an important activity. In its heyday – its first decade – it was one of the best-informed outlets for information on life, conditions and politics in the USSR. Apart from direct communications from individual Mensheviks still at large and active in Russia, there were numerous points of contact between official Russia, people who retained some sympathy with Menshevism, and the Menshevik emigration. Taken together, these informal networks provided a steady stream of information. As former party comrades of the Bolsheviks, Mensheviks could claim a good insight into the mindset of Russia's rulers, and as Marxists, they had a ready analytical framework for interpreting Bolshevism. These were assets they used in politics, in journalism and in the academic sphere.

Menshevik émigrés were well represented in the socialist and labour movements of Europe and North America. Some, like the Paris-based émigré Oreste Rosenfeld, to a greater or lesser extent 'went native', and concerned themselves more with the politics of their new homelands than with Russia. Others saw their role as first and foremost the voices of Russian social democracy in the West. Within the international movement, the RSDRP generally aligned itself with the left; it had been one of the parties involved in creating the 'Vienna Union' in 1921. After that body merged with the Labour and Socialist International (LSI) in 1923, the Menshevik delegates did their best to help shape the policies of member parties towards the USSR. Personal connections played an important part here; relations with the SPD in Germany were particularly extensive, while links with the socialist party in France, the SFIO, were greatly assisted by the fact that from the late 1920s onwards, one of the closest collaborators of its leader, Léon Blum, was Oreste Rosenfeld.[98]

British Labour, on the other hand, showed little interest, either in Menshevism or the LSI. It was often receptive to Soviet approaches, and was generally very resistant to Menshevik entreaties not to be taken in. The veteran British trade unionist Ben Tillett, for example, was reported in the Soviet press at the end of 1924 as saying that the Mensheviks were in the pay of French capital. Cases like this elicited a flurry of letters from the Delegation Abroad to the party concerned and the LSI seeking a retraction.[99] This was to little avail; for all British Labour's domestic anticommunism, it did not pay much attention to Russian socialist critiques of communist rule.

The Menshevik contribution inside Soviet Russia

The contribution of former Menshevik party members who remained in Russia – which was most of them – is easy to discern but harder to quantify. As we have seen, even before the party was driven completely underground many of its members occupied responsible positions, particularly in the burgeoning Soviet economic apparatus. Dvinov recounted a bizarre episode in the summer of 1922 when a Cheka agent came across a session of the Menshevik CC in Moscow and could still be convinced that this was actually a meeting of senior state employees to discuss economic questions.[100] However, by this stage the number of active Mensheviks was tiny in comparison to the number of former members. Some of those former members repudiated their erstwhile convictions and joined the Bolsheviks in order to remain involved in political life. Many others abandoned politics altogether and retreated into private life. A third group simply gave up party activity while retaining their fundamental political and ideological outlook. Some of these were to play an important part in the 1920s as specialists in the Soviet economic apparatus.

The New Economic Policy introduced in Soviet Russia from 1921 involved a shift away from a militarised siege economy, coordinated largely through physical force, towards the use of economic incentives and mechanisms. In some respects, it resembled the policy that the Mensheviks had been recommending during the civil war, and had been attempting to apply in Georgia.[101] At the same time, the first attempts at laying the basis for a planned economy were being undertaken with the foundation of Gosplan, the State Planning Commission, in February that year. Former Mensheviks played a very prominent part in this work. For example, Gosplan's work on devising the methodology for a single economic plan was led in its first years by Stanislav Strumilin (a Menshevik until early 1921, although he joined the Communist Party in 1923 and fully adopted its outlook),[102] Vladimir Groman (the Mensheviks' leading economic expert who only left the party in February 1922),[103] and Vladimir Bazarov (a dissident Bolshevik up to 1917, but a frequent contributor to Martov's journal *Mysl'* in early 1919).[104] Economic institutions and commissariats at all levels had former Mensheviks in responsible posts on their staff. So long as NEP continued, their generally gradualist approach to the development of a socialised, planned economy was in keeping with state policy, and they were often respected and influential specialists.[105]

The end of Menshevik influence

This changed rapidly after 1928, when the Bolshevik leadership again chose to resort to physical force as one of the main levers in its economic policy. This shift in policy was accompanied by an increasingly bitter campaign in the Soviet press against real and imaginary 'Menshevik' ideas and specialists, culminating in the show trial of the 'All-Union Bureau' of Mensheviks in March 1931. In this trial, which coincided with the height of the Communist International's campaign against social democracy as 'social fascism', Groman, Sukhanov and twelve others were tried and convicted on a variety of charges, chiefly conspiracy to engage in economic sabotage at the behest of Anglo-French imperialism. Although the charges of conspiracy and wrecking were baseless, it was certainly true that the defendants represented a group of people with a distinct social and political outlook who had been opposed to Stalin's reversion to physical-force economics. Interestingly, the one political group of Menshevik-minded economists which *had* existed in the 1920s, the 'League of Observers' around Groman between 1923 and 1927, was never mentioned at the trial. Its existence remained secret until it was revealed in 1956 in the memoirs of Nikolay Valentinov.[106]

The shrill press campaign against 'Menshevik wreckers' heralded a wave of arrests of former Mensheviks across the Soviet Union at this time on charges of 'sabotage'. Some of the absurdities of this campaign are nicely illustrated in the memoirs of N. B. Bogdanova, the daughter of Boris Bogdanov, one of Dan's colleagues in the leadership of the Menshevik group in the Petrograd Soviet in 1917. In the 1920s and 1930s, Bogdanov was periodically arrested, imprisoned and then exiled, and in each place of exile he was given responsible work in the local economic administration. In 1928 he was exiled to Simferopol', and shortly thereafter found responsible work in the Crimean planning organisation 'Krymplan'. In early 1931 he was arrested again in connection with the forthcoming 'Menshevik' show trial of alleged saboteurs. After another spell in prison, in 1932 he was exiled to Tomsk – and almost immediately put in charge of the planning department of 'Shakhtstroy', the body responsible for constructing mines in Western Siberia.[107] Bogdanov, who survived numerous imprisonments and exiles, was one of the 'last of the Mohicans' in the USSR. Finally rehabilitated in 1956, he died in Moscow in 1960, aged 76, never having renounced his political convictions.

MENSHEVISM IN HISTORY

Menshevism was a product of its time, of the early history of Marxism in Russia and of a set of expectations about Russia's post-revolutionary development – through capitalism, political democracy, the maturation of the labour movement and then eventually towards socialism. Those expectations overall turned out to be quite false; Russia's history took a very different path. Menshevism was dead as a political movement long before the last individual Mensheviks inside and outside the USSR either died or abandoned the struggle. There was no new generation to step forward and replace them; the post-war emigration from the USSR was largely unreceptive to any forms of socialist politics. How to relate to the new emigration, and whether to take part in an émigré 'Union of Struggle for the Liberation of the Peoples of Russia' with non-socialists and even former soldiers from A. A. Vlasov's wartime collaborationist army, was the main issue over which the Delegation Abroad collapsed in 1951.[108] A tiny group around Solomon Schwarz continued to bring out *Sotsialisticheskiy vestnik* until 1965, but by this time the remaining Mensheviks were mainly preoccupied with recording history rather than trying to make it.

They had a free run: the Bolshevik anathematisation of Menshevism ensured that very little serious work on the party or its leading figures appeared in the Soviet Union for more than seventy years, until the late perestroika period. In official histories, they were always the foils for the invariably correct positions of V. I. Lenin. The *History of the Communist Party of the Soviet Union (Bolsheviks)* from 1938 was typical in portraying the Mensheviks as nothing but 'opportunists', 'anti-party' factionalists, and worse.[109] In the post-Stalin era, however, they did not become simply unmentionable in the way that Trotsky and many of the Bolshevik leaders of 1917 did. Although most Soviet authors found it easiest to deal with Mensheviks by simply citing at length what Lenin had said about them at different times, there were a few works, intended for an academic readership, which discussed aspects of their history more intelligently.[110]

Overall, though, the dearth of serious Soviet-published works meant that the historiography of Menshevism – and to a significant extent, of the Russian revolutionary movement as a whole – would be shaped in the West, first and foremost by the émigré Mensheviks themselves. Writing history was nothing new for the Menshevik leaders. For example, between 1909 and 1914 they had produced four weighty volumes surveying social movements in Russia around the time of the 1905 revolution mentioned above, to which Dan, Martov, P. P. Maslov, Potresov and others all contributed articles.[111] Martov had prepared a history of social democracy in Russia in 1917-18, and a much more detailed pre-history of the movement which appeared in 1922,[112] while Maslov in 1914 had published a general course book on economic history from ancient times to the twentieth century.[113]

In the post-revolutionary period, memoirs were probably the most important literary form in which Mensheviks presented their own history. The first volumes of Sukhanov's *Zapiski o revolyutsii* (Notes on the Revolution) appeared in 1919, when he was still in the RSDRP; over the next five decades many Mensheviks in emigration, not least Dan, followed Sukhanov's example in writing memoirs. The greatest fillip to this process of gathering and publishing reminiscences was the creation in 1959 of the Inter-University Project on the History of the Menshevik Movement at the Hoover Institution, Stanford University. Under the leadership of Leopold H. Haimson, for almost two decades this project collected and published reminiscences, organised interviews with surviving émigrés and collected an archive, now held with Haimson's papers at Columbia University.[114]

The outstanding figure of Menshevik historiography was Boris Nicolaevsky. Before the war he had worked as an archivist at the Marx-Engels Institute and then the International Institute of Social History. After emigrating to the USA in 1942 he continued amassing materials; his collection at the Hoover Institution is one of the major repositories on the Russian revolutionary movement.[115] Nicolaevsky's writings from the 1930s included a biography of Marx and a study of the tsarist police double agent Evno Azef. After the war, he was the joint author, with another Menshevik émigré, David Dallin (Dalin), of *Forced Labour in Soviet Russia* (1947), one of the first studies of the Gulag system. In the post-war period, several figures from the Menshevik emigration, particularly its right wing, made a major contribution to the emergence of 'Sovietology' as an academic discipline in the USA. Naum Jasny, a colleague of Groman in 1917, published several studies on the Soviet economy; Solomon Schwarz produced books on the 1905 revolution and on Jews in the Soviet Union, and in 1962, shortly before his death, Raphael (Rafail) Abramovitch's *The Soviet Revolution 1917-1939* appeared. Although all these authors continued to regard themselves as on the political left, and in most cases as Marxists, the story they told was not one many Western leftists wanted to hear. For those leftists prepared to accept criticisms of the USSR, Trotskyist critiques, which kept the romantic image of October 1917 intact, were generally more palatable.

The post-war sidelining of Menshevik ideas from socialist debate had a curious consequence in the decades after 1956, as reform communism, then eurocommunism and finally perestroika slowly began to develop within the world communist movement. The reformers' perspective of democratising Soviet-style societies to rejuvenate socialism, both within those societies and more widely, was remarkably similar to Dan's left Menshevism of the 1930s and 1940s. Yet they were almost certainly quite unaware of this precedent.

TWO YEARS OF WANDERING

Like Menshevism itself, Dan's memoir is very much of its time. Although at the time he wrote it (mid-1922) his party's organisation had been effectively destroyed in Russia, many Mensheviks did not imagine that the Bolshevik regime could last for long – they regarded it as chaotic, brutal and above all, destructive. They could see no constructive potential in Bolshevism. The economic policies which had characterised it up to early 1921 had demonstrably failed, but NEP was yet to show its potential as a framework for reconstructing the economy. Dan's immediate verdict was harsh – 'not one iota of economic progress, and rapidly developing moral and political disintegration', (p. 186) – and stands in contrast to his later observation about the same period, in which he referred to 'the visible successes of the New Economic Policy'.[116]

However, it is the immediacy of this book which makes it so valuable. It has not been censored or reordered with the wisdom of hindsight, nor is it a considered work of history in which events and impressions have been selected and reworked in order to demonstrate a thesis. It is one man's fresh account of his experiences, impressions and observations. It presents a vivid picture of life in the red heartland of Soviet Russia during the civil war. Dan travelled widely around Bolshevik-held territory, and met a wide variety of people, both in his political and in his work capacity. His ambiguous position as insider and outsider meant that, on the one hand, he was dealing with people at the very top of the Bolshevik state, while on the other hand, he experienced some of the squalor in which ordinary people had to subsist. In the latter part of the book, he provides first-hand descriptions of life in Soviet prisons and accounts of some of the people who ended up in that system, both as jailors and jailed. Among the people Dan encountered in jail were the sailor Petr Perepelkin, one of the leaders of the Kronstadt rising against Bolshevik rule in March 1921, the Finnish communist Voitto Eloranta, allegedly the instigator of a factionalist massacre of Finnish communist leaders, and the US socialist Adolf Carm, denounced as a provocateur by 'Big Bill' Haywood at the founding conference of the Profintern (Red International of Labour Unions) in Moscow and immediately arrested by the Cheka.

But perhaps the most interesting aspect of this memoir is the light it sheds on the formation of the Soviet one-party state, from the standpoint of a leader of a party which is being forced out of existence. The tensions and ambiguities of this process are brought out very well. At the same time that the Cheka was arresting Mensheviks across Russia, Dan was being invited to come to Moscow and address the Seventh and Eighth All-Russia Congresses of Soviets in 1919 and 1920. Moreover, in relation to the Mensheviks at least, there remained a great deal of ambivalence in Bolshevik circles – were they in some way 'comrades' or not? Dan remarks that in 1919 'in Moscow there had never been any major swoops on members of our party without some anonymous well-wishers telephoning me or Comrade Martov to warn us' (p. 74). Even in early 1922, Dan records one of the Chekists involved in expelling him from Russia saying: 'Do you imagine that we can just forget that we used to be in the same party as the Mensheviks and used to work together? We shall never have the same attitude to the Mensheviks as, say, to the SRs and anarchists.' (p. 187)

Although Dan's memoir clearly shows that the Bolsheviks initially had no 'grand plan' to establish a political monopoly for their party, it no less clearly illustrates the logic of the process which led to that monopoly. In the course of their political struggle, the Bolsheviks had damned the Mensheviks, and every other significant socialist current apart from themselves, as 'counterrevolutionaries' and 'enemies of Soviet power'. A large body of political police, operating with few constraints, had been created expressly for the purpose of dealing with such elements. The system built by Lenin and Trotsky in the civil war proved organically incapable of accommodating any kind of legal opposition. The full implications of this were something that oppositionists within the Communist Party itself, and those accused of supporting them, would discover soon enough in their turn.

CONCEPTION OF THIS EDITION

When Dan wrote this book, the places, names and events it recounts would have been familiar enough to his intended audience of Russian émigrés. Some of them will be less familiar to an English-speaking audience almost a century later. I have included explanatory footnotes where this seemed necessary. In the index I have included full names and dates for people mentioned in the text, wherever information is available. Although there are remarkably few errors in Dan's account of episodes where details can be verified, I have corrected occasional slips where they have come to light.

There are several other documents now available which add further detail or insights to Dan's story. In the appendices I have translated some of the leaflets and appeals of the Petrograd Mensheviks in early

1921 concerning the Kronstadt rising, the protocol of Dan's interrogation by the Cheka in April 1921, a review of Dan's book in the Bolshevik press, and Viktor Chernov's own account of his speech to the British workers' delegation in May 1920.

ACKNOWLEDGEMENTS

Several people have assisted me in this project by answering queries, tracking down obscure information, or making helpful comments on drafts. In particular, I would like to thank Gleb Albert, John Biggart, Tim Davenport, Richard Deswarte, Mikhail Strakhov and Reiner Tosstorff.

NOTES

1. N. N. Sukhanov, *Zapiski o revolyutsii t. 2*, Izdatel'stvo politicheskoy literatury, Moscow, 1991, p. 54.
2. These editions are: V. Tchernov, *Mes tribulations en Russie soviétique*, Povolozky, Paris 1921; Viktor M. Tschernow, *Meine Schicksale in Sowjet-Russland*, Der Firn, Berlin, 1921; V. Tzernov, *Mina oden in Sovjet-Russland*, Tyders, Stockholm, 1921. The translation of Chernov's speech in this volume is from the French edition.
3. Tchernov, *Mes tribulations*, p. 85.
4. Yu. O. Martov, *Zapiski sotsial-demokrata*, ed. P. Yu. Savel'ev. ROSSPEN, Moscow 2004, p. 169.
5. For this and other details of Dan's biography, I draw heavily on two biographical essays: Boris Sapir, 'Fedor Il'ich Dan (1871-1947). Ocherk politicheskoy biografii', in Theodore Dan, *Letters (1899-1946). Selected, annotated and with an outline of Dan's political biography by Boris Sapir*, Stichting Internationaal Instituut voor Sociale Gescheidenis, Amsterdam, 1985, pp. xxxvii-lviii, here p xxxix; and B. L. Dvinov 'F. I. Dan' in G. Ya. Aronson, L. O. Dan, B. L. Dvinov, B. M. Sapir, *Martov i ego blizkie*, Rausen Bros, New York, 1959, pp. 118-137. Available online on http://socialist.memo.ru/books/perli/martov/martov08.htm.
6. Details from Sapir, 'Dan', p. xxxviii.
7. Ibid., p. xxxix.
8. Dvinov, 'Dan', p. 120.
9. See Claudie Weill, *Marxistes russes et social-démocratie allemande, 1898-1904*, Maspero, Paris, 1977, p. 51.
10. The ongoing correspondence between Dan and Kautsky can be found in Dan, *Letters*.
11. Dvinov, 'Dan', p. 121.

12. Dan, *Letters*, p. 165.
13. Ibid., p. 184.
14. Ibid., p. 184.
15. F. I. Dan, 'Proletariat i russkaya revolyutsiya', *Golos sotsial-demokrata* No. 3, March 1908, reprinted in S. V. Tyutyukin, compiler, *Men'sheviki. Dokumenty i materialy. 1903-fevral' 1917 gg.*, ROSSPEN, Moscow, 1996, pp. 296-297.
16. Ibid., p. 297.
17. On Potresov's attitudes at this time and his differences with Dan and Martov, see e.g. Boris Sapir, 'The Mensheviks before the Revolution of 1917', in Leopold H. Haimson (ed), *The Mensheviks. from the Revolution of 1917 to the Second World War*, University of Chicago Press, Chicago,1974, pp. 356-358. On the attitudes of Mensheviks in Russia, see also Martov's article 'Spasiteli ili uprazdniteli' from 1911, republished in Yu. O. Martov, *Izbrannoe*, Moscow, 2000, p. 270.
18. Rossiyskiy gosudarstvennyy arkhiv sotsial'no-politicheskoy istorii (RGASPI), f. 36, op. 1, delo 11, ll. 235, 271.
19. The bare details of this journal can be found on http://feb-web.ru/feb/periodic/pp0-abc/pp2/pp2-1671.htm.
20. See Dan to A. Martynov, 19 November 1910, in Dan, *Letters*, pp. 233-234. Of the projected six volumes, four actually appeared: L. Martov, P. Maslov and A. Potresov (eds), *Obshchestvennoe dvizhenie v Rossii v nachale XX-go veka*, Vols 1-4, Obshchestvennaya pol'za, St. Petersburg, 1909-1914.
21. A brief account of these arguments is given in I. G. Tsereteli, *Vospominaniya o fevral'skoy revolyutsii*, I, Mouton, Paris, 1963, p. 9.
22. 'Soviet Appeal to the Peoples of All the World', 14 (27) March 1917, in Robert Paul Browder and Alexander F. Kerensky (eds), *The Russian Provisional Government, 1917, Documents*, Vol. II, Stanford University Press, Stanford, CA, 1961, p. 1078.
23. For the text of the Zimmerwald Manifesto, see: www.marxists.org/history/international/social-democracy/zimmerwald/manifesto-1915.htm.
24. The dilemmas faced here are well described in N. N. Sukhanov, *Zapiski o revolyutsii t. 1*, Izdatel'stvo politicheskoy literatury, Moscow, 1991, pp. 53-54.
25. Sukhanov, *Zapiski t. 1*, p. 329.
26. Ziva Galili and Albert Nenarokov (eds), *Men'sheviki v 1917 godu. t. 1. Ot yanvarya do iyul'skikh sobytiy*, Progress-Akademiya, Moscow, 1994, p. 348.
27. Ibid., p. 348.
28. See André Liebich, *From the Other Shore. Russian Social-Democracy after 1921*, Harvard UP, Cambridge MA, 1997, p. 65.
29. Sukhanov, *Zapiski t. 2*, p. 52.
30. Ibid., p. 52.
31. Ibid., pp. 52-53.

32. Albert Nenarokov, *Pravyy men'shevizm. Prozreniya rossiyskoy sotsial-demokratii*, Novyy khronograf, Moscow, 2012, p. 122.
33. Sukhanov, *Zapiski t. 2*, p. 53.
34. 'The policy of a general democratic peace had one basic flaw – it could only justify itself if it could give *rapid* results … ', F. Dan, 'Voprosy voyny i mira', in B. Gorev, A. Dalin, F. Dan, A. Ermansky, L. Martov and Finansist, *Za god. Sbornik statey*, Kniga, Petrograd, 1919, pp. 5-6.
35. See B. D. Galperina, V. I. Startsev (eds), *Petrogradskiy Sovet Rabochikh i Soldatskikh Deputatov v 1917 godu, t. 3*, ROSSPEN, Moscow, 2002, p. 314.
36. For an account of the discussions around this demonstration and Dan's role, see I. G. Tsereteli, *Vospominaniya o fevral'skoy revolyutsii*, II, Mouton, Paris, 1963, pp. 242-252.
37. Sukhanov, *Zapiski t. 2*, p. 53.
38. See S. E. Rudneva, *Demokraticheskoe soveshchanie, sentyabr' 1917 g. Istoriya foruma*, Nauka, Moscow, 2000, pp. 38, 40-41; Ziva Galili, *The Menshevik Leaders in the Russian Revolution: Social Realities and Political Strategies*, Princeton University Press, Princeton NJ, 1989, p. 384.
39. For details of this see F. Dan, 'K istorii poslednikh dney vremennogo pravitel'stva', in S. A. Alekseev (compiler), *Oktyabr'skaya revolyutsiya*, Gos. Izdatel'stvo, Moscow/Leningrad, 1926 (reprint: Orbita, Moscow, 1991), p. 120.
40. Ibid., p. 128. See also Kerensky's account of the same episode in A. F. Kerensky, 'Gatchina', in W. Astrov, A. Slepkov and J. Thomas (eds), *An Illustrated History of the Russian Revolution*, Volume 2, Martin Lawrence, London, 1928, pp. 371-373.
41. For a contemporary account of the crumbling of Menshevik support and organisation in the second half of 1917, written by an internationalist journalist, see Rafail Grigor'ev, 'The Disintegration of the Minority', translated from *Novaya zhizn'*, 28 September/11 October 1917, on www.korolevperevody.co.uk/korolev/grigorev.htm.
42. Unfortunately, the stenographers at the congress, on secondment from the city duma, also walked out with the Mensheviks and SRs. Consequently no stenographic report of the congress was ever produced. A collation of newspaper reports from different standpoints was published in 1997 – all accounts of Dan's brief opening speech coincide. See A. S. Pokrovsky and E. Yu. Tikhonova (compilers), *Vtoroy Vserossiyskiy s"ezd Sovetov rabochikh i soldatskikh deputatov (25-26 oktyabrya 1917 g.) Sbornik dokumentov i materialov*, Arkheograficheskiy tsentr, Moscow, 1997.
43. See Ziva Galili and Albert Nenarokov (eds), *Men'sheviki v 1917 godu. t. 3. Ot kornilovskogo myatezha do kontsa dekabrya. Chast' vtoraya. Ot Vremennogo Demokraticheskogo Soveta Rossiyskoy Respubliki do kontsa dekabrya (pervaya dekada oktyabrya – konets dekabrya)*, ROSSPEN, Moscow, 1997, p. 606.

44. Nenarokov, *Pravyy men'shevizm*, p. 275.
45. Galili and Nenarokov, eds, *Men'sheviki v 1917 godu. t. 3 ch. 2*, p. 270.
46. Ibid., p. 271.
47. Ibid., pp. 515, 523.
48. Ibid., p. 428: Dan's speech as reported in *Novyy luch*, 3 December 1917.
49. According to Radkey, the Mensheviks secured 1,384,826 votes out of a total poll of 41,686,876 across Russia, and 569,362 of those votes were cast in Transcaucasia. See Oliver H. Radkey, *Russia Goes to the Polls. The Election to the All-Russian Constituent Assembly*, Cornell, Ithaca, NY, 1989, pp. 18, 81.
50. Cited in Vladimir N. Brovkin, *The Mensheviks after October. Socialist Opposition and the Rise of the Bolshevik Dictatorship*, Cornell University Press, Ithaca, NY, 1987, p. 119. Brovkin provides details of the Stalin-Martov case on pp. 110-117.
51. Ibid., p. 121.
52. Published in *Dekrety Sovetskoy vlasti t. 2*, Gos. izdatel'stvo politicheskoy literatury, Moscow, 1959; available on www.hist.msu.ru/ER/Etext/DEKRET/18-06-14.htm.
53. F. I. Dan's theses 'On the policies of the party in Soviet Russia', in D. Pavlov (compiler), *Men'sheviki v 1918 godu*, ROSSPEN, Moscow, 1999, p. 707.
54. Ibid., p. 708.
55. F. Dan, 'Oborona revolyutsii' (Defence of the Revolution), republished in D. Pavlov (compiler), *Men'sheviki v 1919-1920 gg.*, ROSSPEN, Moscow, 2000, pp. 271-274, here p. 274.
56. RGASPI, fond 17, op. 3, d. 259, l. 5. Politburo minute No. 82.
57. RGASPI, fond 17, op. 3, d. 242, l. 17. Politburo minute No. 84.
58. Boris Dvinov, *Ot legal'nosti k podpol'yu (1921-1922)*, Hoover Institution, Stanford CA, 1968, p. 72.
59. Dan's deposition in TsA FSB RF, d. N 1379, ll. 7-9 ob.; republished in V. P. Naumov, A. A. Kosakovsky (compilers), *Kronshtadt 1921*, Mezhdunarodnyy fond 'Demokratiya', Moscow, 1997, p. 267. See appendix IV of the present volume for the full text.
60. See the entry on Sergey Osipovich Ezhov-Tsederbaum in P. V. Volobuev et al. (eds), *Politicheskie deyateli Rossii 1917. Biograficheskiy slovar'*, Bol'shaya Rossiyskaya Entsiklopediya, Moscow, 1993, pp. 109-110. Also available on www.hrono.ru/biograf/bio_ye/ezhov_so.php.
61. For details of the 'Martov line' and its problems, see Liebich, *Other Shore*, pp. 83-88.
62. Cited in Thomas Reißer, *Menschewismus und Nep. Diskussion einer demokratischen Alternative*, Lit Verlag, Münster, 1996, pp. 226-227.
63. For an account of the debates around this question, see Liebich, *Other Shore*, pp. 193-199.
64. See ibid., p. 217.

65. Otto Bauer, Théodore Dan, Amédée Dunois and Jean Zyromski, *L'Internationale et la guerre*, Éditions Nouveau Prométhée, Paris, 1935, p. 10.
66. Ibid., p. 22.
67. See A. Nenarokov (compiler), *Men'sheviki v emigratsii. Protokoly Zagranichnoy Delegatsii RSDRP, 1922-1951 gg.* chast' 2, ROSSPEN, Moscow, 2010, p. 42.
68. Ibid, p. 49.
69. See Sapir, 'Dan', pp. liv-lviii for an account of Dan's final political initiatives.
70. See Theodore Dan, *The Origins of Bolshevism* (translated and edited by Joel Carmichael), Secker & Warburg, London, 1964, pp. 438-439.
71. See B. M. Sapir, 'Lidiya Osipovna Dan', in B. M. Sapir (ed), *Iz arkhiva L. O. Dan*, IISG, Amsterdam, 1987, p. xxiv, note 27. Sapir observed that everyone who could have shed light on this episode was no longer alive.
72. See secretariat minutes of 6 February 1924 in A. Nenarokov (compiler), *Men'sheviki v emigratsii. Protokoly Zagranichnoy Delegatsii RSDRP, 1922-1951 gg.* chast' 1, ROSSPEN, Moscow, 2010, pp. 157-158.
73. See Sapir, 'Lidiya Osipovna Dan'. This is also discussed in Svetlana Jebrak, *Mit dem Blick nach Russland – Lydia Cederbaum (1878-1963). Eine jüdische Sozialdemokratin im lebenslangen Exil*, Dietz, Bonn, 2006.
74. Here, as in many other respects, Georgian Menshevism went its own way. Noe Zhordania, recounting events around the time of the 1905 revolution, observed that unlike the Russian social democrats of both factions, the Georgians 'brought the workers and peasants together and made one army out of them, to create a single socio-political order and change the old one'. See Noah Zhordania, *My Life*, Hoover, Stanford CA, 1968, p. 44.
75. See Leopold Haimson's interviews with Denike in Leopold H. Haimson with Ziva Galili y Garcia and Richard Wortman (eds), *The Making of Three Russian Revolutionaries*, Cambridge University Press, Cambridge, 1987, here p. 337.
76. Report in *Edinstvo*, No. 5, 5 April 1917, in Galili and Nenarokov, *Men'sheviki v 1917 godu. t. 1*, p. 178.
77. For an account of this initiative, see Francis King, 'Between Bolshevism and Menshevism: The Social-Democrat Internationalists in the Russian Revolution', *Revolutionary Russia* Vol. 9 No. 1, 1996, pp. 1-18.
78. See for example the resolution of the Mensheviks' Fifth Extraordinary Congress on 6 December 1917, Galili and Nenarokov (eds), *Men'sheviki v 1917 godu. t. 3. Chast' vtoraya*, p. 514.
79. The increasing use of administrative measures against inconvenient soviets is detailed in Brovkin, *The Mensheviks after October*, chapter 5.
80. For more on this see Brovkin, *The Mensheviks after October*, chapters 7 and 8. An excellent annotated volume of the documents and materials of

the movement is D. B. Pavlov (compiler), *Rabochee oppozitsionnoe dvizhenie v bol'shevistskoy Rossii 1918 g.*, ROSSPEN, Moscow, 2006.
81. For details of this episode see E. A. Ermolin and V. N. Kozlyakov (eds and compilers), *Yaroslavskoe vosstanie 1918*, Materik, Moscow, 2007, pp. 11, 28-30.
82. D. Pavlov (compiler), *Men'sheviki v 1918 godu*, ROSSPEN, Moscow, 1999, p. 591.
83. See ibid., p. 600.
84. See ibid., p. 624.
85. Ibid., pp. 616-617.
86. A participant in the rising and administration in Votkinsk, the Menshevik foundry worker I. G. Upovalov, later in emigration, wrote an account of events with a bitter assessment of the failure of the Menshevik CC to support the rebels. See I. G. Upovalov, *Rabochee vosstanie protiv Sovetskoy vlasti* on www.istprof.atlabs.ru/1319.html.
87. See the RSDRP CC appeal 'What is to be done?' in D. Pavlov (compiler), *Men'sheviki v 1919-1920 gg.*, ROSSPEN, Moscow, 2000, pp. 230-237, here p. 231.
88. See 'Theses of the Right Mensheviks' in Pavlov, *Men'sheviki v 1919-1920 gg.*, pp. 241-247. An English translation is on www.korolevperevody.co.uk/korolev/right-men-19.html.
89. D. Dalin, 'Gryadushchaya epokha' (The Coming Epoch), *Mysl'*, May 1919. Republished in Pavlov, *Men'sheviki v 1919-1920 gg.*, pp. 200-209, here p. 203.
90. F. Dan, 'Oborona revolyutsii' (Defence of the Revolution), republished in ibid., pp. 271-274, here p. 274.
91. Letter of Yu. O. Martov to P. L. Lapinsky, RGASPI, f. 275, op. 1, d. 64, ll. 4-6.
92. Boris Dvinov, *Ot legal'nosti k podpol'yu (1921-1922)*, Hoover Institution, Stanford CA, 1968, p. 144.
93. Ibid., p. 103.
94. In a letter of 2 June 1918 to the Menshevik CC in Moscow, Zhordania and I. Tsereteli set out in detail the events which led them to declare independence. See D. Pavlov (compiler), *Men'sheviki v 1918 godu*, ROSSPEN, Moscow, 1999, pp. 512-516. An English translation is available on www.korolevperevody.co.uk/korolev/gruzine.htm.
95. For an account of Georgian Menshevism and its origins, see Stephen F. Jones, *Socialism in Georgian Colors: The European Road to Social Democracy, 1883-1917*, Harvard UP, Cambridge MA, 2005. For Zhordania's own account of his life (in Russian) see Zhordania, *My Life*. For a rather idealised contemporary portrayal of Georgia under Menshevik rule, see Karl Kautsky, *Georgia: a Social-Democratic Peasant Republic*, International Bookshops, London, 1921.
96. See J. Shaphir, *Secrets of Menshevik Georgia. The Plot Against Soviet Russia*

Unmasked, CPGB, London, 1922, and Voronsky's review in the present volume for examples of this.
97. A thought-provoking analysis of this process is provided in Scott B. Smith, *Captives of Revolution: The Socialist-Revolutionaries and the Bolshevik Dictatorship 1918-1923*, University of Pittsburgh Press, Pittsburgh PA, 2011, pp. 163-176.
98. For details of Rosenfeld and his role in the SFIO, see Liebich, *From the Other Shore*, pp. 175, 225-228 and ff.
99. See A. Nenarokov (compiler), *Men'sheviki v emigratsii. Protokoly Zagranichnoy Delegatsii RSDRP, 1922-1951 gg.* chast' 1, ROSSPEN, Moscow, 2010, pp. 185-188 and ff. for the Tillett case.
100. Boris Dvinov, *Ot legal'nosti k podpol'yu (1921-1922)*, Hoover Institution, Stanford CA, 1968, pp. 142-143.
101. See for example the motion the Menshevik fraction at the Seventh All-Russia Congress of Soviets proposed in December 1919 in D. Pavlov (compiler), *Men'sheviki v 1919-1920 gg.*, ROSSPEN, Moscow, 2000, pp. 310-314. An English translation can be found on www.korolevperevody.co.uk/korolev/mensh-19-7-cong.htm.
102. For the date Strumilin left the Menshevik organisation, see D. Pavlov (compiler), *Men'sheviki v 1921-1922 godu*, ROSSPEN, Moscow, 2002, p. 321; for a sketch of the rest of his biography, see the *Bol'shaya sovetskaya entsikopediya* article on e.g. http://slovar.cc/enc/bse/2045462.html.
103. See Pavlov, *Men'sheviki v 1921-1922 godu*, for Groman's letter of resignation from the RSDRP, on the grounds that he had begun to 'reexamine the basic ideas of Marxism', p. 446.
104. For a biographical essay on Bazarov, see Francis King, 'Vladimir Aleksandrovich Bazarov (1874-1939): One of the first dissident communists', *Socialist History*, 34, 2009, pp. 20-35.
105. See Naum Jasny, *Soviet Economists of the Twenties: Names to be Remembered*, Cambridge University Press, Cambridge, 1972; Francis King, 'The Russian Revolution and the Idea of a Single Economic Plan 1917-1928', *Revolutionary Russia* Vol. 12 No. 1, 1999, pp. 69-83.
106. See N. Valentinov, *Novaya ekonomicheskaya politika i krizis partii posle smerti Lenina*, Sovremennik, Moscow, 1991, chapter 1, for an account of this group. Its main intellectual project was to monitor the fate of the ideas which had underpinned the October revolution.
107. N. B. Bogdanova, *Moy otets – Men'shevik*, Memorial, St. Petersburg, 1994, pp. 141-145, 148.
108. See Liebich, *From the Other Shore*, p. 291 for details.
109. See for example CPSU CC Commission (eds), *History of the Communist Party of the Soviet Union (Bolsheviks)*, FLPH, Moscow, 1939, p. 44, for these charges in the passage dealing with Menshevism's first appearance.
110. For example Yu. S. Tokarev, *Petrogradskiy Sovet Rabochikh i Soldatskikh Deputatov v marte-aprele 1917 g.*, Nauka, Leningrad, 1976, provides a

worthwhile account of the early days of the Petrograd Soviet in 1917 and the main figures involved. But the print-run of his book was only 2200 copies, which was very small for those years.
111. See L. Martov, P. Maslov and A. Potresov (eds), *Obshchestvennoe dvizhenie v Rossii v nachale XX-go veka*, Vols 1-4, Obshchestvennaya pol'za, St. Petersburg, 1909-1914.
112. See 'Istoriya rossiyskoy sotsial-demokratii' in Yuliy Osipovich Martov, *Izbrannoe* (compilers D. B. Pavlov, V. L. Telitsyn), Moscow, 2000; Yu. O. Martov, *Zapiski sotsial-demokrata*, ROSSPEN, Moscow, 2004.
113. This work has been republished, 101 years after its first appearance. P. P. Maslov, *Obshchedostupnyy kurs istorii narodnogo khozyaystva. Ot pervobytnykh vremen do XX stoletiya*, Lenand, Moscow, 2015.
114. See http://findingaids.cul.columbia.edu/ead/nnc-rb/ldpd_6909647/print for a brief description of this collection.
115. See http://oac.cdlib.org/findaid/ark:/13030/tf7290056t/ for the catalogue of the Nicolaevsky collection.
116. Dan, *Origins of Bolshevism*, p. 417.

1
An 'Official' Exile

In May 1920, a British workers' delegation visited Moscow. Every trend in the British workers' movement was represented in that delegation. There was Robert Williams, who at that time had not yet been labelled a 'traitor' and was regarded as an orthodox communist; he was honoured with special banners and kept himself apart from other members of the delegation. There was Wallhead, chairman of the ILP [Independent Labour Party], there were Labour Party members, Fabians, simple trade unionists, socialist writers – Ethel Snowden, Tom Shaw, Skinner, Buxton and others – and there was even a Christian communist, Russell.[1] Two trade unionist workers came separately as delegates from factory committees.

As is the custom in Moscow, from the outset the Bolsheviks attempted to build an impenetrable wall around their valued guests. They were put up in the 'Delovoy Dvor' hotel. This hotel maintained a standard of luxury which afforded a bizarre contrast with the unimaginable wretchedness of the lives of ordinary Muscovites at that time. The guests were furnished with cars, interpreters and guides, while downstairs, at the entrance to the hotel, Chekists were installed to demand 'passes' from anybody wishing to make contact with the 'representatives of the international proletariat' who had come to the 'world proletarian capital'. In other words, in time-honoured fashion, the Bolsheviks made every effort to take their guests into their warm smiling embrace, to show them only what it was useful for them to see, and to make them hear through Bolshevik ears and see through Bolshevik eyes, painstakingly insulating them from any 'external' influence.

This operation – or, to put it crudely, this eyewash – had frequently succeeded with less perceptive or already much more sympathetic foreign guests. Many of these distinguished, or even far from distinguished, foreigners left Russia with the pleasant conviction that, in general, everything is fine. The economy is 'getting sorted out', culture and education are blossoming as never before, the workers revere the

Bolsheviks and invariably vote for them unanimously ('we saw and heard it for ourselves!'), and even the tales about the appalling material situation in Russia, about the hunger and cold, are greatly exaggerated. Certain people, it must be said, even brought material proof of Russia's well-being back with them in the form of expensive fur coats, samovars and suchlike pleasant 'souvenirs' given to them by the Bolsheviks. This is not to mention the fairly large number of foreigners who act as the permanent courtiers of the Executive Committee of the Third International. The splendid Hotel Lux on Tverskaya Street is reserved for them, and they have no reason at all to complain of the harshness of life in communist Moscow ...

The British, however, turned out to be the sort of people who could not easily be deceived by the crude Asiatic methods of their Bolshevik hosts.[2] They came with the intention, first and foremost, to ascertain the 'facts', and to ascertain them with their own hands and eyes. Therefore they had compiled in advance a short list of questions which they wanted answered, and had decided in advance to make contact not only with the Bolsheviks, but with representatives of other parties as well. They began to press for this, with typically British insistence, from the day they arrived in Moscow. Additionally, one of the delegation, Buxton, who had acquired my address from P. B. Aksel'rod in London, sought me out on his arrival, and through me made contact with the Central Committee of our party. Although the Bolsheviks tried to devise an itinerary for the delegation which would have made it physically impossible to meet anybody outside the officially prescribed circle of people, the British quickly succeeded in winning the right to go where they pleased, and to use their own interpreters and guides. We provided two of these interpreters, and thanks to this the British guests learned a great deal on official visits as well, which under other circumstances would have been concealed from them. Our interpreter was present even on their visit to the notorious Cheka, which in this instance turned out to be very useful. Incidentally, this breach in the Bolshevik 'blockade' was greatly assisted by the 'non-party' interpreter provided by the Bolsheviks, the trade unionist Yarotsky, who did not foresee that in the very near future he would find it expedient to become a most rabid communist. There was a slight fault in the mechanism!

For its part, our Central Committee had prepared certain materials for the arrival of the delegation. Some of these materials had been prepared even earlier, in anticipation of the – abortive – commission elected by the Berne Conference (Kautsky, Adler, Longuet, MacDonald).[3] Purely factual material had been chosen on the Bolsheviks' general and economic policies, mostly from their own press, with brief explanatory notes. In addition, we had compiled a memorandum which described our party's situation under the Bolshevik regime, and which set out its programme and tactical position. Comrades Martov, Abramovich, Yudin and I visited the delegation in its hotel on behalf of the Central Committees of our party and of the Bund.[4] The delegation itself attended two sessions of our Central Committee. It should be stressed that individuals and groups on the delegation were careful to avoid any kind of surreptitious or separate discussions with different parties or organisations, and loyally informed all members of the delegation without exception of any forthcoming meetings. Nonetheless Robert Williams did not wish to meet our Central Committee or any of its individual members even once.

The Bolsheviks showed the British a great deal, including Red Army parades. But there was one thing they did not want and were not able to show them: a free workers' meeting. There was a simple reason for this – the attitude of the Moscow workers at that time was not one about which they could boast. So we did what the Bolsheviks would not do: the leadership of the printers' union, which consisted mainly of members of our party, took advantage of the embarrassment of the Bolshevik authorities in the presence of their foreign guests and called a massive workers' meeting in the large hall of the Conservatory. The tickets were numbered, and the audience of over 3000 consisted almost entirely of ordinary workers. This was the only workers' meeting the British were able to see but – I should add, running ahead somewhat – it was also the last such meeting in Bolshevik Moscow.

Among the speakers at the meeting were Mensheviks from the leadership of the printers' union (Chistov and Kamermakher), and Bolsheviks – Tikhonov from the Polygraphical Department of the Supreme Council for National Economy and Mel'nichansky from the Central Council of Trade Unions. There was simultaneous translation of the speeches for the British delegation. However, even without any translation, from the way the audience reacted to the speeches of the Mensheviks and the Bolsheviks, the foreign guests could clearly tell that the Bolshevik regime enjoys little sympathy among the workers.

I spoke on behalf of our Central Committee. In my speech I stressed that we did not look upon our guests as judges, to decide between us and the Bolsheviks, but as comrades in struggle with whom we wanted to share our experience. They would have to face the same problems as us, and like us, would have to choose between two methods of struggle for socialism: the Bolshevik way of a terroristic dictatorship of a minority, or the social-democratic, Marxist way of the rule of the conscious majority. I cited a series of facts to illustrate the results of the Bolshevik method. The end of my speech I devoted to a protest against the intervention and to an appeal to the British workers to struggle to lift the blockade against Russia.

The meeting was already coming to a close, when a man of medium height with a long beard reaching almost to his waist came onto the stage from a side door and approached the chairman. The chairman then announced that there would be a speech from a representative of the Socialist-Revolutionary Party. It was only once the orator had begun to speak that I realised to my astonishment that it was Chernov – his long beard had changed him so much! Chernov had taken an enormous risk in appearing at this meeting, since at that time he was being hunted by the Cheka. Chernov's speech was not a great success. He compared the teachings of socialism to the teachings of the early Christians, and the Bolsheviks to the degenerated Christian church. This speech was far too abstract and literary, and failed to inspire this audience of workers, who responded with only weak applause.

The situation was saved by the Bolsheviks. The moment they realised that the speaker was Chernov, they were unable to remain quietly in their seats. Mel'nichansky, who was sitting next to me, fidgeted in his chair as if he were about to jump up and run somewhere. I called to him scornfully, 'You want to call the Cheka?' Forgetting himself, he replied angrily, 'Yes, of course, they should be informed immediately!' Other Bolsheviks also began to get agitated, and it was only our fixed stares and scorn which restrained them from running to the telephone to tell the Cheka what was happening. Instead, as soon as the speaker had finished, the Bolsheviks began to call out, 'What is your name? Make him say who he is!' Chernov stood up and gave his name. The results were not what the Bolsheviks had hoped for. Their zealous police work and cries of 'arrest him!' simply caused the hall to burst into thunderous applause for the quarry. The Bolsheviks lost their heads, and in the general pandemonium Chernov was able to disappear unnoticed, just as he had appeared.

The Bolsheviks were mortified by that meeting. The damage they sustained in the eyes of a foreign workers' delegation with that display of the real sentiments of the Moscow proletariat was only made worse by a pitiful demonstration they organised after the meeting, in which just 100 to 150 people marched from the meeting place to the building of the Moscow Soviet. They had not realised that with that sort of number it would have been better not to have gone ahead with that demonstration. From that day on the avenging hand of the Bolsheviks was raised against the initiators and the active participants of that meeting, and they simply waited for an opportunity to deal with these 'criminals'. A vicious campaign was immediately launched against the leadership of the printers' union. It was soon broken up, and a 'red' administration forcibly installed in its place, while the members of the old leadership were sent to jail. It was soon to be my turn ...

At that time I was 'on active service'. In June 1919, following a three-month spell in Butyrki prison, I had been mobilised by the Bolsheviks in my capacity as a trained doctor and seconded to the People's Commissariat of Health, where I was put in charge of the Surgical Subsection of the Department of Medical Supplies. This is a lowly position in the hierarchy, but it had real importance in the provision of medical services in Russia. The Surgical Subsection was concerned with providing the republic with medical instruments and supplies for patient care. This was not an easy task, as stocks were not very large, and many things could not be made in Russia at all. Even attempts to produce those items which could be manufactured in Russia met with almost insurmountable obstacles – the general chaos, the 'nationalisationary' policies of the Bolsheviks, the constant interference of organs of the Cheka, and finally, it must be said, the surreptitious sabotage of various glakvi (economic departments) which were conserving their stocks for the 'owners', whose return they anticipated in the more or less near future. Afterwards, one of the specialists who had been in charge of one of those glavki at the time openly admitted this to me. Apart from that, the way was blocked by monstrous corruption. There were glavki, government economic organs, from which we, also a government institution, could get nothing at all. However, private firms (there were two or three which I am convinced continued to exist until they were finally liquidated at the end of 1920) and speculators trading on the black market were able relatively easily to get those items we needed but could not obtain, by liberally greasing the palms of the right people at the right time. The interference of the Cheka was at best useless, and usually made the situation even worse, either by preventing medical institutions and the population from obtaining the articles they needed, albeit at an inflated price, from private traders, or sometimes by increasing the 'costs' of traders and speculators.

Bribery, or, at least, the receipt of 'gifts' in state institutions for fulfilling requests not only from private individuals, but also from other state institutions, became the norm. I can recall a curious example of this. I was approached by a representative of Glavryba (the fisheries department) to let them have some microscopes for a laboratory they were setting up. At that very time we had just received a few dozen microscopes found in Arkhangel'sk after the British troops had withdrawn from there. Thus I was in the unusual position of being able to satisfy the requirements of Glavryba in full, and just two days later their representative was the lucky recipient of this 'order'. Having taken delivery of them, he came up to me, leaned towards my ear and furtively asked me for my address. I asked him, in amazement, why he needed it. 'Since you were so helpful to us, we will deliver some fish to you at home.' I could only shrug my shoulders …

We could barely satisfy one hundredth of the real need. Nonetheless, those who had dealings with our Subsection, especially those working in the provinces, frequently expressed their surprise at finding an institution which tried as much as it could to meet their requirements, to reduce the endless red tape as far as possible and generally get things done. This was highly unusual for Soviet offices in general, and for an office dealing with any kind of material supply, 'real values', in particular!

It was virtually impossible to get anything done as far as organising production was concerned for the reasons outlined above. Even orders to handicraftsmen were reduced to almost nothing when, as a result of the 'principles' of economic policy in operation at that time, it was forbidden to pay for such orders in cash. Having brought us some item from some provincial town which had taken a week to make, the producer then had to spend the next week chasing round Moscow so that finally, having passed through dozens of departments, he received a chit entitling him to receive his starvation wages from the Narodny Bank. The purchase of hidden stocks from private individuals also virtually ceased once all the supply organs received a secret order from the Cheka to the effect that if they purchased any item from a private individual for more than 5000 rubles, they should immediately inform the Cheka of the transaction, indicating the name and address of the seller, so that he could be caught and the money confiscated. Naturally, I categorically refused to go along with this. This 'most strict' order was circumvented by the supply organs thus: if they purchased an item for, say, 100,000 rubles, 20 chits for 5000 rubles were made out for different periods or to different persons. Nonetheless, the red tape involved in this, and the whole 'Chekist' atmosphere this created, put an end to almost all private supply for a long time. As for orders from abroad, this was all still a distant dream. Targets were set, estimates were made and so forth, but in reality, the whole time I was in charge of the Surgical Subsection we received just a couple of kilograms of dental instruments, sent by aeroplane from Germany. The aviators crashed twice on the way, so the cost of two ruined aircraft has to be counted in the price of the thirty kilograms of cargo received, which consisted mainly of alkaloids.

We were therefore in an appalling situation as far as replenishing our stocks was concerned, and we were heading rapidly towards their complete exhaustion. Nonetheless, we were able, with great effort, to make headway in collecting, accounting for and storing appropriately the little that was available, and in speedy and equitable distribution of the instruments among the many claimants to them. This was not much, but it was enough to ensure that I was highly valued in my post and was considered almost 'irreplaceable'.

The peaceful course of my official service was, however, interrupted in an unexpected way. In the last days of May 1920 I used two days' holiday to take a trip with my wife in the area around Moscow, to Zvenigorsk and Voskresensk, the most beautiful places in the Moscow gubernia. Having seated ourselves in a railway carriage on the Alexandrovsk line in order to travel to Golytsino station, I opened the newspaper and was amazed to find some incredibly malicious official announcements and articles about the Mensheviks and Socialist-Revolutionaries. At that time the war with Poland had just broken out, and an announcement by the Cheka declared that we were traitors who were assisting the Polish army, disorganising the Russian economy, blowing up bridges and setting fire to warehouses! It concluded by threatening us with all manner of scorpions. An adjacent article showered compliments on former tsarist generals who had, in the national interest, decided patriotically to support the Bolshevik government.

I had read many slanders which had poured from Bolshevik pens before then, and have read many more since, but none of them have induced such feelings of revulsion in me as that one. This might be because in this provocation of nationalist pogroms against us as 'enemies of the motherland', combined with 'patriotic' flirtation with tsarist generals (some of whom, of course, are personally honourable people), I sensed the beginnings of the shameless 'new policy'. This policy now permits our 'communist' government to consort with and embrace all kinds of foreign and domestic stock-jobbers, speculators, swindlers, and suchlike shady characters, while keeping in jail or in exile thousands of socialists and non-party workers who have been so bold as to doubt the divine infallibility of the Bolshevik authorities, with all their fantasies, scandals, petty tyranny and occasional 180-degree turns.

Two days later I returned to Moscow, still feeling a burning sense of outrage. Without seeing or consulting any of my comrades, I wrote a declaration to the member of the board of the People's Commissariat of Health in charge of the Department of Medical Supplies. In this declaration I stated that the malicious official insinuations about setting fire to warehouses made it impossible for me to remain in charge of an institution which held considerable stocks of irreplaceable medical supplies, of great significance for an army which had been sent to war. I declared that these insinuations undermined any trust in members of our party in the eyes of their subordinates and officials of other institutions, and made it unthinkable for me, as a member of the Central Committee of that party, to occupy a responsible position and successfully to fulfil the difficult tasks it placed upon me. I therefore asked to be transferred to some ordinary post in a medical institution, since, as I had been mobilised, I could not refuse government service altogether.

That very morning I delivered this declaration to the member of the board. Like other high officials, he tried all means to persuade me to withdraw my declaration, and to convince me not to take the Cheka's slanders seriously. I, however, remained unmoved. The document went from office to office, and for two or three days I did not receive any response. Then I telephoned Dr Semashko, the People's Commissar of Health, and asked him what his decision would be. He started by trying to persuade me to withdraw the declaration, assuring me that there was no question of mistrusting me, and that he trusted me completely. I thanked him for that expression of confidence, but remarked that it was not a question of whether or not he personally trusted me, but that this official slander, not officially repudiated, gave any person or institution I had to deal with in an official capacity every right to mistrust me.

The 'honourable minister' evidently felt insulted by my ingratitude and by my impertinent underestimation of the 'highest' trust he had so graciously bestowed upon me. His tone betrayed his wounded pride: 'Fine, I will release you from your post, but will pass you over to the Committee for Struggle with Labour Desertion'.

That was so boorishly stupid that I replied: 'That is your business.'

'But think of the position you are putting your wife in.'

'Please leave it to me to worry about my family affairs,' I replied, and hung up the telephone.

The next day some well-wishers from the Moscow Military Medical Authority informed me that it had been decided to transfer me to work in the Urals. I did not want to believe this, but I was soon summoned and was officially informed that Semashko had decided to transfer me to Ekaterinburg, to the Urals Military Medical Authority, and that I had to depart within 24 hours.

To leave in 24 hours meant not only abandoning my party and domestic affairs to the whims of fate, but also completely disorganising the important official task the Bolshevik government had entrusted to me. The work was complicated, I had no assistant, it would be necessary to find a new person and introduce him to the job. This required time. For my replacement they seized upon the first young doctor who passed by, who was not at all suited to the work. The member of the board, along with all my other immediate superiors, asked me to start handing over to him, reckoning that they could get a stay of one week for this purpose. The Military Medical Authority agreed, in view of the request of the board member and in anticipation of Semashko's answer, not to insist that the order be carried out to the letter.

The news that I was to be transferred to Ekaterinburg quickly travelled round Moscow. It was clear to everybody that this transfer had not been dictated by the needs of the job, and that it was a form of masked exile. Many, even among the Bolsheviks I knew, did not want to believe that such savage reprisals were possible, and that something as important and painstakingly established as medical supplies could be disrupted in order to gain revenge. One Bolshevik had tears in her eyes when she talked to me about Semashko's unworthy behaviour. Our Central Committee protested against this reprisal, which was evidently intended to disorganise our party. Certain Bolsheviks also got involved, requesting that the exile be revoked and that I be left in Moscow, albeit in a different job. Nothing helped, and it soon became apparent why. The matter which Semashko had started was taken up by the Politburo of the Central Committee of the Russian Communist Party. The petty wounded pride of the People's Commissar for Health had become intertwined with the high state politics of the group of five who dictatorially ran Russia. They seized delightedly upon the chance to get back at me 'for the British delegation'. It is clear that this was the real reason for this reprisal, because only I was affected by it. Almost all members of our party who occupied more or less responsible positions in government institutions had, at the same time as me, sent to the Presidium of the All-Russia Central Executive Committee and distributed a collective declaration. In this declaration they protested against the slanderous official insinuations and said that they were not themselves resigning from their posts because they did not want completely to disorganise the republic's already chaotic economy, but stated that if the Bolsheviks did not sack them from their positions, then this would testify to the complete mendacity of their accusations and to their most repugnant hypocrisy. The Bolshevik government took this public slap in the face in silence …

All this time I was quietly occupied with handing over to my designated successor and preparing him for his new post. Four or five days passed. The board member did not get round (or maybe did not want) to discuss with Semashko any official postponement of my departure. Suddenly, on the 10th or 11th of June, I cannot remember exactly, around 3 o'clock in the afternoon the same well-wishers from the Military Medical Authority telephoned to inform me that the Authority had received a furious note from Semashko who, having discovered that I had not yet gone, gave the Authority a most severe reprimand and demanded that I be taken that very day under armed guard to the station and sent to Ekaterinburg. I was warned that within half an hour someone would arrive with all the necessary papers, would put me on the train and would not leave me until the train departed at 6 o'clock that evening. I exploded with rage at this news. I grabbed the receiver and telephoned Enukidze, the secretary of the All-Russia Central Executive Committee. Without mincing my words, I told him that I would never submit to this sort of savage wilfulness, and would ensure that the affair became a major scandal. Enukidze was confused, and tried to calm me down; he was clearly embarrassed by his own 'ministers'. He promised to sort everything out.

At the same time, a man in military uniform arrived with papers and a railway ticket. I explained the situation to him and asked him to wait for a while. And indeed, half an hour later the Military Medical Authority telephoned to say that they had received another telegram from Semashko, cancelling his note of that morning. The armed guard left, and the next day I 'freely' boarded a train to Ekaterinburg.

NOTES

1. The 'Christian communist Russell' referred to by Dan was almost certainly Bertrand Russell (who was neither a Christian nor a communist). Russell was not part of the delegation; he was in Russia at the same time on his own fact-finding mission. For details of the British group, see *British Labour Delegation to Russia, 1920: Report*, Labour Party and TUC, London 1920.
2. Here Dan expresses the commonplace view of Russian Marxists at that time that the backward aspects of Russian life reflected the 'Asiatic' side of their society's heritage.
3. The Berne Conference was convened in February 1919, under the chairmanship of the Swedish social-democrat Hjalmar Branting, as one of the first post-war attempts to refound the Socialist International.
4. The General Jewish Labour Bund within Russia became increasingly divided after 1917. One section aligned itself with the Bolsheviks and eventually merged with them, while the other section retained a social-democratic ideology.

2

In Ekaterinburg

My journey was very comfortable. One of the 'powers that be' had taken the trouble to secure me a place in an international-class sleeping car. My travelling companions were two 'specialists' being sent by the Supreme Council of the National Economy (VSNKh) to 'sort out' coal mines in the Urals and Siberia, and an actor from Chelyabinsk, who had been attending a conference of theatrical workers in Moscow.

The lapels of the actor's jacket were adorned with some small red badges bearing portraits of Marx, Lenin and Trotsky. He went on incessantly about his theatrical triumphs on the one hand, and about the delights of communism, which protected the arts and looked after actors, on the other. He was evidently one of those luckless characters who had encountered many misfortunes in his time travelling all over Russia, and had at last found refuge in the Chelyabinsk agitation and education apparatus and the local party committee. When he was neither boasting of his own successes nor praising Bolshevism, he talked just as enthusiastically about his wonderful house in Chelyabinsk, his fine cow and his splendid garden. He was, he declared, his own man everywhere, especially among the regional transport, i.e. railway, Cheka, and could offer protection and assistance to anybody who wished to take advantage of the relative cheapness of supplies in Chelyabinsk and settle there.

The specialists were people of a different type altogether. It was clear that neither of them supported the Bolshevik regime. However, one of them was restrained, while the other, a more nervous character who, judging by some of his words, was annoyed at having been sent away from either his wife or his girlfriend, argued from time to time with the actor. The arguments themselves were fairly pointless. The actor understood very little about communism, socialism, revolution, the workers' movement and suchlike things of which he spoke with such pathos, and he occasionally interspersed his elevated world-historic observations with moving remarks about the rations he was now receiving and the esteem he enjoyed 'even among the railway Cheka'. The specialist was also no expert in politics, and his 'criticism' was essentially a tedious and ill-tempered list of all the privations and grievances he had had to endure. However, these arguments were excellent for whiling away the time, and, having traded insults for an hour or two, the disputants opened their bags, pulled out some food and began to eat, calmly offering one another white rolls, butter and whatever other delicacies they happened to have.

At one stage the argument with the specialist was joined by a young man from the next compartment. He wore high boots, riding breeches, a service jacket, a helmet with a huge red star and other items of military paraphernalia and, as it later transpired, had some position with the railway Cheka. This fellow was politically completely illiterate, and the argument became ridiculously pointless – the discussants did not listen to each other, they talked about quite different things, and jumped from subject to subject. Finally, the young soldier despaired of ever defeating his opponent verbally and demanded, 'tell me, are you a Menshevik or an SR?'

'I am non-party.'

'Why didn't you say that long ago? I wouldn't have bothered talking to you! I know how to argue with Mensheviks and SRs – we've been taught that! But non-party people – you never know where to start with them!' And, with a wave of his hand, the gallant polemicist left our compartment.

At the stations there were crowds of peasant men, old women, and children selling bread, milk, butter, curd cheese, cooked meat and poultry. Occasionally some of them were seized by men bearing rifles and arrested, at which the other traders scattered. However, they soon reappeared, approaching the train again more cautiously with their goods hidden in their skirts, or they went around the back of the station building or across the road, beckoning their customers over. There were some depressing scenes: there was one ragged boy who had been caught with a few pieces of cooked mutton crying 'Let me go!', as some unbending militiaman, food requisitioning agent or some such dragged him off to jail, and there was the pale, confused railway worker who had been caught at the scene of the 'crime' with two cans of hempseed oil. In general, however, everything was well arranged: the bodies of armed men guarding the 'economic policy' of the time, and the traders who were violating that 'policy' had managed to reach a modus vivendi. And in some towns, such as Vyatka, the station itself housed a large bazaar with a fair selection of foodstuffs on sale.

It was very difficult to buy anything from the peasants or old women at the stations for money. They wanted manufactured goods, soap, salt, matches or tobacco in exchange for their foodstuffs. There was a particularly great demand for tobacco, or makhorka.[1] The men even occasionally accepted well-used old pipes in exchange for their goods, in order to clean them out and smoke the scrapings. To run ahead somewhat, when I made the return journey two and a half months later and, on the basis of my first trip, stocked up with makhorka to trade for food, I was sorely disappointed. Nobody wanted it any more; the men declared scornfully that they no longer needed tobacco as they had planted and harvested their own. Green stripes of flax plants were also very noticeable against the background of the now yellowed fields. This was yet another little illustration of how the countryside could respond to an 'economic policy' that did not suit it by reverting from a commodity economy to a natural one …

We arrived at Ekaterinburg between three and four o'clock in the afternoon. I was told to apply to the accommodation department of the local Soviet to secure a hotel room. I went there, and after an hour's wait, checks on my status as a mobilised worker, and several telephone conversations between the young lady on duty and various hotels, I was given a voucher for a room at the Palais Royale. All the hotels had imposing-sounding names, like Grand Hotel or Palais Royale, and their new official titles – First Soviet Hostel, Second Soviet Hostel and so on – were not used even in the Soviet institutions themselves. I went to my 'hotel', left my things at the reception and went with the receptionist to view my room. The stairways and corridors were filthy with spit and cigarette ends, which did not lead me to expect anything much good. However, when I saw my room I gasped with shock – there were five trestle-beds in a medium-sized room, covered with overcoats, travel bags and suchlike personal effects. All were evidently occupied by someone. In astonishment I asked my companion where I was supposed to sleep in that room. 'Here, for the moment,' he replied, pointing to a tiny, sagging couch with filthy stuffing, springs and bits of rope poking through the torn upholstery. He explained that there were still five delegates to a Red Army congress staying in the room, but that the congress would finish soon …

It was certainly impossible to remain there, particularly since anyone could see that the overcoats and beds were crawling with bugs and lice. What was I to do? I had known before I had left Moscow that our party organisation in Ekaterinburg had all been arrested at the time of the local Soviet elections, along with Comrade Dalin, a member of our Central Committee who had come to Ekaterinburg for two weeks on both official and party business. The haste with which I had left Moscow had meant that I had not been able to furnish myself with any other, non-party addresses where I might lodge. Moreover, I did not really want to put non-party people at risk by associating with a seditious character like me in a provincial town, where everything can be observed, and where the local Cheka reigns supreme. Where was I to go? I had firmly decided to spend the night on a chair in the reception, or even on the street, but on no account to sleep on the bed I had been 'officially' allocated.

Happily, I recalled that N. N. Sukhanov, who was then still one of our party comrades, was in Ekaterinburg. Trotsky, who at that time saw labour armies as the way to save the situation, had taken Sukhanov there in his train and had persuaded him to work in the local Sovtrudarm (the Labour Army Soviet of the Urals Okrug, of which more later) as a representative of the People's Commissariat of Agriculture. I set off to find him. I went to the Sovtrudarm, but work there had finished for the day, and I was directed to the Atamanovsky Rooms, lodgings that were considerably tidier than my miserable Palais Royale, but which were reserved exclusively for visiting notables and local ones without their own apartments. However, Sukhanov was not there: he had gone with his family to a dacha in Shartash, about seven kilometres from the town. Fortunately I found M., a friend of Sukhanov. This young man had travelled with him to Ekaterinburg and had also got stuck in the Sovtrudarm. He now cursed the turn of fate that had led him into this hole and into such a useless, pointless institution. M. was kind enough not only to tell me where to find Sukhanov, but also to take me there himself. There were several cabs operating in Ekaterinburg, so we took one, at a very steep price for those times, and travelled along a wonderful wooded road to the Shartash lake.

I arrived at Sukhanov's dacha towards seven o'clock in the evening. He rubbed his eyes in amazement to see me, and it was with difficulty that I explained to him how I had come to be in the Urals. His hospitable family immediately took me in, and for a time I was based at the dacha. It turned out that Dalin was here as well. He had recently been released, and had been applying to various institutions for the release of other arrested comrades. Fairly soon they were all indeed released, one after the other.

It took a few days for me to get started in my new 'service' and, with the greatest difficulty, to find a tiny room in town. The general housing 'crisis' was raging in Ekaterinburg as well, owing to the presence of a large number of troops and a mass of state institutions which took up a great deal of space. It was certainly not a result of any growth in the local population or of a boom in local industry and trade.

The gemstone works in the town had ceased operating altogether. The former mint was being used for some other branch of production and employed just a few workers. The massive Verkhne-Isetsk works was almost totally idle. It seemed that virtually the only enterprises operating were a tiny repair shop for medical instruments housed in the gemstone works, two workshops making rubber stamps, and a couple of tailor's shops. Everything, apart from the rubber-stamp makers and some tailors, had been 'nationalised' – right down to hairdressers and canteens. 'Free trade' took place at the bazaar, to which peasants brought various foodstuffs, and on the streets, where people crowded to buy and sell bread, pastries, lumps of sugar, matches, tobacco, and all kinds of new and – more often – second-hand junk: boots, shirts, tunics and so forth. The traders in these crowds were often soldiers, who were trying to sell sugar or makhorka from their rations in order to buy bread. While I was there the prices of everything rose incessantly, but at the same time as a pud[2] of flour was fetching 3 – 4000 rubles in Ekaterinburg, in Kurgan, an uezd[3] town in Ekaterinburg gubernia, it was selling for just 300 rubles. It was the same with butter and other foodstuffs. However, it was forbidden to bring food in, and there were food detachments on the roads to enforce this.

During the two-and-a-half months I was in Ekaterinburg, the bazaar and the street flea market were raided by the authorities about three times. The enormous square would suddenly be surrounded by troops, a hue and cry would break out, the peasants would quickly pack their goods onto their carts, and, whipping their horses, try to escape. The rest of the public, both traders and purchasers, would run off in panic. Those who were caught were sorted individually: those with the correct assortment of papers were released; those without were sent to the militia to have their identities confirmed. These raids invariably netted a mass of deserters from military and labour service. 'Rationed' foodstuffs were confiscated, and those on whom such goods were found – mainly women – were sent off for a few days to perform 'forced labour' as 'parasitic' elements. Incidentally, this constantly incensed the workers, whose wives were frequently brought, under one pretext or another, directly from the bazaar to work. Following these 'raids', the bazaar and flea-markets were quiet for two or three days, then everything gradually returned to normal, except the prices, which had suddenly shot upwards.

The town's native population had fallen sharply during the civil war years. Some had been killed, some had retreated with the whites, and others with the reds each time the town changed hands. Whenever I stopped people in the street to ask directions, I would get the same answer: 'I don't come from round here, I haven't been here long.' It was even difficult to locate government offices, including for the locals, because almost every street had been renamed, and the old nameplates had been taken down. Streets on the outskirts of town had been given the names of fallen heroes of world socialism such as Rosa Luxemburg and Karl Liebknecht, or of local civil war leaders: Leonid Vayner, the worker Roman Zagvozkin, the sailor Khokhryakov and so on. The two main streets, as was the custom, were named in honour of the still-living Lenin and Trotsky. Their names, along with that of Dzerzhinsky and others, also adorned clubs and suchlike places.

The abundance of the military and the comparative rarity of civilians gave the town the air of a military camp. Many of the best buildings right in the centre of town had been taken over for Red Army posts or other military institutions. From morning to night different divisions marched about the town singing soldiers' songs:

> For Soviet power
> We'll bravely face combat
> And will die as one
> In the struggle for that!

I would go to bed late at night and wake early in the morning, and that song could constantly be heard somewhere in the distance. Then on one occasion I beheld a curious sight: an enormous column of men was marching towards me, singing those very same Soviet-patriotic words. As the column approached, I realised that it consisted of 100 to 150 deserters from the Red Army being marched under armed guard, and that they were declaring their readiness to die 'for Soviet power' under orders from the commander. Officialdom could debase anything which had once expressed real and sincere, albeit naive, enthusiasm ...

In the very centre of town were the premises of the Cheka, or, rather of two Chekas: as a garrison town, Ekaterinburg had not only the usual Gubernia Cheka (Gubcheka), but also a Special Department of the Cheka. Although both organisations were headed by the same person – one Tunguskov, an unusually crude and cruel man – each had its own staff and premises. The Special Department was mainly concerned with the army and with rooting out the former officers of Kolchak's forces, while the Gubcheka dealt with the other citizens. The Gubcheka already occupied several buildings, but before I left Ekaterinburg I heard that it was asking to clear out and take over two or three neighbouring buildings, as it was getting short of space. Those who had been arrested by either Cheka were held in the basements. The window of the Gubcheka's basement opened onto the street, and in the summer, when the windows were open, one could look into the depths of that terrible place. There, in unbelievably cramped conditions, the prisoners sat, their faces pale and wracked with hunger, their bodies covered with all kinds of parasites. One of the local Communists I knew told me (and I repeat it for what it is worth) that executions took place in the courtyard of that building, under the prisoners' windows. He also stated that all members of the local Communist organisation were mobilised in turn to take part in these executions. I thought better of asking him whether his turn had come yet ...

While I was there the Cheka staged, as a propaganda and intimidation exercise, a public trial of some people accused of large-scale embezzlement. The trial was held in the municipal theatre, which could hold several hundred people. It passed judgement on some engineers, managers of warehouses and suchlike, and these unfortunates were sentenced to the firing squad. What sort of public attended this trial, and how it conducted itself, I cannot say. Enormous posters had been stuck up to advertise this spectacle, but I did not have the stomach to go and watch it ...

When I first arrived at Ekaterinburg, the town had been spruced up: there were colourful posters, and here and there hastily-erected triumphal arches rose from the streets. These had been made of wood covered with painted canvas. They had been left over from a recent visit by Trotsky, and when I left the town these decorations, now washed-out and tattered by rain and wind, were still in place. Two of the arches were especially bizarre. One of them – on Lenin Street – sported portraits on its four upper corners. On one side were Lenin and Trotsky and on the other the leaders of the 'International' – from the First, Karl Marx, and from the Third … Grigori Zinoviev. On the pediment between them was a pile of shot, rifles, machine guns and cannon muzzles. Poor old Marx! He was also made to suffer on the other arch, which had a picture of Red Army men climbing a cliff, on the top of which stood Karl Marx in a red shirt, wide Cossack trousers and high boots, carrying a banner inscribed 'Red Urals'. This arch had been erected on the exit from People's Vengeance Square, on the cliff above which stood the mansion of the merchant Ipat'ev, in which Nicholas II and his family had been killed, and which had since housed a Communist club.

Numerous monuments and statues had been put up around the town. There was a bust of Marx on a marble socle in People's Vengeance Square, and monuments to the Commune, the victims of the struggle against Kolchak, the *Urals Worker* newspaper and so forth. Most of these monuments had been carved by Er'zya, a noted sculptor of Mordvin peasant stock, who had been well known to the Russian émigré colony in Paris in 1910-12, and who had even won a prize in Rome. For all that, most of the sculptures which adorned Ekaterinburg were not a success. This was especially true of the monument to the victims of the struggle against Kolchak. This was an enormous globe of sheet iron, on which a naked female figure lay with her back turned to the small cemetery in which those who fell in that struggle were buried. More successful was a completely naked male figure gazing into the distance, which had been erected in front of the cathedral. But this work was spoilt by the fact that the socle it stood on, which had previously borne a bust of Catherine II, was far too small and quite unsuitable. In addition, the statue offended religious believers – a naked man in front of the cathedral, with his back to it to boot!

By the time I had arrived in Ekaterinburg, Er'zya was no longer there. He had been squeezed out by more 'left' artistic elements, who took upon themselves the decoration of the town. This decoration consisted, in the main, of massive, brightly coloured canvas posters plastered all over the walls of buildings and around the streets, screaming their slogans for various agitational purposes. There were some permanent posters, such as those which assured passers-by that 'the peasant will give the worker bread, and the worker will give the peasant goods'. Other posters lauded the Red Army, and depicted a soldier with his boot on a prostrate, bleeding, fat general wearing epaulettes and medals, and so on. There were also temporary displays – to mark the 'week of aid to the peasant', the construction of the Kazan'-Ekaterinburg railway and suchlike. All this was very unsophisticated, but it was colourful, and to an extent offset the miserable appearance of the town, in which almost 90 per cent of the inhabitants were dressed in dismal khaki. Most importantly, presumably, such work kept people fed and occupied.

But living in that town was totally boring. Our party work had been reduced to a minimum, at first by the arrest of the entire local committee, and then, once they had been let out of jail again, as a result of impossible police conditions and widespread worker apathy. There was not the slightest hint of freedom of the press, of speech, of assembly, or of trade unions. It was impossible to get two dozen people together without the local Cheka hearing about it straight away. Committee members and I were constantly followed – the spies watching me usually sat on the bench opposite my windows, and were sometimes stupid enough to question my neighbours, who then informed me of this. All these conditions meant that our organisation was only ever able to conduct any mass work on special occasions, such as elections to the soviets, and paid for this each time with the subsequent arrest of its members. The trade unions in no way resembled those of Europe or America. They occupied a spacious building – the former district court, which had been ostentatiously renamed 'Palace of Labour' – but in reality they were just drab, quiet offices. If workers ever set foot in there, it was almost always to be tried for 'labour desertion', 'shirking' and suchlike offences in a 'comradely disciplinary court', which would sentence them either to forced labour or to a more or less lengthy stretch in prison.

It was impossible to get hold of books anywhere. There were no libraries, the bookshops had nothing but bare shelves, and only sold anything at all to institutions with special orders. The local newspaper,

Urals Worker, was a pathetic, politically illiterate sheet. In this total absence of intellectual nourishment, even the Moscow papers *Pravda* and *Izvestiya*, which I was able to get regularly thanks to the high position occupied by Sukhanov, seemed to be a delicacy. As for those few books which I occasionally got from Moscow – what more can I say?

Contacts with Moscow were the only source of intellectual life. However, these contacts could not be established immediately. One had to wait for 'occasions', since it was impossible to rely on the post – even official correspondence was frequently lost. The secret behind these missing letters was explained to one of our comrades in jail by a girl who had worked in the Cheka 'black office'. Her boyfriend had wanted his relations in Omsk to send him some boots. He knew that letters were held up in the black office prior to despatch, and frequently never left there at all, so he gave his letter directly to this girl to send. The girl could not help telling her friends about this, and as a result both she and her boyfriend ended up in jail. According to this girl, the mail was intercepted in the following way. All incoming and outgoing letters were taken from the post office to this Cheka black office, and then distributed in packs of several hundred among the staff there, most of whom were very green youngsters. The instructions to the staff were to remove from the packs: 1) all envelopes addressed in very neat handwriting (assumed to be 'white guard' correspondence); 2) all envelopes written in very poor handwriting (assumed to be correspondence between Red Army men and their home villages); and lastly, 3) a certain proportion of other envelopes on the off-chance – in addition, of course, to letters to addresses for which examination was mandatory. As for the intercepted letters with 'seditious' content, the staff were specially instructed to present a written report to their superiors, who would then finally decide which letters to retain, which ones to copy, which ones merited initiating 'proceedings', and so on. In order to reduce the amount of work they had to do, the youngsters in the office simply destroyed a certain proportion of the letters, since nobody had counted them. In their boundless provincial naiveté they then stamped the intercepted envelopes with an oval stamp alongside the normal round postmark. Indeed, looking through the letters I received, the envelopes always bore that oval stamp, dated two or three days after the date on the ordinary postmark.

The highest organ of power in Ekaterinburg, formally speaking, was the Sovtrudarm, the Soviet of the Labour Army. After the army group deployed in the Urals (the Third Army, if I am not mistaken) was put onto a 'labour' footing, the intention had been to construct the entire administration of the Urals kray on that basis.[4] At least, those were Trotsky's plans, who imagined that in his 'labour armies' he had discovered a new and most effective way to 'save Soviet Russia'. The conversion of armies into 'labour' armies was carried out with great pomp; the newspapers were full of telegrams of greetings, solemn resolutions, laudatory leaders and even a daily list of the works these armies were undertaking. Alas, this was just another scheme which burst like a soap bubble. Who ever recalls or mentions labour armies today, even though they still exist, at least on paper? When our party criticised this 'labour-army utopia', and predicted that nothing would come of this venture except another monstrous waste of our national resources and more suffering, Bolshevik papers used this criticism as yet another example of our 'social treachery' and 'betrayal'. However, no number of inflated accounts by bureaucrats wishing to please their bosses by exaggerating short-term successes could change the sad fact that from the very outset the productivity of the labour armies was minimal, while the costs of maintaining them were enormous. Peasants from distant gubernias, dragooned into working in labour armies in the Urals, were quite unable to understand why now, when the war with Kolchak was over, they had to chop wood, cut hay and so on, far from home, under military command, but they could not do the same things freely at home. Consequently, they deserted en masse, while the local peasants, infuriated at these strangers coming in and lording it over them, set fire to the piles of wood and haystacks built by the labour armies. The entire plan was an unworkable bureaucratic fantasy.

This was already evident by the time I first arrived in Ekaterinburg, and it was openly spoken about inside the Sovtrudarm. But Communists needed to keep the faith, and therefore publicly and in the press 'everything was going fine', and the noisy campaign continued. The attempt to turn the Sovtrudarm into something like a Urals oblast' government also continued. However, since the whole edifice was built on rotten foundations, not only did the Sovtrudarm not become an organ of power, it withered away day by day. The real power in the oblast' was concentrated in the hands of the Oblast' Bureau of the Central Committee of the Russian Communist Party, and on a local level, in the hands of the local CP committee.

The Sovtrudarm was made up of representatives of the different commissariats, nominated from the centre. N. Sukhanov had been a member, as the representative of the Commissariat of Agriculture. However, not long before I arrived, our party committee was arrested and Sukhanov's premises had been searched. He, a member of the 'highest government institution', had been searched by the Cheka which was ostensibly subordinate to that institution. He therefore sent a declaration to Trotsky announcing his resignation from the Sovtrudarm, and stating that he would only be fulfilling his duties as a representative of the Commissariat of Agriculture in the expectation that there would be some delay in sending his replacement.

The Sovtrudarm was housed in a very large building, with a portrait of Lenin above the porch. This icon was illuminated day and night by an electric light. I had no close contact with other members of the Sovtrudarm, or with any of the local communists or bureaucrats. I was too well known as a 'seditious' figure in this town, where everything was visible, for any person in an official position to risk a closer acquaintance with me. And I spent too little time in Ekaterinburg to form any clear picture of the local ruling group from a distance.

It is time, however, to write about my 'work service'. Once I had reported to the Military Medical Administration, I learnt that Semashko had sent a telegram instructing that I be kept in Ekaterinburg itself. In the circumstances, this was an unexpected pleasure. The head of the administration was a Communist, Dr A., a young man who was unusually hard-working and ascetic, but dry and unbelievably formal. He beavered away at his 'business' from morning to late at night, but on closer examination this 'business' was just a mass of futile paperwork, to run a cumbersome bureaucratic machine which, alas, produced no tangible results at all. This was because everything was in short supply: there were no medicines or surgical instruments; there was not enough food, bedding or clothing for the sick; there were no materials for repairing hospital buildings; and so on and so forth. The less of these confounded 'materials' was to be had, the more unmanageable the volume of 'correspondence' about these materials became. Thus A. had an ever-increasing amount of 'business' with which to occupy himself, as he conscientiously observed every form, schedule, allocation and time-limit. A.'s assistant was Dr G., a doctor of the old school who knew all the orders, circulars, instructions and so on ad nauseam. The tedium of this work had worn him down, but he was afraid to show any signs of independence in front of all the communists who were watching him like hawks.

The question immediately arose of what to do with me. I refused to work as a doctor, as I had not practised at all for many years. Dr A., who, to be fair to him, was trying to find me the most congenial position possible, suggested that I worked in the health education department, lecturing to Red Army men. That did not appeal to me very much, as I realised that it would be difficult to talk about health issues in present-day Russia without dealing with general economic and social conditions, which could have led to ... After I had talked to A.'s political assistant, I categorically refused that work. As a Communist, A. was himself a political commissar (politkom), but for that area of his work he had to have an assistant (pompolitkom), responsible for political surveillance of all the office and medical staff working for the Administration. This assistant himself had an assistant, whom I dubbed in jest 'pompompolitkom'. Both of them were pharmacy students. After talking to one of these young pharmacists, who had tactfully instructed me in what 'spirit' I should give the lectures, I thought it wise to refuse point blank to work in 'health education'.

Then they made me the assistant to the chief of the medical department. The chief, my immediate boss, was Dr L., a young man of about 28. He was a Communist, but his communism was of a rather peculiar type. I learnt from him that he was a 'wartime' doctor, that is, that his training had been accelerated. He had been sent straight from university to the front. After the revolution he had intensely disliked 'all these army committees', as he put it, which poked their noses into everything and undermined subordination and discipline. The Bolsheviks, on the other hand, he liked for having dispersed 'all these committees', put a stop to 'democracy' and reintroduced firm discipline. But in his regiment discipline and respect for rank had always been preserved. And L. told me some fantastic story about how, after October 1917, his regiment had gone over to the Bolshevik side and decided to abandon the front, but had done so in an 'organised' and 'disciplined' fashion. They had acted under the command of their officers, who, in spite of the Bolshevik decrees, had retained their shoulder-straps. They had seized entire trains and moved around Russia, here and there forcing their way through, fighting skirmishes with other groups of soldiers on the move who also called themselves

Bolsheviks, and seizing each other's wagons and engines. Who was fighting whom, L. himself was not quite sure, but eventually the regiment ended up in its home area, and all its members gradually made their ways home.

Not only had L. never been involved in the workers' or even the revolutionary movement, he was not even interested in it. With a touching naiveté he would sometimes cautiously ask me, 'Who was Jaurès then?', 'What was Bebel famous for?' and so on. He had become a Communist solely because it was expedient from a career and a personal point of view, and because he liked the Bolsheviks' strictness and lack of 'slobbering humanism'. However, on one occasion he tried to explain the 'ideological' basis of his communism: when he had lived alone as a bachelor, he had not been well fed, but now he had formed a 'commune' with some other comrades it was all very comfortable, with hot meals and so forth.

He had no idea who I was or what Mensheviks in general were – he had just heard vaguely that we were 'traitors'. Overall, apart from his political ignorance, what struck me about this product of the era of Third-Duma reaction and war was his extreme unintelligence overall, his complete lack of intellectual interests. And this was a doctor, and moreover, the son of a professor!

On everyday matters L. was a good-natured and obliging lad. We 'worked' together without much friction. But what 'work' it was! We would send out innumerable forms and questionnaires to all medical institutions, which, once completed, would come swarming back to us. They would be bound together, and would then either get lost without trace in office cupboards, or be assessed, converted into tables and sent on to the Chief Military Medical Administration. There they would either be quietly bound into dossiers, or be used as the basis for questionnaires for us to complete or send on to our subsidiary institutions and so on. It was a vicious bureaucratic circle which did not have the slightest purchase on reality. Now and again this monotonous 'work' would be interspersed with the production of 'drafts' on orders from above, such as draft orders from the Military Medical Administration, or a draft plan for a 'network of public baths' and suchlike. Commissions would meet, an ideal plan for the construction of a network of baths and laundries of an ideal type would be drawn up, costed and so forth in the full knowledge that there was not the slightest chance that the necessary buildings could be constructed, equipped, or even supplied with soap and linen. But the bureaucratic machine ground on, there was not enough time to get things done, compulsory overtime was decreed, 'matters were in hand', and the leadership was happy.

I must admit that I could not acquire a taste for all this whistling in the wind. The task of the head of department and of myself, as his assistant, was to 'lead' this paper chase and to write the 'draft plans' mentioned above. As a 'writer', who was supposed to be good with a pen (a highly-prized skill in Soviet institutions), it fell to me in particular to compose these drafts. But however I tried to overcome the unbearable boredom of all this organised idleness, I could not spend more than one hour a day on all the 'tasks' I was given, however conscientiously I performed them. They could have been done by any village scribe. I did not have the slightest desire to waste my energy on 'initiatives', which would have meant creating new heaps of purely paper 'work'. Had I had enough books and newspapers, I could have usefully spent my time at work reading. But as there was very little reading material available, I had no choice but to try to start work as late as possible and leave as early as possible. But despite all this my boss was amazed at how quickly I had 'got to grips' with such difficult and important paper-shuffling.

However, my 'skiving' did not pass unnoticed. The 'political department', in the person of the above-mentioned pompompolitkom, was paying close attention to 'labour discipline' – that is, that everybody arrived at work and left it exactly at the appointed hour. For this purpose every day there was a sheet of paper which every employee had to sign in person, and five minutes after the start of work the sheet would be removed and taken to the bosses. Those employees who really wanted to please their superiors even turned up early. These people also volunteered to go after work on Saturdays to take part in the *subbotniki* organised by the communist authorities, that is, they would go somewhere outside the town or to the station to load logs or unload wagons. Those who did not attend the *subbotniki*, including me, were looked upon askance by the pompompolitkom.[5]

This pompom, a certain M., was a young man with the features and intellectual capacities of a horse. When I had first arrived, he had cheerfully said to me 'If you would give up your Menshevism, Comrade Dan, and join our party group, you could lecture to us!', and had been very upset when I declined this honour. M. assiduously monitored the 'mood', had his informers and poked his nose into everything. It was he who decided to take radical measures to sort out 'labour discipline'. One day, as I arrived at work, very late as usual, I saw a huge placard on the wall, divided into two halves. On one side was written in red ink 'Glory to honest workers!', with a list of the surnames of the most assiduous bureaucrats underneath. On the other side, in black letters, was the heading 'Shame on idlers and slackers!', and my surname was the first on the list. At the bottom of this placard was M.'s signature. I was genuinely highly amused to be labelled a 'slacker' in my forty-ninth year! Naturally, I did not change my habits in the slightest, M. did not speak to me about anything, but the red and black charts stayed up right up to the time I left, covering me in 'shame'.

At the beginning of August, the military authorities decreed that on a certain day all employees of military institutions, apart from invalids with a doctor's certificate, should take part in cutting firewood. Everyone was given a target of one cubic sazhen' (about 10 cubic metres).[6] This procurement was to take place on Saturdays after lunch and on Sundays, about 10 or 12 kilometres from the town.

On the first designated Saturday, the square in front of Ekaterinburg II station filled from all sides with detachments from different institutions. In all about 3000 people gathered. On their backs they had knapsacks with supplies of food. One echelon after another embarked on the goods trains which had been supplied for the purpose. Our turn came, and we got on the train and left. When we disembarked in the middle of the woods, we lined up and marched about two kilometres. The clearing, full of men and women, old and young in picturesque disorder, resembled a Gipsy camp. Bonfires smoked, kettles whistled, while horses harnessed to wagons neighed. On the edge of the wood a military orchestra played. It was all very lively and even cheerful. It got worse when the work started.

We were summoned to work according to our institution, and were divided into groups of six. Each group was allocated a number of axes and one saw. The foresters had set aside a patch of land for each group on which we were supposed to build a one-sazhen' cube of firewood. These patches were all next to each other. We had to cut down a tree so that it fell in a certain direction, chop off the branches, saw it up, put the firewood into the correct cube and pile up the branches. This was extremely hard work for those who were not used to it, and here were not only men who had never even held an axe, but hundreds of women and girls – typists, office workers and so on. There were very few gloves available, and within an hour people's hands began to be covered with scratches and blisters. We had to spend the night out there in the forest, in order to continue work on Sunday, and the nights were already getting cold. There were also a number of accidents – one girl was killed by a tree that fell the wrong way, another worker broke his thigh, there were masses of more minor injuries – and a dressing station had to be set up to deal with them.

Some of my party comrades came to help me, as I had my own workgroup, and we worked together to try to fulfil my allocation. When our turn came around, it was already seven o'clock, and we started work in the twilight. Fortunately, among my comrades were people who had been compelled by harsh Soviet conditions to cut wood before this for their families, so they had already had some experience. We worked until four in the morning with only brief tea breaks. Then we put out the fire, slept around it for about two hours, then worked again until midday. In that time we had managed to put half a cube together. Having decided to put off the second half for another Saturday, we obtained a chit from the forester for the amount of work we had done, and set off back home on foot to Ekaterinburg.

However, we never had to complete that cube of firewood, because my period of vegetation in Ekaterinburg was about to be cut short unexpectedly.

I knew that our Central Committee had called a party conference for 20 August. The conference had been called perfectly legally, and had even been announced in the Soviet papers. Formally, our party existed and operated quite legally. We had no press, our local organisations were constantly being rounded up by the Cheka, and searches and arrests of members never ceased. But at that time in Moscow the Central Committee had official premises with a club in which members of the Moscow organisation would meet, sometimes as many as 200 or more people. From time to time, the Cheka would raid the premises and seal it, seizing papers and arresting those present. But our party did not abandon its positions. Whenever it was necessary and feasible, we would print leaflets and proclamations of the Central Committee with the help of the printworkers, ignoring all the Bolshevik prohibitions. We would speak on behalf of our party at congresses, meetings and rallies, and would use all possible methods to defend our right to work openly. And, at least in the centre, in Moscow, the Cheka was not in a position to deal with us once and for all. A significant proportion of the Bolsheviks themselves, particularly the working-class Bolsheviks, realised deep down that to persecute our party was to attack the most conscious, revolutionary-minded workers, and that such persecutions were an indelible stain on the record of the Communist Party, which claimed to be a workers' party. Consequently, those who were arrested tended to be released within two or three months, as happened in March-June 1919, when I and other comrades were first arrested by the Bolsheviks. Premises would be unsealed again, and the life of the organisation got underway again. I should say that in Moscow there had never been any major swoops on members of our party without some anonymous well-wishers telephoning me or Comrade Martov to warn us. This was despite the fact that the Cheka had threatened more than once to 'catch and shoot these scoundrels', whose telephone conversations with us were no secret – our lines were constantly tapped, conversations were recorded and sent to the Cheka, who did not flinch from producing these transcripts in the course of interrogations. But we were in the habit of expressing ourselves freely over the telephone, as if nobody else was listening – without mentioning, of course, those names, addresses and special conspiratorial details we did not wish the Cheka to know ...

Anyway, the August conference was organised quite openly, and in corresponding with Moscow we arranged that the Central Committee would take measures to try to get me the opportunity to take part. One day, shortly after our woodcutting weekend, Sukhanov brought me a telegram from Martov to say that I had got permission to travel to Moscow for the conference and that a telegram to that effect had been sent to my bosses. Only a few days remained before the conference, and the journey would take three days. Nothing had been said to me at work about any telegrams having been received, and I began to fear that I would be late. I decided to sort it out.

The administration head, Dr A., was in Moscow at the time. The administrative side of his work was being carried out by Dr G., and the political side by the notorious pompom M. When I enquired about the telegram, both of them told me that nothing had been received. Two more days passed, and then one of the employees informed me that the telegram had indeed arrived, but that M. had sent some query about it to Moscow by post. This put me in a difficult position: to say that I knew about the telegram would cause problems for my informant, and to keep quiet would mean that I would certainly be too late. A reply to an enquiry by post would take at least eight to ten days, and the conference was scheduled to open in three to four days.

I had to resort to cunning. I went to see M., and said that I had heard in the Sovtrudarm that they had been told of the decision of the Moscow authorities to call me to Moscow, that instructions had been sent to the Military Medical Administration, and that members of the Sovtrudarm were surprised that this instruction had not been carried out. This frightened M., who admitted to me that there had been a telegram from Semashko authorising me to take an immediate two-week break to go to Moscow. However, since in wartime (the war with Poland was then in progress) all leave for military employees was forbidden, he had sent a written enquiry to Moscow, asking how the telegram should be understood, and could do nothing until he received a reply. When I demanded that instead of 'leave' he authorise a 'business trip', he refused.

Sukhanov and I then ran to find M-v., a Communist and former Moscow worker, who at that time was acting chairman of the Sovtrudarm. It was already 3.30, so there was just half an hour until the end of the working day. M-v., to whom we told the whole story and explained why my departure could not be postponed, was annoyed at the pompom's obvious sabotage. He immediately sent a note to the district military commander, who sent the following instructions to the Military Medical Administration which arrived at five to four: 1) to authorise this very day my trip to Moscow 'on a matter known to the Sovnarkom'; and 2) to place M. under arrest for seven days for obvious red tape and non-compliance with the instructions of the leadership.

What the unfortunate pompom thought about this unexpected outcome to his attempt to get at the 'subversive' I do not know, but at seven o'clock that evening I received all the necessary papers. I was only able to leave, however, the following evening, as there was no room on the train that day.

On my arrival in Moscow I learnt that the pompom's red tape had done me a favour. Before the first session of the conference had even opened, the delegates who had assembled on the premises of our party club had been arrested. The only ones who had slipped through the net were those who had arrived late or had been warned by members of our Youth League, who had immediately mounted pickets on all the surrounding street corners, and had also had two or three people fall victim to the Cheka. It is true that within three or four weeks all the arrestees were released, but, had I not been late thanks to the efforts of the pompom, there would have been yet another page in my prison biography ...

What all these contradictory antics by the Bolsheviks meant, I still have no idea. Was it a conscious provocation, particularly in relation to me, who had been granted the possibility of travelling to a 'conference' by decision of the Central Committee of the Communist Party itself? Or did the Cheka once again want to show that it was in charge, and did not take orders from anyone? I repeat, I do not know. But the conference did not take place. The life of the Moscow organisation was paralysed for a few weeks. Yet at that very time Martov got permission to travel abroad, and our Central Committee hastened to send him to take part in the congress of the German USPD [Independent Social-Democratic Party of Germany] in Halle,[7] at which the question of its attitude to communism and affiliation to the Third International was to be decided ...

NOTES

1. Makhorka (*nicotiana rustica*) was widely used in lower-grade smoking products in Russia at this time. Its nicotine content is considerably higher than that of common tobacco (*nicotiana tabacum*).
2. A pud was a pre-metrication measure of weight used in Russia, equivalent to 16.38 kg or 36.11 lb.
3. A Russian province (gubernia) would typically be subdivided into between three and seven uezds. The 'uezd town' was the centre of administration in each uezd, and typically gave the uezd its name.
4. A kray was typically a large region of the Russian empire located at or near the borderlands.
5. *Subbotniki* were days of organised, ostensibly voluntary, socially-useful work. They were typically, but not invariably, on Saturdays (hence the name, from the Russian *subbota*).
6. An old Russian measure of length, the sazhen' was standardised in the mid-nineteenth century at 2.16 metres.

7. The Halle congress of the USPD, in October 1920, had to decide whether to affiliate to the Communist International or not. The debate was addressed by Grigoriy Zinoviev for the Bolsheviks and Martov for the Mensheviks. In the event, the pro-communist section broke away to join the Spartakusbund in forming the United Communist Party of Germany. The texts of the speeches are in Ben Lewis and Lars T. Lih, *Zinoviev and Martov: Head to Head in Halle* (2011).

3

To the Front!

I spent about three weeks in Moscow. There was talk of returning me there for good, and this was requested by my former superiors at the Commissariat of Health. Our Central Committee also demanded it. Nothing helped. Semashko granted me an audience, at which he expressed his great offence at the way I had rejected his concern for the welfare of my family. He declared that he could not allow me to remain in Moscow, and even assured me that this was for my own good, hinting that I would be subject to continual arrest by the Cheka. However, he did agree not to send me back to the Urals, and allowed me to choose to continue my service anywhere except Moscow.

The choice, however, was not great. I could not go to any of the large cities in the South – Kiev, Khar'kov or Rostov-on-Don – because the distance from Moscow would make it very difficult for me to stay in to touch with our Central Committee. Any of the Central Russian cities would have been no better than Ekaterinburg in any respect: the same enforced idleness, the same dead atmosphere, and the same ever-worsening arbitrariness of petty provincial dictators …

I thought for a bit, and decided to request a transfer to the Russo-Polish front. At least there I would get a new environment and some new impressions, which would do something to enliven the miserable greyness of provincial life. I even wanted to take a look at the Red Army. I realised, of course, that the Bolshevik atmosphere of terror, spying and informing would prevent me from having very close contact with Red Army men and finding out what they really felt about things; that I would have to limit myself to the role of a 'passive observer', but still …

There were no objections from Semashko, and, once all the necessary formalities had been completed, I travelled to Minsk, where the headquarters of the front was then located. In my pocket I had a letter from the head of the Chief Military Medical Administration to the head of the Military Medical Administration of the Western Front, requesting that I be given some administrative post. I was again lucky with my travelling arrangements. Through people I knew I got a place in one of the 'private' carriages which various institutions had in large number. It was a fourth-class carriage, but it was clean. It had a little stove, on which the conductors boiled water and even prepared meals. There were only twelve of us on it, and we travelled very comfortably.

I arrived in Minsk towards the end of September. Following its rout near Warsaw, the Red Army had retreated a long way, and from my first day there I heard talk that Minsk might soon be evacuated.

In its external appearance Minsk was very different from Ekaterinburg. However strange it might seem at first, despite its proximity to the front and the abundance of military institutions, Minsk had much less of a 'military' appearance, and was not a uniform khaki colour. It gave the impression of having a stable, settled population, which had been living here yesterday, was living here today and would still be living here tomorrow without being swallowed up by the bureaucratic-military tidal wave. The streets were lively. Many shops were open – and this was another strange thing: at a time when clothing, footwear and hardware stores had already been closed up and 'nationalised', food shops remained open and were trading freely. Everywhere else in Soviet Russia the food shops had been the first victims of 'communism'. Presumably the closeness to the front and a desire not to annoy the Red Army men played some role in this 'connivance'. And the range of goods available in these shops was amazing for any Soviet citizen from the rest of Russia: butter, sausage, meat, white bread and rolls, sugar, pastries and even Swiss chocolate! It was all very expensive, but buyers could be found for everything. Red Army men were prominent among them. Many of them seemed to have a great deal of money – from where, I have no idea. I was told that many Red Army men were receiving a mass of money from the countryside, where whole piles of Soviet banknotes had accumulated. The exchange rate for these banknotes fluctuated wildly. At that time in Minsk the real unit of currency was the 'tsarist' ruble. But the currency exchange, although illegal, somehow managed to function quite regularly, and every day at midday the rate of the 'tsarist' ruble was known precisely, and appropriate adjustments were made to the prices of goods.

It was very difficult to get a flat, or even a room, in Minsk. Everywhere had been taken up by frontline institutions and their innumerable staff. Moreover, significant parts of the suburbs of Minsk, along with the factories, had been destroyed. I was told that they had been deliberately torched during the retreat of the Poles, who had hampered attempts to put the fires out. However, I was lucky in this respect, thanks to the recommendations I had brought with me from Moscow and the assistance of my party comrades: the very next day after my arrival I had found a magnificent room.

It turned out that there were several of my comrades in Minsk. There were, on the one hand, natives of Minsk, mainly from the local groups of the social-democratic Jewish Bund, and on the other hand, social democrats from Smolensk, who had been mobilised by their party for the war with Poland and were working in various frontline institutions.

The local Menshevik organisation was in a fairly poor shape. Many of the Jewish workers, the main contingent in the local proletariat, had been won over en masse to communism. As I was able to tell from my observations and conversations, there were sufficient objective reasons for this. The position of people working at home or as petty handicraftsmen – like the majority of Jewish workers – had not deteriorated during the first phase of the Bolshevik regime. It may even have improved somewhat. It would be difficult to talk of deterioration in a situation where the standard of existence was on such a low level, where sweated labour predominated, and where technical and economic backwardness, combined with a lack of national rights, weighed down so heavily on the heads of the Jewish proletariat. Bolshevism emancipated the slave of cottage industry and handicrafts, turning him into a worker, working directly for the state. It also freed him from national humiliation and directly raised his social position. Lively, intelligent Jewish workers, with a long history of urban culture behind them, now had access to all kinds of administrative posts. Bolshevism had not yet had time to display all its negative facets in Belorussia. Its detrimental effect on the economy expressed itself in the incessant price rises, but at the same time large amounts of money were pouring into the community through the army. The bourgeoisie, who had had their enterprises confiscated, and the peasants, who had suffered requisitioning of foodstuffs and livestock, were of course already groaning under the weight of communist policies, and it was felt too by the few workers in heavy industry, which had come to an almost complete standstill. But for the mass of Jewish handicraft workers the roses of Bolshevism were more obvious than the thorns. It is not surprising that Bolshevism still enjoyed broad sympathy among those masses, and that when the Bund split the great majority of organised workers went with its communist part.

To be sure, some signs of a morning-after headache were already apparent. A prominent figure in the communist Bund told me with bitterness how the communist Jewish battalion, mobilised by their party and comprised of the flower of the organised Jewish proletariat, was almost annihilated in its first battle. He believed that this massacre was partly the result of 'politics', which had given the military command the idea of entrusting this inexperienced force, which had never before come under fire, with a task which was clearly beyond its capabilities, thereby condemning it to destruction. Members of the communist Bund (Vaynshteyn, E. Frumkina) had joined the Belorussian government. This did not restrain the official press from persecuting the communist Bund in exactly the same way that the papers of Soviet Russia were persecuting the social democrats, for wishing to retain a separate organisation, thereby revealing their bourgeois and treacherous nature. Every day the papers carried letters from people who had 'matured', had left the ranks of the Bund and declared their adherence to the Bolshevik party. The Bundists felt that the ground was being cut away from under them, and that it would not be long before their organisation was destroyed. As we know, that happened soon enough. On a decision of the Comintern the Bund was dissolved, and its members joined the Russian Communist Party. And, a little while later still, during one of the party 'purges', many of the Bundists were excluded from the RKP as 'former Mensheviks'. Others were removed from the places where many years of work linked them to the local proletariat. Vaynshteyn, for example, one of the oldest and most experienced Bund activists, is now (1922) the chairman of the Executive Committee ... of the Bashkir Republic.

The Smolensk comrades (about ten of them) were working, as I have already said, in frontline institutions, often in highly responsible capacities. The bosses rated their work highly, but their own mood was depressed. The Smolensk organisation, like all our party, had mobilised its members readily when Poland had started the war with Russia, with clearly aggressive intentions and the evident encouragement of the Entente imperialists. But, when the Bolsheviks had used their initial military successes in order, in their turn, to go onto the offensive, when the assault on Warsaw had been declared and a 'revolutionary committee' was created and brought from Moscow in order to 'Sovietise' Poland, when the Bolshevik press started talking about the Rhine as the place where the final and decisive battle with international capitalism was to be fought, when, in a word, the aim evidently became 'to bring communism to the peoples of the West' on the bayonets of the Red Army – then, of course, the attitude of our party members changed significantly. We had not the slightest desire to support *this sort of* 'foreign policy' or *this sort of* war, as we openly declared in a CC resolution.

The mobilised members of the Smolensk Menshevik organisation shared the general attitude of the party, and as soon as I had arrived in Minsk some of them were concerned with the question of whether, in view of the changed circumstances, the party should demobilise its members. On thorough consideration we answered that question in the negative: the assault on Warsaw had been pushed back, the Red Army was in continual retreat and, from another quarter, the south, the gentry and generals' reaction was advancing again in the shape of Wrangel. Under such circumstances demobilisation would have been unacceptable from our party's point of view.

Personally, I thought at the time, and still do, that the defeat of the Bolsheviks near Warsaw was something much more significant than a mere military failure. It seemed to me that this defeat showed beyond all doubt that the idea that the Red Army, essentially a *peasant* army, could be used as a means of implanting communism in socially and economically more advanced countries was an illusion. That army was, is and will remain invincible when it is a question of defence, of protecting the peasants' revolutionary gains against encroachments from domestic reaction or foreign imperialism. To defend the land he has seized against the possible return of the landlord, the peasant Red Army man will fight with the greatest heroism and the greatest enthusiasm. He will advance bare-handed against cannons, tanks, and his revolutionary ardour will infect and disorganise even the most splendid and disciplined troops, as we saw with the Germans, the British and the French in equal measure. A Red Army man can just about be used in wars of a 'colonial' type, where he is coming up against an 'alien' population with a quite different, pre-capitalist culture, where strong resistance is not likely, and easy and rich pickings beckon. Khiva, Bukhara and to an extent Georgia provide examples of this. But the idea of Bolshevik communism is so alien and even hostile to the mindset of the peasant Red Army man, that he can neither be infected by it himself, nor can he infect others with it. He cannot be attracted by the idea of war to convert capitalist society into communist society, and this is the limit of the Red Army's potential for the Bolsheviks. Looking at the question more broadly, this is also the limit of the potential of the Russian revolution as a whole. It can provide a stimulus to world social and political processes only as a 'peasant' revolution, albeit one which is strongly influenced in its course by proletarian ideology and politics, but not as a directly socialist revolution.

The assault on Warsaw should have sufficed to demonstrate that even to the blindest person. An army which had just thrashed the Poles wherever they tried to advance into Russia began to experience defeat after defeat the moment it was set a quite different task – that of making Poland 'red' with a view to then 'communising' Germany etc. The Polish population, peasants, petty bourgeois, and also workers, are people of a higher cultural level. They were not at all ideologically susceptible to the elemental backwardness of their assailants. They left their homes en masse as the Red Army advanced and retreated together with the Polish troops. But not only did the Polish armies fail to disintegrate under the influence of the Red Army men, the Red Army itself began to disintegrate, as it lost interest and faith in the usefulness of the cause for which it was fighting. This process of disintegration was assisted, of course, by the poor organisation of material supplies – another expression of the fact that the economic base of a backward and exhausted country was quite unsuited to the grandiose task set it by the Bolsheviks – the social transformation of the entire world.

As result, the further the Red Army advanced on Warsaw, the more it became separated from its supply trains. Although there was a special supply organ for the front (*Oprodkomzap*), in fact the army lived entirely by requisitioning from the local population. This caused massive resentment and annoyance, and the Red Army's ranks increasingly melted away as soldiers began to desert. Desertion reached colossal proportions. A little later, in Smolensk, I heard a Red Army escort in conversation with some of his comrades who had been arrested in Mogilev and were being escorted to a gathering point. He joked that of the 'three-million-strong Red Army' one million were deserters, another million were in jail, and the third million were catching the deserters and bringing them back. Despite all the threats of severe punishments, interspersed with 'deserters' weeks', where those who returned voluntarily were promised a complete pardon, desertion from the ranks did not stop, and only during those 'weeks' did the deserters return, in order to get a change of uniform before disappearing again.

The Warsaw campaign demonstrated beyond all doubt that the Red Army could not fight an offensive 'communist' war, and in that respect represented a turning point in the Bolsheviks' foreign policy. Indeed, the cost to Russia of this unsuccessful attempt was the Treaty of Riga! But almost immediately thereafter this same Red Army, which had proved helpless when it was attacking Poland, displayed phenomenal courage and invincibility in the war against Wrangel, that reactionary remnant of tsarism and the nobility! What can be clearer than this historical example? And what can show more strikingly that the real victor in all the civil wars of the Bolshevik period has been the Russian peasant, and him alone?

Let us, however, return to our story.

I reported to the Military Medical Administration. The person in charge turned out to be a former Bundist turned Bolshevik, Dr L., a fairly limited individual. So far as I could tell, he was quite unequal to the task that had been entrusted to him – to run wartime medical services for the entire front – especially given the unimaginable chaos in transport and supplies. He desperately tried to observe 'discipline' and defer to rank, and he would latch on to petty details, but he could not grasp the overall picture. Moreover, as I had cause to discover in the course of my work, he was unable to look his superiors in the eye and tell them the whole truth. I have always been strangely struck by the way that people can degenerate so quickly into the sort of bureaucrats who report that 'everything is fine'. Just the previous day they had been comrades in the underground struggle, and seemed very far from any kind of bureaucratic style. It is clearly something running in the veins of the people of Russia …

L. received me in a very friendly fashion and, having learned that I wanted to stay in Minsk, gave me a job in the Military Medical Administration's reserve staff and directed me to the evacuation department. But I did not get to start work straight away. For about two days the head of the evacuation department could not decide what task to give me, and by that time the question of evacuating Minsk, which until then had just been a matter of rumours, became a real issue. There were confused reports that the Poles were advancing on Minsk, and the inhabitants began to get agitated and started whispering to one another in the street. Finally, it was announced that the frontline institutions were leaving Minsk. It was decided that we would relocate to Smolensk. Everybody began hastily to sort out and pack up their 'files'. Billeting officers sped to Smolensk to look for accommodation. It was all done in a desperate hurry, because it was feared that the Poles would cut the railway line at Borisov.

My bosses in the evacuation department were, of course, in no position to induct a new person into the job. There was absolutely nothing for me to do in Minsk. I had no desire at all to risk being taken prisoner by the Poles, if the route to Smolensk were actually to be cut off. I decided to go straight away, without waiting for our department to gather itself together and depart. They readily gave me travel papers and left me to my own devices.

The whole town was in chaos. Almost none of the locals was leaving, but all the military and some of the civil institutions were setting off straight away. Crowds of Red Army men were making their way to the main station. Carriages, carts and lorries were rumbling along in an unbroken chain. They were packed to the top with all sorts of bits and pieces: office desks and chairs, trestle-beds, bundles of 'files' in folders, stacks, packs and barrels of all kinds of goods, together with luxury soft furnishings, hangings, paintings, massive mirrors, upright and grand pianos! It was clear that many of those who were being evacuated were taking furnishings from those 'bourgeois' apartments where they had been billeted as 'souvenirs'. There was even an unpleasant incident related to this involving one of the Smolensk comrades, Dr G. Together with other members of the Military Medical Administration staff, he had been living in the apartment of a member of the district court, Petrusevich, who had left Minsk along with the Polish troops. Petrusevich had previously worked in the Russian workers' movement and had even, as a participant in the First Congress of the Social-Democratic Party, been one of its founders. Although he had subsequently given up party activity, he had still been doing all sorts of favours for the local social democrats. His flat had been furnished tastefully, with numerous paintings, statuettes, vases and so forth. Some of the uninvited inhabitants of Petrusevich's flat seized part of this collection and the furniture to take to Smolensk. G. was very distressed to think that Petrusevich might return, discover who had been living in his flat and consider G. to have taken part in the looting. He therefore decided to leave a note in the flat for Petrusevich, expressing his sorrow about the havoc in the flat and assuring him that he, G., had had nothing to do with it. But the anticipated occupation of Minsk by the Poles did not happen, and a special commission of the Cheka was sent there. They discovered the letter in that flat, and G. was arrested. He got off reasonably lightly: he was imprisoned for a couple of weeks, but the Cheka clearly had no wish to look into this 'sensitive' matter.

It was complete bedlam at the station: shouting, noise, swearing, crushing, children crying. There were several trains standing, almost all composed of goods wagons and platforms, some of them still without engines. It was hard to work out which train was allocated to which institution, and absolutely nobody had any idea when they were going to depart. It was freezing cold, especially at night, but almost everyone had to find space for themselves in unheated goods wagons or on the open platforms between piles of goods and furniture. And the journey would take two, three or even four days. Some even took a week to get there; it all depended on whether they could get through the double-track section at Borisov quickly and whether they got locomotives in time.

Certain 'former Mensheviks' who had gone over to the Bolsheviks and occupied very prominent positions in the life of the front, got me a place in a first-class wagon – one of the 'special' carriages reserved for a particular institution. To complete my good fortune, this carriage was attached to the last fast train leaving Minsk. However, it was only 'fast' relatively speaking; the journey still took two days and nights.

Apart from me, the only passengers in our carriage were staff of the institution that had reserved it and their families. There were relatively few passengers, because everybody had a couchette. But I must admit that these material comforts had never weighed so heavily upon me as they did then, in that chaos, where soldiers, old people, women, children and the wounded were crowded together in goods wagons with stoves and on open platforms, freezing and loudly cursing the few fortunate ones who had settled into the higher class carriages.

There were not many of those carriages in our train, only about three or four, and one of them was an international one marked 'for delegates to the Third International'. What delegates these were I have no idea, but there were only a few people in that luxurious carriage. Unfortunately, though, the crowd, and especially the Red Army men, were most annoyed by the carriage into which fate had brought me.

The problem was this: the head of transport for the institution that had reserved this carriage – a very hard-working and selfless person, as I discovered – was sending his family away in it, including a one-year-old child who was unwell. They knew there was no chance of getting any milk during this journey, and the child was in a bad way. So his father had hit upon the ill-fated idea of sending a goat along with the family to provide milk. No sooner said than done, and the goat was found a place in the corridor of the carriage. All the time the train was moving, there was no problem. But whenever the train stopped, the accursed animal would put its front paws up on the window-ledge, show its face to the good people outside and start to bleat loudly! The reaction can hardly be described. The Red Army men went wild, waved their fists, shouted that this was a scandal – a goat travelling in first class while the wounded were lying on the roofs of carriages etc. At times it looked as if the crowd was going to smash up the carriage, at which point other passengers, many of whom were transporting wagonloads of goods, started shouting that the goat needed to be thrown out, at which point the child's mother would begin to fret. I just wanted to jump out of that carriage, and could hardly wait for this nightmare journey with our inconvenient four-legged companion to come to an end.

We got to Smolensk early in the morning. There was the same chaos and confusion here as in Minsk, just the other way around. Carts, vans and lorries were rushing away from the station, cars were sounding their horns, the air was thick with cursing. For this small, picturesque town, spread out on hills, this was like Baty's Mongol invasion. Where was this horde of people and institutions going to go? Each of them wanted to be accommodated with all facilities, in view of their importance to the needs of the front. The crowding and stuffiness in the premises of the billeting troika were enough to make one faint. The people demanding flats were shouting, the people who were being squeezed up or evicted to make room for them were shouting, or sometimes crying. Everything had to be done 'within twenty-four hours', whole families were being thrown out onto the street with the right only to take a little furniture with them, or were being squashed into one room. The troika had no time to go into any detailed examination of individual cases, it was giving out billets right and left, and as a result men found themselves moved into rooms occupied by women, and typists and office girls were being squashed into rooms occupied by some Smolensk notable or other. People were running about making complaints and were just getting shouted at in reply. Everything more or less settled down and sorted itself out in the end, although numerous petty or less pushy office workers ended up spending the night in the office they were working in.

I was personally offered accommodation by one of our party comrades, a native of Smolensk. The accommodation was not luxurious: it had no windows, just a partition glazed at the top, separating my section from the one at the front, and moreover, it was a thoroughfare. But we even had to fight tooth and nail to keep this accommodation out of the hands of the billeting officers and other sundry claimants, taking our case almost to the highest level.

A building was allocated to the Military Medical Administration that had previously been used for training 'red commanders'. And here is a characteristic detail: all the walls were covered with monarchist and anti-Semitic graffiti! As a politically 'unreliable' person it was not easy for me to mix either with rank-and-file Red Army soldiers or with their commanding officers. But I would come into contact with Red Army officers in state institutions, on the street and in carriages, and this was enough to give me a quite definite impression of them. In their way of talking, their interests, their thuggish swagger and so on, they were not much different from the officer corps of the good old days. I could not help thinking that here was a fully-fledged officer caste for the coming Bonapartism. On one occasion I even heard one young thug remark: 'Trotsky would make a great dictator – pity he's a Yid!'

The Poles' assault on Minsk was delayed, and the evacuation process became less feverish. Our administration did not arrive in Smolensk for about another ten days. I did not have much to do during that time, so I looked round the town and got to know our local party group. Despite the constant repression, the group had firm roots among the town's workers, was represented in the soviet and had a small meeting-place. The seals on the doors of this meeting-place, put there the last time the Cheka had raided it, had been removed just before my arrival. With the return from Minsk of Smolensk citizens who had been mobilised, the life of the group picked up a bit. Members' meetings were organised, at which I reported on the situation in the party, the Polish-Soviet war and so on, but any public activity – apart from speeches in the Soviet, which convened very rarely – was impossible.

Soon after the front institutions had transferred to Smolensk, military action ceased, an armistice was agreed and talks began which were to lead to the Treaty of Riga. Minsk was not occupied by the Poles, but the front administration remained in Smolensk. The evacuation department, where I was employed, was largely preoccupied with removing and accommodating patients with typhus and relapsing fever. There were tens of thousands of these patients, and there was nowhere to put them. There were towns where typhus patients were laid out in their hundreds and thousands on the floor, with almost no care or attention. There were cases where entire barracks were declared to be 'hospitals', because almost all their inhabitants were ill, and there were neither enough hospitals to accommodate them, nor enough transport to move them. The telegrams and reports that poured into the centre hardly improved the situation, because everything was in short supply. But, nonetheless, our work was less of a purely paper exercise than in Ekaterinburg.

At the beginning of October it was announced that employees were to be given two weeks leave to return home and get warm winter clothes. I made use of this break to travel to Moscow, where I spent about three weeks. The question of my transfer back to Moscow was raised here again. Semashko told me that 'in principle' he no longer had any objections, all that was needed was to 'finish Wrangel off', and in no more than a month I would be back in Moscow. And with that I returned to Smolensk.

There was a surprise waiting for me when I got there. It turned out that on the very night I had left for Moscow, the Cheka had visited me and almost every other Smolensk social democrat and carried out a thorough search. Nobody had been arrested. The Chekists were sorry that I had not been there, one of them affirmed that I was an 'old acquaintance' from party congresses. In their conversations with the landlords, they expressed their belief that I had not 'simply' moved to Smolensk, but that I probably intended ... to organise a Belorussian government in order to overthrow the Bolsheviks and join with Poland!

There was no follow-up to the search, and my life resumed its usual tedious routine as I awaited my return to Moscow, when suddenly my time in Smolensk was cut short, just as unexpectedly as my time in Ekaterinburg had been.

A comrade returning from a business trip to Moscow informed me that the CC of our party had received an invitation from the CEC

Presidium to send a delegation to the forthcoming Eighth All-Russia Congress of Soviets. The CC had elected me as part of this delegation, and the Presidium Secretariat had undertaken to send a telegram to Smolensk requesting that I be immediately given leave to visit Moscow.

This news was unexpected for me. It was true that the previous year we had received an invitation to send a delegation to the Seventh Congress and had made use of it. Martov and I had made speeches at the congress and set out the platform of our party. But this was the time of Denikin's advance, when the Bolsheviks were seriously frightened. Moreover, although my speech at that Seventh Congress, which reaffirmed our readiness to support the Bolsheviks in their struggle with Denikin, was generally to the communists' taste (in the official report in *Izvestiya* it was even spelled out that 'Lenin and Trotsky joined in the applause'), they noisily expressed their dissatisfaction when Martov set out our platform in the course of his speech. A year had passed since then, a year filled with the most malicious repression against our party. Peace had already been concluded with Poland, and Wrangel had been routed. Under such circumstances a repeat invitation to us to attend the congress seemed improbable. But, since it had happened, our CC decided to make use of the opportunity, uncommon in Soviet Russia, to publicise social democracy's point of view from an All-Russia tribune.

There was no time to lose. There were just two or three days before the congress. We had to draft motions on every point of the agenda – of course, without the slightest hope of getting them adopted by the congress, but in order that they should be included as official documents in the published reports of the congress and could serve as materials for social-democratic agitation. For this reason it was necessary to leave for Moscow immediately, without waiting for telegrams which, by the time they had made their way around various offices, might only reach Smolensk on the eve of the congress itself. I therefore went to see L. that very evening and explained all the facts of the matter to him, asking him to give me leave to travel now, not waiting for the official telegram from Moscow. L. agreed, and the next day I left Smolensk, taking all my things with me, since on the basis of previous conversations with Semashko I was sure that I would not have to go back there. This was some time after 20 December 1920.

4

At the Congress of Soviets

Having arrived in Moscow, I called on Semashko on work business and got his formal assurance that there would now be no obstacles to me moving back to Moscow. The question of what post to give me in Moscow was set aside until after the congress. My old bosses in the medical supplies department of the People's Commissariat of Health were convinced that I would be returning to the surgical subsection, which was already in a state of regular chaos.

Now I had to plunge head-first into party work, as there was little time remaining before the congress opened. As well as work on the Central Committee (CC) preparing for the congress, there was work to be done in the local party organisation: our premises were open again and were hosting meetings of up to 150 people.

The congress, as usual, resembled a huge meeting, but a meeting which had been carefully selected beforehand. There was a small non-party grouping of around 250 people, and all the rest were communists. There were communists in the stalls where the congress members were seated, there were communists on the benches and in the galleries, where members of the Moscow Soviet, the Moscow factory committees and the trade union leadership sat. The massive hall of the Bolshoi Theatre was packed. One of the 'directors" boxes was set aside for 'diplomats', but, apart from the representatives of the Azerbaijan Republic,[1] there did not seem to be anybody there. The 'Tsar's' box opposite the stage was occupied by the Third International, and the stage itself was taken by the Central Executive Committee (CEC). There were also places here for us and other similar delegations: the social-democratic Bund, the 'Narod' SR group and so on.[2]

The area around the theatre where the congress gathered presented a familiar picture: a thick military cordon surrounded the square, only allowing those fortunate enough to hold valid tickets through, with endless ticket checks at all the entrances and exits etc. In the evenings, illuminated hoardings on the roof of one of the neighbouring buildings blazed with communist maxims and slogans, as well as paeans to foreign communists. These days [1922] both the Englishman Robert Williams and the Italian Serrati have long since joined the ranks of the 'social traitors', but back then all Moscow was emblazoned with 'Long Live Robert Williams!' and 'Long Live Serapio!' – this was how the name of the esteemed Italian socialist had been rendered by the hoarding designer, whose grasp of international spelling was shaky. The mistake was rectified after a few days.

It was of course very noisy in the conference hall and the lobbies. But there was no sense of life at the congress. Like all the rest of the Soviet apparatus, from the local soviets right up to the All-Russia CEC, Soviet congresses had long been crushed by the fact that everything important was always decided at the meetings of the Bolshevik group, which was always assured of a majority beforehand. All the other groups had been forcibly excluded from the soviets, and at all ostensibly elected or representative gatherings the Bolshevik group was faced with just an insignificant, unorganised and intimidated bunch of non-party people. The whole Soviet machine had started to smell putrid, and all its sessions, meetings and suchlike were becoming just tedious pageants which followed a set formula. These pageants had worked somehow while there was still some enthusiasm left, or while some simple, basic task – like the struggle against Denikin – had bound the Bolsheviks together through fear of a common danger and the need to strain all their efforts to remove it. Now, after the conclusion of peace with Poland and the victory over Wrangel, this psychological bond had weakened, and no trace remained of their previous enthusiasm or belief in their cause. There was a sense of crisis, and for the first time the disagreements which had been tearing the Bolshevik party apart from within broke out into the open. These disagreements also leaked out into the press, accessible to everyone. In the guise of arguments about the role and significance of the trade unions, about bureaucratism, about the party leaders and the rank and file, one could see sharp divisions on questions of economic and general policy. These divisions stemmed from disillusionment with the results of previous policies, and had been artificially channelled into the inner-party debates. We got hold of some literature on these questions intended 'only for RKP members'. Here the questions were posed more sharply than in the newspapers. They were discussed in fractional meetings even more pointedly, and all Lenin's efforts were devoted towards formulating and pushing a sort of 'middle' line. It made verbal concessions first to one side, then the other, while actually trying to keep everything as before, somehow ironing out the difficult points and distracting the party's attention from those questions that were knocking at the door ever more insistently.

This was not an auspicious position for pageantry. Both before and during the congress, the Bolshevik leaders had to spend time and effort working behind the scenes to reconcile irreconcilable contradictions. For this reason, the opening of the congress itself was postponed from day to day, then there were long breaks in proceedings, sometimes lasting as long as two days. Reports presented at the congress would be discussed in meetings of the communist fraction alone, and in the fraction itself there was an additional report on Zinoviev's report on the struggle against bureaucratism and 'workers' democracy' – an event that was probably without precedent in the annals of any representative institution.

Virtually all that remained for the congress's infrequent and brief official sessions were reports to the effect that 'everything is fine', which inspired nobody. There was also voting – or, rather, pushing through resolutions, drafted in the RKP fraction and imposed by its Central Committee. These resolutions were passed, even though the great majority of the delegates fundamentally disagreed with them! Lenin recounted how good everything was with the republic's domestic and foreign position, and how successfully food requisitioning was going, Trotsky and Emshanov reported on the splendid effects of the notorious decree No. 1042 on repairs to locomotives and rolling stock,[3] Rykov recited the successes of state planned economy, while Zinoviev spoke touchingly about how workers would come to the trade unions for all their needs – for benefits, for chits entitling them to footwear, and even for a coffin for a deceased mother. And the audience, who had come from the provinces and knew well from their own experience the failure of requisitioning, the inflated nature of all of Trotsky and Rykov's figures, and the falsity of the idyllic pictures painted by the city boss of Petrograd – this audience dutifully listened to the official speeches, dutifully voted for the resolutions and dutifully met and accompanied their 'leaders' with applause.

This last feature struck me, even in comparison with the last year's congress, as an indicator of the changed situation and changed public mood. The audience did not greet Trotsky, or even Lenin, with that genuine, albeit naive enthusiasm which we had seen in the past. There was an obvious coolness in the air. So, in order to create the impression of an 'ovation', Lenin resorted to a theatrical trick of which, I admit, I would not have thought him capable. He waited behind the scenes, and came out onto the stage at the very moment that the orchestra started to play the Internationale and the whole 4000-strong crowd stood up. It was impossible to tell whether people had stood up and then applauded for the anthem, or for the person of the leader. If I am wrong, and that most effective entry was made inadvertently, then it certainly turned out very well for Lenin …

In the conference hall itself the most crushing boredom reigned supreme. It would be no exaggeration to say that the only times the audience woke up and listened with interest and attention were when the opposition was speaking. From our delegation Dalin spoke on the report on economic policy, and I spoke on Lenin's report. Despite the fact that the rules only gave me ten minutes to speak, at the audience's request my time was extended four times, which meant that I spoke for about an hour in total. I was told that certain Bolsheviks were disappointed that the tone of my speech was not sharper: 'after all, don't we abuse each other like that within our own fraction'?

Of course, the motion I put forward on behalf of our delegation managed to get only a few dozen votes. But there was a surprise waiting for me the next day – two congress delegates, a worker and a peasant, unknown to me, approached me in the street. They took me to one side and said: 'Please don't be annoyed that we didn't support you, Comrade Dan. All of us non-party delegates agreed with your motion, and even several of the communists told us that they wanted to vote for your motion, but we were frightened of the consequences when we got back home. But rest assured that when we get back we will tell everything about the congress and will try to convey all that you said as widely as possible, so that it won't have been pointless.'

I must admit that these and similar declarations that I got to hear from other delegates gave me great satisfaction. They brightened up a really onerous party obligation – that of speaking at Bolshevik-dominated congresses, where the most elementary rights of dissenters were so crudely violated, where everything was so cynically and shamelessly rigged to suppress freedom of speech and discussion. Making speeches at the Central Executive Committee (Fourth Convocation) and at various Soviet, trade union and other congresses during the Bolshevik epoch will always remain in my memory as the party activities which required the greatest effort of will and moral courage. This will be understood by anyone who knows what it is to get up to speak in front of a selected audience, specially poisoned against you, with a pre-prepared decision; to get up to speak in the knowledge that you have just a few minutes, after which two, three or four speakers will pour filth over you, make the most startling slanders against you, without you or any of your co-thinkers being able to object or nail the lie, get the chairman to come to your defence, or even just publish a 'letter to the editor'. One must give the Bolsheviks credit where it is due; the cynicism of their methods of shutting the mouths of their opponents has beaten all world records. And the fact that, despite all this, I still managed to give an hour-long speech at the Eighth Congress of Soviets, showed that 'something was rotten in the state of Denmark'.

The congress was clearly dying on its feet. The sessions took place ever more rarely. Voting on resolutions was postponed while the battles behind the scenes were still going on. Something had to be done to keep the congress occupied and reinvigorate it, and so an unplanned diversion was dreamt up: a new bit of Bolshevik theatre called 'electrification'. The Bolsheviks had had many miraculous recipes for instantly establishing communism: there had been 'subbotniki', Committees of the Rural Poor, labour armies, food requisitioning, Order No. 1042 and sowing committees. Each time it had been solemnly declared that a most effective means had at last been discovered for curing all ills. The grandiose prospects offered by this latest 'great initiative' would be sketched out, plans of action would be compiled, telegrams would fly about reporting great successes, right up to the point where it became clear that this 'initiative' was just another soap bubble. Then a new 'slogan' would be launched, with exactly the same degree of success.

It was just the same now. All their previous cards had obviously been trumped, so a new one was dreamt up – electrification. Once Russia was covered by a whole network of powerful hydroelectric stations, there would be no need to worry about shortages of coal or oil. Plants and factories, electric ploughs and threshing-machines, electric trains – when all this was set in motion, Russia would at last become a verdant communist garden! 'Communism is Soviet power plus electrification', proclaimed Lenin, and there were enough fools around who believed, or pretended to believe, that drivel. Of course, no thought was given to the fact that there is no trace in Russia of the material, technical, social and cultural prerequisites for electrification. On paper it was all worked out and was set out neatly. The delegates all received a fat volume of reports. An enormous map of Russia was dragged in, speckled with different-coloured electric bulbs representing the projected 'regional power stations'. G. Krzhizhanovsky, the main producer of this mystery play, spent two full hours drumming into his audience the full glories of our future electric prosperity, and all the while the little multi-coloured bulbs twinkled away on the map, like illuminations in honour of the coming triumph.

Alas, this fantasy play did not create the impression its authors had counted upon. 'Electrification' was immediately redubbed 'electrofiction', and that was the term that spread round Russia. And then ... who now remembers Lenin's celebrated 'plus electrification'?

The congress came to an end. Its complete futility was shown less than three months later, when the 'New Economic Policy' was suddenly proclaimed, thereby demonstrating the falsity of all the official assurances that all was going well that had been fed to the delegates at the congress. But for me personally, that congress was very significant indeed, in that my intervention at it had some definite consequences.

A few days after the close of the congress Semashko informed me that my transfer back to Moscow, which we had thought had already been decided, was now encountering some obstacles. He claimed that he had personally long been prepared to transfer me at any time, but the CC of the Communist Party was blocking it. Our CC got in touch with Krestinsky, who was at that time the secretary of the Bolshevik CC, about the matter. Krestinsky swore that this had nothing to do with his CC, and that the whole business was in the hands of Semashko. Semashko, in his turn, shrugged his shoulders and swore to God that the matter was not up to him. This nonsense carried on for about two weeks. Krestinsky declared more than once that he had phoned Semashko or would do so, but was careful to put nothing on paper. But Semashko affirmed that Krestinsky had not spoken to him on the phone about anything. Both put on surprised expressions and talked about some kind of 'misunderstanding'.

The morality governing relations between the people's commissars and the ruling political fivesome on the Bolshevik CC was well illustrated by a curious conversation that I got to have with one of the ministers, who was outraged by the vindictive way I was being treated. When I had told him about the farce of being sent from Pontius to Pilate and back, he told me he would get to the bottom of it, and that he would even speak to 'Lenin himself'. A few days later he told me in some embarrassment that nothing had come of his discussions, and that I was not to be allowed to remain in Moscow. I was interested to discover what lay behind this continual exile – was it my speech at the congress? To that my interlocutor replied, with a pleasant smile, 'Do you imagine they tell us that sort of thing? They don't consider us, with our limited sense, able to understand high affairs of state. Everything is decided up there, on Olympus, and they tell us what we need to know and carry out without explanation.' I could only just restrain myself from asking how, under such circumstances, people with any degree of self-respect could not only remain in their 'ministerial' posts but even fight tooth and nail to cling on to them ...

I had to abandon the idea of being transferred to Moscow and find myself a new base of operations. There was no point in returning to Smolensk, because the front institutions were being wound down and staffing was being cut. Moreover, I wanted to be closer to Moscow, in order to take a more active part in the work of our CC. Besides Martov, Abramovitch had also gone abroad, and Dalin was preparing to leave. We had few forces left.

Semashko offered me the chance to choose any place except Moscow. I said that I would like to work on a hospital train, calculating that I would be able to return to Moscow after every journey and spend a week or two there. However, on the draft order Semashko compiled outlining my assignment he stated that I was to be given any available hospital train, excluding those based in Moscow. After that, of course, I lost all interest in working on the trains, and I refused that assignment. I needed to choose a place to live. Having roamed around the provinces, I had no desire to go back there again, and, after much thought and discussion with my friends, I decided to put in for Petrograd.

I was well aware of all the problems associated with living in the fiefdom of Zinoviev – the most repugnant and dishonourable of all the Bolsheviks – and also knew the risk of being arrested very soon. But there was no choice. In my position, even in the provinces I always had to reckon with the possibility of arrest. I could not go 'underground' for two reasons. First, because that would go against the interests of our party, which had adapted all its tactics to the struggle for an open existence despite all the Bolshevik terror. Moreover, because of my previous record I was too well known personally to a very wide circle of Bolsheviks and Cheka agents. This would have meant that I would have had to go very deep underground indeed, and with the housing, transport, postal etc. conditions which obtained then, I would still have had to reduce my party activity to the barest minimum. But there was also another reason for not going underground. I had been drafted. Going into hiding was desertion. I did not think that I could give that sort of trump card to Bolshevik demagogy and put myself in a position where I could be sentenced to imprisonment on the strictest formal basis as a common criminal. I therefore had to opt for Petrograd and risk being rapidly arrested. Moreover, as one old Bolshevik assured me, that I had no reason to fear arrest in Petrograd. 'You know, Zinoviev is a democrat now', he ironically remarked about the pathos-laden tirade that 'Grishka Interplut' (as the Jews of the North Western province called him) had made against bureaucratism at the last Soviet congress.[4]

So, after five weeks in Moscow, on 1 February I again boarded the train to Petrograd.

NOTES

1. Although Azerbaijan had lost its independence following its occupation by the Red Army at the end of April 1920, the Azerbaijani SSR still preserved some of the trappings of sovereignty at the end of that year.
2. The 'Narod' group was a small splinter from the SR party, founded in October 1919 on a platform of co-operation with Soviet power. It lasted in various guises until the spring of 1922. See V. V. Shelokhaev et al., *Politicheskie partii Rossii. Konets XIX – pervaya tret' XX veka. Entsiklopediya*, ROSSPEN, Moscow, 1996, pp. 380-382.
3. Order No. 1042, decreed by Trotsky on 22 May 1920 in his capacity as acting transport commissar, envisaged a massive programme of locomotive repair over four-and-half years. The resources with which this was to be achieved were not indicated.
4. Literally 'Greg Interswindler'. This play on words involves a diminutive form of 'Grigoriy', a reference to Zinoviev's role as head of the Communist International, and an assessment of his moral qualities.

5
Petrograd

This was the second time I had returned to my native city since the Bolshevik seizure of power, and the same sense of sadness overcame me. The streets were deserted: when I had been in Petrograd in the autumn of 1919, many of them had been covered with grass. There were few passers-by and even fewer carriages. The buildings looked sullen and lifeless, with peeling paint and bright patches – the shop signs which, unlike in Moscow, had survived almost untouched. It gave the impression of a city in a state of torpor, like the enchanted town of Kitezh, just awaiting the hour of its awakening. Once that hour strikes, then all the sealed doors and windows of the shops will open again, and all these countless little shops – bakers, grocers, clothes and shoe shops – will be filled with goods. Nevsky Prospekt will be bustling with crowds, and old Petersburg will come back to life again. But in the meantime the incomparable beauty of all those squares, embankments, palaces and bridges just caused a strange kind of heartache. I had never felt that austere magnificence of Petersburg as strongly as I did then, when that great city barely showed any signs of life. Without the distractions of the hubbub of everyday life, I could not help but dwell on its grandiose appearance.

There was a mass of handcarts at the station, and their owners were vying with each other to carry my luggage. The few trams that still ran stopped at six in the evening. There was no sign of any cabs: horses and carriages, just like cars, had become the exclusive privilege of the ruling class. It was not uncommon to see a man pushing his sick wife or a son pushing his aged mother about on a handcart: there were no other means of transport. Every single shop was closed. But street trading, despite all the bans and mass round-ups, was winning out step by step. On Sennaya Square traders and customers moved about in a dense crowd. 'Everything' was on sale here: bread, meat, butter, sugar, cigarettes, and manufactured goods. All the goods were dusty, dirty and thoroughly mauled. And right next to all this was the fine building of the former market, derelict, with its doors smashed in. The crowd had turned it into a public toilet. On the corner of Nevsky and Ligovka they were also buying and selling small items – cookies, cigarettes, dubious-looking sweets and chocolate. There was also a mass of prostitutes here plying for trade, and an increasing number of them seemed to be underage girls. While I was in the city, in order to root out this trading, the authorities in their wisdom gave the order to demolish and remove the numerous local marketplaces that the city had built in various districts. They set about this 'work' with gusto. Several marketplaces were razed to the ground. And this was about a month before free trade was declared legal again!

As soon as I arrived I had to get busy with work matters. The Military Medical Department had been racking their brains for some time trying to decide what job to give me. In the event I was given a very comfortable position as doctor at the 7th Rozhdestvensky sports club. This institution was part of the system of youth training before call-up. It offered gymnastics, military drill and ski sports etc. In reality the club was barely functioning. My duties consisted in making a brief visit to the club about three times a week and keeping an eye on the fel'dsher [paramedic] charged with administering first aid for any minor injuries sustained during gymnastics. I was also supposed to examine any youngsters who declared they were ill and unfit to exercise. Just at the time I took on this position, a 'communist' Red Army company was being formed at all sports clubs from boys who had just joined the Komsomol, and it fell to me to give them their medical examinations.

Overall, I was quite happy with this work placement, because it took up very little time and freed me from having to waste time hanging around in offices.

At that time, the economic and food-supply situation in Petrograd was desperate. In November and December, in accordance with the 'economic programme', several plants and factories had been reactivated. Raw materials and fuel were 'allocated' to this programme, but within two months it turned out that there had been a 'little error' in the programme – the 'allocated' fuel and raw materials existed only on paper. One after another the enterprises stopped working again. The 'fuel weeks' that were declared did not help matters at all; they just annoyed the workers who were sent out into the forests tens of kilometres away, without any warm clothing, any bread to eat, any axes or saws or any hope of transporting the small amount of fuel wood they managed to cut.

The food supply situation also got worse day by day. All that was given out on ration cards was between half and one pound of bread and occasionally a little granulated sugar. Even bread – and what bread! – was not available every day. It was also impossible to get anything on the free market. Not everyone could get to Sennaya Square, and in fact there was not even a lot there. The blocking detachments were getting more ferocious, and at times even the black marketeers had nothing to sell at any price. The position with bread was particularly bad.

Workers were starving. Red Army men were also going hungry. I used to have to pass a barracks on the way to work. Each time I would be stopped ten or so times by Red Army men, literally pleading for 'a little bit of bread' or offering me a piece or two of sugar from their meagre rations in exchange for bread.

People were beginning to get restless in the factories and plants. Workers called meetings to discuss the situation, and all their demands centred on the question of removing the blocking detachments and permitting free trade in foodstuffs. They did not want to hear the communists who got up to speak at the factories and plants. The workers dragged them out of their cars on the street, and some of them were threatened with beating. By 20 February the movement had taken the form of a general strike. At first, the Bolshevik press tried to maintain a strict silence about the movement, and then tried to conceal its real extent and nature. Rather than call the strike a strike, they came up with new terms like 'fuss' and 'row' and so on. The newspapers printed resolutions protesting against the movement from 'red students'. They insisted that all the 'fuss' stemmed from a misunderstanding, that all the workers wanted was more shops in their localities so they did not have to spend so long in queues, and that the Mensheviks were deceiving the workers by imposing their slogans on them.

However, the movement could not be stopped by this official lie, and – especially on Vasil'evsky Island – the movement began to spill out on to the streets. Huge crowds of workers would gather, together with sailors from the naval vessels moored on the Neva (including the famous *Aurora* which had fired on the Winter Palace in October 1917) and Red Army men. Impromptu speeches were made, and the crowds made their way to the factories that were still working to bring the workers out. Besides the demand for free trade, other slogans gradually began to be advanced: the abolition of the communist party cells ('komyacheyki') in the plants and factories, which had a purely police function and had been dubbed 'komishcheyki' (communist police dogs) by the workers; freedom of speech; free elections to the soviets; and so forth. The movement was so massive that it got a response right across the city. Just like in the former days of the revolution, small groups began to form on the Nevsky Prospekt, where people loudly criticised the Bolshevik regime with newfound courage. The more effusive people even claimed that the spirit of 'February 1917' was in the air.

The Bolsheviks responded to the movement with repression. The Komsomol was given the dirty work of spying: the youth was tasked with seeking out the flats where the workers were holding meetings and leading the Cheka there to make arrests. Not every member of the league consented to play that shameful role. Even the Bolshevik newspapers were obliged to admit that the youth league proved to be 'not up to the task', and that many young communists played a most active part in anti-Bolshevik demonstrations. Later on, at the remand prison I personally met a fifteen-year-old young communist. He had been arrested because, instead of sniffing out workers' meetings, he had warned the workers when the Cheka was about to raid.

The movement nonetheless continued to grow, and it was decided to use military force against it. But the authorities could not count on the Red Army men. The attitude among the military units was such that the authorities preferred to keep them locked up in their barracks. Indeed, a source I have no reason to doubt told me that in many regiments the Red Army men had had their boots taken away, under the pretext of inspecting them with a view to replacing them, in order to ensure that the men did not leave their barracks on their own account.

It was exclusively the cadet officers – those Bolshevik Junkers – who were sent into action against the workers. From my window I could see how units of foot and mounted Junkers, with their artillery, moved down the Nevsky Prospekt on to Vasil'evsky Island, while the public looked on in sullen silence. Nor were the cadets themselves happy about it. The whole spectacle was uncommonly vile. A few hours later, approaching the Senate building, which houses the historical revolutionary archive where I was working, I heard the sound of gunfire coming from Vasil'evsky Island. Soon people began to arrive, screaming that they were shooting workers on the island, and that there were many dead and wounded. Happily, that report turned out to be false. The Junkers, too, refused to shoot into the crowd, and instead shot into the air. Naturally, this merely encouraged the workers, and meetings and demonstrations broke out in other parts of the city.

The Bolsheviks had no alternative other than to make concessions. At a hastily convened session of the Petrograd Soviet it was resolved that the food-blocking detachments around the city be lifted and that workers and their families be allowed to travel into the countryside in search of food. At the same time there were emergency distributions of meat, footwear and manufactured goods in the factories.

With these concessions and benefits, the atmosphere became somewhat more relaxed. The movement began to decline. The Bolsheviks used this to carry out mass arrests of 'ringleaders' as identified by the 'komishcheyki'. No fewer than 500 workers were thrown into prison during those days! At the same time, our organisation was broken up. Our organisation had been existing in Petrograd under extremely difficult circumstances. Arrests had been carried out systematically on the basis of old membership lists seized during one of the raids. Thanks to this, those arrested included people who had left the party a long time ago and even some who had abandoned politics altogether. And, conversely, comrades who had joined the Petrograd organisation after the list had been lost remained untouched. This circumstance was very helpful for conserving the organisation during the most difficult times. And the true selflessness of certain old party workers, who time and again would resume party work as soon as they were released from prison, and would walk for ten or more kilometres in order to be at some small workers' meeting, did the rest: the organisation did not die. The fact that some experienced workers, with wide contacts among the masses, took part in our party's central organisation sometimes even brought us considerable success.

When I arrived in Petrograd, the majority of our members had only recently come out of prison – at the end of December and the beginning of January. They had had to start almost everything again from scratch. Meetings of the committee were convened clandestinely in private flats – just like in the good old days! – and we resolved that as far as possible we should refrain for the time being from making agitational speeches at factory meetings and so on. The position in Petrograd at that time was that almost every such speech led to the immediate arrest of the speaker. We decided to start by working in small circles, in order to bolster the scattered links that we had, and thereby create firm bases in the factories. If we succeeded in doing that, then individual arrests would not prove to be as damaging as they had been hitherto.

However, the force of circumstance proved stronger than our good intentions. We could not stand aside from the mass disturbances which were breaking out, so we had to deviate from our intended line of organisational work.

Our attitude to the disturbances themselves was fairly sceptical from the very outset, and we did not expect great results from them. It was clear that a strike in itself would not worry the Bolsheviks too much, since the factories were already shutting down because of the lack of fuel and raw materials. It presented an immediate danger only inasmuch as it demoralised the Soviet apparatus and, in particular, the Red Army, and, had the Red Army men joined with the workers, it could have led to an attempt at an armed overthrow of Bolshevik rule in Petrograd. There were optimists – mainly among former social democrats who had left the party and called themselves 'Plekhanovists' or the 'Edinstvo' group – who imagined that the workers' movement was consciously and definitely marching under the banner of the Constituent Assembly. These optimists, along with some ordinary citizens, believed that a movement comparable to the February revolution was being reborn, and that the working class would be leading, and setting the political agenda for, all the other forces hostile to the Bolshevik regime. Therefore they were prepared to fan the flames of this movement so far as to start open street clashes with the authorities, and did not shrink from becoming involved with all sorts of dubious elements in the anti-Bolshevik camp.

There was no chance of any such mood in our organisation. We could see very well the enormous difference between that mass movement and the movement of early 1917. Here we had the working masses, but they were atomised, disorganised, tortured by four years of suffering and privation. They had seen their illusions cruelly dashed, they had lost faith in their own strength and had no clear political goals. These were masses whose thoughts went no further than satisfying their most elementary needs for food and warmth, and who were thoroughly penetrated by the police network of 'komyacheyki'. They had no old party organisations, capable of uniting and leading the whole mass movement. Subsequent developments showed just how correct we had been in our assessment of the situation, and how outlandish the optimists' illusions had been: the Kronstadt movement found no support at all among the Petrograd workers. And this was because the Soviet's concessions and emergency distribution of foodstuffs, clothing and footwear mentioned above had given the workers hope that their material position, which had driven them to strike, would improve.

A conversation I had with a member of Edinstvo, whom I met by chance at somebody's house, gave a characteristic picture of the masses' mood. He was enthusiastically talking about his meetings with a workers' circle which supported the demand for a Constituent Assembly. The circle assured him that the movement would not stop until the Bolsheviks had been overthrown, and requested speakers for workers' street meetings. 'Just don't send us any Jews', the circle had asked. So it would seem that a movement, supposedly capable of bringing even openly counter-revolutionary elements along into the struggle for democracy, had itself succumbed to the danger of falling under the influence of reactionary anti-Semitic demagogy.

To imagine that a spontaneous workers' movement could act as the political leadership for all the other anti-Bolshevik forces under such conditions was to fall victim to the grossest illusions. In fact, we needed to be worried about the opposite: how could a turbulent surge of the working masses, driven to desperation by hunger and cold, not be used politically by counter-revolutionary forces? From our perspective, there was nothing positive to be expected from the movement going over to open rebellion either. If the Red Army men had joined with the workers, they may have been able to overthrow Soviet power in Petrograd. But in those circumstances, in a city without any stocks of food or fuel, the victory of this spontaneous mass movement would inevitably have led to the looting of stores and private flats, before finally being drowned in blood. It would merely have strengthened the hand of the privileged military caste, to whom the honour would have fallen to save the city from 'anarchy'. I will not dwell further on the details of our analysis of the situation at that time. In any case, our organisation resolved not to fan the flames of the movement under any circumstances, to recommend that the workers be satisfied with partial concessions, while using the events to explain to the masses the connection between their present sufferings and the overall policies of Bolshevism. We were to stress the need to abandon the system of total nationalisation of everything, the need to reach agreement with the peasant small producers and to liquidate the party dictatorship. Free elections to the soviets (not 'soviets without communists', as the Bolsheviks later claimed we had said) as the first step to replacing dictatorship with democracy – that was our general political slogan. That was the spirit in which our speakers spoke at factories, and it was the spirit of the leaflet I wrote 'To the hungry and cold Petersburg workers' and the motion I composed to be moved at meetings.

Our organisation worked feverishly. Two of our comrades (Kazukov and Kamensky) were arrested immediately after making successful speeches at factories. This was an indication of our impending collapse, but it did not diminish the energy of those who remained. With the help of printworker comrades we were able to run off 1000 copies of our proclamation and 500 copies of a one-off newspaper devoted to a 'trade union week' scheduled for the beginning of March. We were able to distribute both the newspaper and the proclamation. That same day, another whole group of comrades were arrested. I knew well that it was just a matter of days before my own arrest. But at that time I had no intention of going into hiding. On the contrary, I used the last few days available to me to do everything I could to ensure that the work would carry on.

I tried to spend my free evenings at the theatre; I could get in freely thanks to certain acquaintances. At this time tickets for the state theatres in Petrograd were not on open sale, but were being distributed solely through official institutions, which meant that visiting the theatre was not generally so easy. Performances at that time, owing to the introduction of martial law in Petrograd, finished early, at 9pm. On 26 February I returned home at 10pm from the Mariynsky Theatre, where I had been listening to Shalyapin in *The Maid of Pskov*. I had a definite feeling that I would be arrested that night. For a brief moment I thought of walking down the road to some acquaintances, make a phone call to discover whether everything was all right at home, and maybe spend the night at their place. But why bother? What did it matter whether I was arrested a day earlier or later? So I just shrugged and went home.

A young man in Red Army uniform opened the door to me: they had been waiting for me! It turned out that Cheka agents had come at four that afternoon, just a few minutes after I had gone out. On learning that I had gone to the theatre, they tried to find out which one, but, on failing to get an answer, they left a Red Army man to wait for me with the order to phone the Cheka immediately on my return. I thanked my lucky stars that I had been able to enjoy Shalyapin's singing for one last time, and awaited my uninvited guests.

They were not long in arriving – two gentlemen in peaked caps with engineer's badges – for some reason, I had noticed, the Petersburg Cheka liked to adorn their caps with that badge in particular. They had already searched my apartment in my absence. It did not take me long to get ready, and around 11pm we were in a car which had been waiting in a neighbouring street, and set off down Gorokhovaya Street. On the way my travelling companions, who called me 'Comrade Dan', expressed their esteem and respect for me and talked in the most humane terms about the difficult situation of the starving workers and peasants, the recent strikes and so on. There was literally not a soul on the streets: martial law was in force. It was strange and terrible to be travelling in a lone vehicle through a completely dead, dark city – electricity shortages had meant that the lighting was turned off in the streets and in buildings at 10pm.

We reached the Cheka premises. It was the old, familiar building of the city hall, where the tsarist okhranka [secret police] had been based in the 1890s. I had been here exactly twenty-five years ago, as a young social democrat, a member of the League of Struggle for the Emancipation of the Working Class. That had been my first arrest, stemming from the energetic activity of our League during the famous textile workers' strike which had inaugurated the era of a mass workers' movement under the banner of social democracy! This was, so to speak, the dawn of that revolutionary movement which had overthrown tsarism and brought the Bolsheviks to power. And now, a quarter-century on – another workers' strike, more hundreds of workers on their way to prison, and again I am with them. But this time we are being persecuted, arrested and interrogated by the Bolsheviks, our erstwhile comrades and brothers in the League, among whose founders and chief figures were Martov and Lenin, and the present-day pillars of communism, and the current Menshevik leaders. What a phantasmagoria! And how many different thoughts crowd into your mind as you enter the familiar vestibule and climb the stairs!

We were met in the waiting room by two old warders. Besides me, the other people who had just been brought in were two bakery workers and an elderly female factory worker. Brief conversations with them revealed that they were perfectly ordinary people, not members of any organisation. The bakers were clearly frightened by the situation and tried to explain to me that they weren't guilty of anything, they hadn't wanted to strike, they had been brought out by the workers of some factory or other. It was as if they were looking to me for protection, and I could already see how demeaned and degraded the spirits of these simple, uneducated workers would be as their Chekist interrogator screamed at them during their questioning and threatened them with all sorts of punishments in order to get their 'honest confessions' and 'remorse'! The woman was in much better spirits, declaring that arrest did not worry her: 'we're all going to starve to death anyway!' She was soon taken away into the neighbouring room, and they started on our 'personal searches'. Everybody had to strip naked. All our pockets were turned out, they checked every stitch and tapped the soles and heels of our boots – here were real masters of their craft at work! Watches, purses, notebooks, penknives, every scrap of paper were put on one side. Once we had been searched, we were led up endless stairs and along winding corridors to be photographed under electric light. Then the workers were led away somewhere, while I was sent, accompanied by a Chekist, to the room of the Cheka Presidium.

Here I found myself among quite a large number of people. A young man was sitting across the table from me. He was about 28, with small facial features. He looked like an assistant in a small haberdasher's shop. I soon discovered that this was 'Comrade Chistyakov', the investigator for cases involving socialists. Afterwards, people told me that he was a former hairdresser's apprentice from the Petersburg side. But he himself claimed that he was a former student who had been a Socialist-Revolutionary and had lived in France and Spain. He was not averse to having 'intelligent' conversations with prisoners and striking romantic poses: he even declared that he did not find working for the Cheka satisfying, that he wanted to 'shake the old world', and that he remained at heart an SR terrorist. He was wondering, perhaps he should go abroad again in order to assassinate Clemenceau, as the head of Entente imperialism. Overall, my conversation with him revealed him to be very unintelligent, politically illiterate, and extraordinarily mendacious and boastful.

There were two other people sitting at another table. One was thick set, with a crude, unrefined face – from what he said, it would seem that he was a sailor, who claimed to have taken part in the July 1917 uprising. The other was a small, fidgety man who called himself Stepanov. That was clearly a pseudonym, as the man was undoubtedly Jewish. The sailor, moreover, insisted that during the July uprising numerous sailors were killed before his very eyes, that he himself buried them etc. etc. I immediately exposed that lie, reminding him that even the Bolshevik papers at the time did not report one single death among the sailors. On the contrary, the sailors themselves had shot at and wounded several people without any cause. But the lad had obviously got so used to his story, which he needed in order to accuse the Mensheviks of 'bloodthirstiness', that he stubbornly clung to his own version.

In addition to these people, there were one or two not very noticeable people of intellectual appearance sitting on a couch, and then the Chairman of the Petrograd Cheka himself arrived – the worker Komarov, a tall, well-fed brown-haired man with a cocky, self-assured expression, dressed in military style with a pistol-holster on his belt.

The conversation was carried out mainly by Chistyakov. He started by saying that the Cheka had only found out about my arrival two days ago, but had already found out where I was working and living. Pointing to our leaflet and the issue of *Rabochaya gazeta* on the table in front of him, Chistyakov asked: 'Presumably it was you who wrote the newspaper and the leaflet?' I replied that it made absolutely no difference who had written them, as a member of the CC I took full responsibility for all the activities of our Petersburg organisation in relation to the strike, including the newspaper and leaflet. After a few tedious remarks about my letter to the Petersburg comrades which had been seized in some raid or other, the conversation moved on to current events, in which not only Chistyakov, but also Komarov, Stepanov and the sailor took an active part. The Chekists, as usual, considered the strike to be the result of Menshevik instigation and declared that it was an openly counter-revolutionary act which needed to be suppressed by force. As for the demand that bread be sold freely, this was a betrayal of the cause of socialism and lackeyism towards the bourgeoisie. There was a lot of clichés bandied about concerning the Entente and the white guards, who were behind the whole movement, deceiving the workers. I replied that not only had the Mensheviks not instigated the strike but, as was clear from the resolution, taken from one of our comrades in a raid and written in my own hand, we had tried to convince the workers that to use the weapon of political strike, given Russia's economic and political situation, would be fraught with danger. We had pointed out to the workers that it was not through outbreaks of strikes, but only through a systematic, stubborn struggle for the right to organise and for free elections that they could ensure that party dictatorship would be replaced by the will of the working people. I also said that all these tales about the Entente and the white guards were rubbish. The real reasons for the workers' disturbances in conditions of economic collapse were the fundamentally incorrect economic policies of the Bolsheviks, especially their policies towards the peasants, which were leading to famine and ruin. 'In any case,' I said, 'once a general strike is a reality, any government that calls itself a workers' government is duty-bound to try to reach an agreement with the strikers. An attempt to crush a workers' movement with military force, especially using privileged military units, is a direct betrayal, a direct attempt at preparing a Bonapartist coup with your own hands.'

I was of course aware that it would have been naive to have hoped to 'convert' the Chekists. But Komarov was a member of the Petrograd Executive Committee and I wanted him to convey my words to the people running Petersburg. I considered it to be my political duty to say, at that critical moment, what I thought. The Chekists, naturally, stuck to their guns, insisting that the workers had simply been led astray, and that once they understood that, they would simply return to their factories, therefore no concessions or compromises were necessary. I was convinced that if there were no concessions made, the matter would end with workers getting shot. Once that had happened, everything would depend on the military authorities, who would not shrink from imprisoning any Bolsheviks who dared express any dissatisfaction with their actions, just as they imprisoned Mensheviks. 'Let's just see what happens in two to three days, if the Executive Committee does not make any concessions to the workers' demands', I said.

'But are these strikers really workers at all?' exclaimed Komarov. 'There are no real workers any more in Petersburg: they all went off to the front, or into food work and so on. These are all scum, self-seekers, and shopkeepers who wormed their way into the factories during the war so as to avoid the call-up. A delegation of Kronstadt sailors came to Petrograd today. They visited several factories, asked the workers about their demands, and told them straight that if they didn't stop these disturbances, the Kronstadters would deal with them!'

I scoffed at this 'Kronstadt' communism, which could call the working class 'scum' and reckon on using the sailors to establish socialism. 'Look, it's only now that you are cursing the Petersburg workers,' I added, 'yesterday your papers were praising 'Red Petersburg' to the skies as the most advanced detachment of communism. Now you're showering praise on the sailors. But that won't last either. Let's see how you curse them if they start creating disturbances!' At the time I had absolutely no idea that the Kronstadt sailors really were on the verge of rebelling. On the contrary, I was convinced that given the privileged position they had enjoyed since October 1917, their loyalty to Soviet power would be unshakable. Our organisation had no links at all with Kronstadt. But, unexpectedly for me, my words turned out to have been prophetic, and within a few days the Bolshevik papers were writing about the rebellious sailors as 'pimps' and 'klyoshniki' (idlers – from the word 'klyosh', the flared trousers much favoured by fashion-conscious sailors at that time). Among the Chekists, my remarks about the Kronstadt sailors and what I had said about what would happen in two to three days if there were no concessions from the authorities gave rise to the legend that 'Dan knew that a rising was being prepared', or even that 'Dan prepared the Kronstadt rising'!

Our discussion in the Cheka Presidium dragged on until two in the morning. After that, they took me to one of the common cells of the Cheka prison. The two bakers I had met in the reception area were also here. We were met by the senior warder in the usual prison warder uniform, with a sabre over his shoulder. He launched himself at us with mouthfuls of abuse against strikers and counter-revolutionaries. After every two or three words he peppered his speech with curses against the Mensheviks and Socialist-Revolutionaries. This made me lose my temper, and I asked him sternly: 'You're a Communist?'

'Yes I am.'

'You should be ashamed of yourself, with your foul language! Haven't your own papers been saying that you can be expelled from the party for swearing like that?'

'And who are you?' he replied. I told him my name. Suddenly his face broke into a cheerful smile: 'Well, well, Comrade Dan! I know you! You know, I'm a Putilov worker, and we and the Mensheviks always worked together standing up for the workers!'[1] But these SRs ...', and again a torrent of abuse poured from his mouth. I tried to shame him again, but he just declared: 'Let them do what they like, let them kick me out of the party, but I can't stop swearing, it's just a habit! You know, I like you; it's just these SRs and white guards ...' I could see that this was hopeless, and simply shrugged.

The workers lay down on the beds. I sat at the table, the warder sat down next to me and had a most friendly conversation about current events, never tiring of mentioning his parents every minute. Gradually a few of the other prisoners began to gather round the table – mainly people arrested for 'speculation' (i.e. trading) – and listened in to our conversation with interest.

I did not want to sleep, and I did not want to lie on a bed without inspecting it thoroughly for lice. The warder suggested getting some hot water for tea. But before he could return, they came for me. I quickly gathered my things, and two officers led me out into the yard, where a lorry full of people was waiting for us.

We travelled along the deserted embankment of the Neva to Shpalernaya Street, to the remand prison.

NOTES

1. The Putilov Works was a major engineering factory in St Petersburg. Its workers had long been in the forefront of the labour and revolutionary movement in Russia.

6
In Peter-Paul Fortress

It was already past three in the morning when our lorry passed through the gates of the remand prison. There were the usual formal questions at the reception, and then our group, which consisted almost entirely of workers, was led through heavy iron gates into a gallery of single cells.

Again I was reminded of how it had been a quarter of a century back, and later, in 1906, when I had come here to visit Trotsky, who had been imprisoned in connection with the first Soviet of Workers' Deputies. At that time Trotsky would talk in agitated and indignant tones about the practice of mass executions which the tsarist regime had introduced. He told me about the young worker Kotlov, who had been sentenced to hang. Trotsky had walked and played leapfrog with him in the prison yard. One night he had disappeared, never to be seen again. But times change, and people change with them …

In one of the galleries we were stopped and subjected to a thorough search. We pointed out that we had been searched already at the Cheka, but that did not help. Our things were turned out, we had to remove our outer clothes, everything was searched and probed. Finally the whole tiresome business was over, and we were to be put in cells. But there were no empty ones available. All the tiny single cells had two or three people crammed into them. They shoved me into a cell where some large person was lying on a bed. He started, frightened, when he heard the noise of the heavy doors.

It was dark in the cell. I sat in my coat on an iron bench affixed to the wall, in front of an iron table. My cellmate sat up on the bed and cautiously began asking me who I was and how I came to be there. Gradually dawn began to break, and I could make out the features of the person I was talking to. He was a tall, thickset man of about 50, with a large bushy beard, a broad face, a fleshy nose, rough worker's hands and frightened, darting eyes. He was wearing a torn coat and torn boots. He told me his story: he was a worker at the Baltic factory, an Estonian, and in his free time – which had not been in short supply in the last few years – he had worked for himself in a little repair shop. But his repair shop had recently been confiscated, and he had come to be classed as one of the 'bourgeois' by the communists. He was not interested in politics, and was solely preoccupied with his domestic concerns, dreaming of returning to Estonia. But as soon as the disturbances had begun, he had been arrested on the instructions of the party cell. He assured me that he was 'not guilty of anything'; he was clearly frightened and did not fully trust me. He had heard of me through the newspapers. Gradually he allowed himself to be drawn into a more open conversation with me. The life of Petrograd workers he depicted was joyless. He told me that at the Cheka he had met arrested workers from the Nobel-Dorofeev factory, who had been found with our newspapers and proclamations.

As morning came, they brought round boiling water. I had some tea and sugar with me, and my cellmate accepted a piece of sugar from me with embarrassment. He had been here one day and had already lost weight: they gave out half a pound of bread a day, and two servings of some cloudy liquid containing occasional pieces of horse lung – and that was all. What is more, this 'soup' contained no salt. I had brought two pounds of bread and a small piece of butter with me, which had happened to be in the house. We shared the bread out between us, reckoning that it should suffice for at least two days, until we were brought some more from home. Having eaten his portion of bread, my neighbour carefully collected all the crumbs from the table into his hand, and put them in his mouth.

We were not kept together for long. In the morning the prison chief, a working-class Bolshevik called Selitsky, came to 'get to know' me, and ordered that my cellmate be moved to another cell, leaving me on my own. Selitsky immediately tried to get me into 'political' conversations of very little interest. It was all the usual thing: the Mensheviks are serving the bourgeoisie by standing for freedom of trade and thus deceiving the workers. The Bolshevik papers and there are no others – had given the line, and the whole Soviet bureaucracy from top to bottom repeated that line … until they were given another line.

The prison cleaners, and the orderlies who brought round the hot water and food, were nearly all working-class 'criminals' who had stolen something or other – what other way was there to survive? Some of them had been involved in political activity in the past. One of them knew who I was, and as a result straightaway I got the chance to make contact with other single cells, where some more of our comrades who had been arrested were being held. I found out the surnames of a lot of people who were being held, and let them know I was there. I got books from the prison library. All the 'senior orderlies' working in the library were inside either as 'counter-revolutionaries' (lawyers, engineers, writers) or as 'speculators'. In spite of the growing efforts at 'weeding out', many of the prison staff were decidedly hostile to the Bolsheviks and, conversely, inclined to sympathise with every prisoner. This all made our situation easier, and the strict prison rules were not always strictly observed.

Every day they gave me a newspaper to read for a quarter of an hour, and in the evenings up to midnight I could hear the sound of music, singing, laughter and applause. This came from the theatre which had been set up in one of the wings for the staff and inmates. But I was never allowed to go there – I was in 'strict' confinement. 'You wouldn't find it interesting anyway', said the assistant prison chief, 'it's just a bit of fun for the bourgeois types and the speculators'.

The electricity was turned off in the cells at 10pm, but Selitsky allowed me to use it without time limits. For something to do I stocked up with novels borrowed from the prison library and sat up till late at night.

On 1 March I got to bed about 1am. I had just managed to doze off when there was the sound of a key in the lock, the door opened, and the chief warder shouted 'Get your things together!'

'Where am I going?'

'You'll see when you get there! But hurry up – they're waiting for you!'

Reluctantly I got up and gathered my things. 'Are you ready?' 'Yes.' They took me out into the corridor, and from there to the prison office. There I met a whole mass of party comrades: Professor Rozhkov, Nazar'ev, Kamensky, Chertkov, Shpakovsky, Dorofeev, Kazukov, Malakhovsky and Glozman. They all had their things with them, and all were wondering – where are we being taken? The office staff said they had no idea. They seemed embarrassed for some reason, and were unusually solicitous. They willingly fulfilled all our requests and hurried to return to us the money and personal items which had been taken from us when we entered the prison. Five women prisoners were also brought in – either Socialist-Revolutionaries or people the Cheka for some reason had decided were members of the SR party. They also had no idea what was going on.

We all sat in the reception area and started talking. We asked each other who had been arrested when, and under what circumstances. Everyone had been taken in the last four or five days in connection with the strike. One comrade told a graphic tale of how a social-democratic meeting near the Moskovskaya Zastava had been tracked down and arrested by a gang of armed youths from the Komsomol. We exchanged our thoughts on where we would be sent to next. Some thought it would be the Kresty (the isolation prison on the Vyborg side), and some thought it would be 'Petrozhid' (the former Petrograd Women's House of Correction).

At last, the sound of lorry engines could be heard in the yard, and the guards entered. Our names were called out, and we were taken out into the yard. We climbed into two large lorries, with armed soldiers positioned in each of the four corners and on the trestles next to the driver. The heavy gates swung open and we drove out. It was already getting light. It was frosty on the streets. There were no people walking about, but from time to time Red Army men with rifles seemed to emerge from the walls. From the driver's cab someone would shout 'friend!' and we would go on further. We went past Liteynyy Bridge – it would seem that we were neither going to Kresty Prison nor to Petrozhid. We started wondering where we were headed. To the Cheka? Or maybe to Peter-Paul Fortress? Someone whispered: 'Are they taking us off to be shot?'

'No', came the reply, 'they do the mass shootings on the Polygon. If we'd been going there they'd have turned and gone across Liteynyy Bridge.'

We turned onto Troitsky Bridge. We became more certain that we were on our way to Peter-Paul Fortress. We stopped on the bridge. Something had gone wrong with the lorry in front, and we were waiting there without moving – a strange and terrible caravan on a deserted bridge, in the morning mist, suspended above the Neva. A car came towards us from the direction of the fortress, containing Chistyakov and some other Chekist. They confirmed our supposition that we were being taken to the fortress, but did not tell us the pretext or purpose. Finally we got started again, and soon the lorries passed through the outer gates of the fortress, then along a long drive to the second set of gates. They nosed through them and came to a halt in between two long single-storey buildings. On the one on the left there was a sign: 'Commandant'.

I had been imprisoned in this fortress in 1896. Then I had occasion to visit it in 1917, when the Tsar's ministers were held here – as the deputy chairman of the Central Executive Committee, I had to make enquiries of Beletsky (former head of the Police Department), Vissarionov (his assistant), General Kurlov (former deputy interior minister) and General of the Gendarmerie Spiridonovich, in order to check some information we had received that a certain prominent political figure had been a provocateur. In our turns, both we, and the Tsar's ministers, had been put in the so-called Trubetskoy Bastion. In 1917, the cell in which I had served time was occupied by the last tsarist interior minister, Protopopov.

But Trubetskoy Bastion is in the very depths of the fortress, behind the Monetnyy Dvor [the Mint]. And our lorries stopped outside the entrance itself. There was another lorry also standing here, filled with people. They turned out to be twelve SRs; they had also been brought here from the remand prison three-quarters of an hour ago, and they were standing and waiting for accommodation to be made ready for our arrival. It turned out that we had not been expected here! It would seem that our transfer had been decided suddenly. What did all this mean?

Another ten minutes or so passed. Chistyakov got the guards to form two lines from the lorry to the building on the right, and first the SRs, then we, walked in single file through the doors, above which a sign still proudly declared: 'food stores'. This had formerly been the premises of the officers' guardroom. But it had been used as the food store and for the whole winter had remained unheated. Now it had been quickly cleaned out for us and the stove had been lit. The large room into which they took us was full of smoke, and the walls were dripping. There were twelve Red Army men here in leather jackets and a tall man with a scruffy light-grey beard, wearing a lambskin astrakhan hat and a grey soldier's greatcoat. He searched us. He took away all belts, braces and shoelaces. I protested that having no braces made walking difficult. 'You won't be needing to walk anywhere!'

We were placed in tiny cells. Their doors opened on to a big room, and they had high barred windows overlooking the yard. The Red Army men in leather, bearing rifles, took up watch in the big room – the guardroom, with a wide plank bed in the centre.

I found myself in a small cell with Rozhkov, Nazar'ev and Chertkov. Although there were four of us, there were only three wooden trestle-beds without any bedding. One of them was under the window, and the other two were perpendicular to it, with a semicircular gap in the middle. It was possible only to sit or to lie down. In this cell it was cold, smoky and damp from the walls, which had been frozen through and were only beginning to thaw out. The door closed behind us and the key was turned. In order to visit the toilet, which was located right there along the corridor, one had to open the little window in the door on to the guardroom and call the attendant, who would arrange for an escort.

We sat down on the benches in our coats and boots and began to consider the situation. We all began to be convinced that we had been brought to the fortress to be shot. But whether it was because deep down we could not quite accept the idea, or whether it was because we were all in it together, not one of us was downhearted – we were laughing and joking. But all the signs suggested that the intention was to execute us – our sudden removal from the remand prison at night, the words of the man who searched us that we would not be needing to walk anywhere, and the complete unpreparedness of the accommodation into which we had been thrown. Running ahead a little, I should say that the administration was so unprepared for our arrival that we did not get any food, bread or hot water until eight o'clock the following evening.

We just could not make out what had brought on this sudden outburst of terror. The most recent news we had available was that the strike wave had been receding. So what had happened to make the Bolsheviks panic so much? Because the mad idea of shooting us would only have entered their heads if they were in a state of panic. It was only two days later that we learned from one of the guards that 'Kronstadt was in revolt', and after that we started to receive the newspapers every day. Then it all became clear to us. Although we had all been ready for death, we had been at a loss to work out the reasons for this unexpected turn of events.

In order to finish with the question of our proposed execution, I shall state what I know about this episode.

In the first days of March, my wife, who was living in Moscow, was telephoned by a very prominent Bolshevik, who said: 'Well, I can reassure you. Fedor Il'ich is not in any danger.' My wife, who at that time knew only that I had been arrested but still did not even know that I had been taken off somewhere from the remand prison, asked in astonishment what was going on. Her caller then told her the following: a telegram had been received from Zinoviev in Petrograd asking for permission to shoot me (our caller was telling my wife about me, but this probably applied to all the people taken to the fortress) as a 'hostage' for Kronstadt. He was refused permission. 'But since I know that this fellow has a tendency to do his villainy in advance and then request permission, I was sure that he had succeeded in having Fedor Il'ich shot already. But now I have made enquiries and am satisfied that all is well', her interlocutor concluded.

More than one year later, Radek confirmed that telephone conversation. At the commission of the Berlin conference of the three Internationals in early April 1922, Radek said that I had not been shot in Petrograd only because 'The Central Committee of the Bolshevik Party had resolved not to shoot the leaders of the Menshevik Party deliberately'. Zinoviev had clearly made a blunder here by not shooting us 'accidentally', perhaps, as they say, 'while attempting to escape'.

Incidentally, I should say that there is no basis for Radek's claim at that same commission that two proclamations issued by our Petrograd organisation during the Kronstadt rising had been the pretext for raising the question of execution. These proclamations took the only standpoint socialists could take. We were faced with an uprising of workers and sailors, a large part of whom had been yesterday's *communists* (almost the entire Kronstadt Bolshevik organisation had joined the rebellion). This was an uprising which even the rebels themselves had not anticipated – they had been driven to armed struggle by the government's haughty and peremptory refusal to consider their demands. Our organisation had demanded that the government should above all try to resolve the conflict peacefully, through discussion and compromise. But, however one might regard the content of the proclamations, and however one might insist that I, although I was in prison at the time they were printed, bear moral and political responsibility for them as for all the activities of our party organisation, Radek was exposed as a liar by one irrefutable fact: we were transferred to the fortress with a view to shooting us on the night of

1-2 March, while the first proclamation of our Petrograd organisation was issued on 6 March, i.e. when the high-ranking caller had already 'reassured' my wife about my fate. They had wanted to shoot us as 'hostages' pure and simple …

Back to my story – it was already light when we, having moved the benches, doubled up somehow and lay down on them to sleep, fully dressed and covered with all the rags that were to hand. We fell into an exhausted sleep, and woke up late.

The first day was very tedious. As I have already said, we did not get anything to eat until the evening, and up till then we were expecting someone to come and take us away at any moment … The little windows in the doors were closed, and the guards strictly ensured that people only went to the toilet one at a time. But in the evening, when they finally brought us a meal and gave out some bread, the atmosphere changed for us. We became sure that we would be *living* here, rather than just passing through these cells on the way to the place from whence nobody comes back …

This change was also noticeable in our guard. We were held by Red Army men from the armoured train, mostly green youths, rather nattily dressed, half of them communists. They did twenty-four-hour guard duty, changing every day, twelve people on each rota. They were commanded by military commissar S. – the same person with the scruffy beard who had searched us when we were taken in. As soon as we had finished our meal, he came up to the little window on our door. He had heard about me, and was curious to 'get to know' me. A conversation, or rather, an argument ensued, since the subject of conversation immediately turned to current events – the strike, that is, as we still knew nothing about Kronstadt. We were not told anything about the rising.

S. was a very curious person in many respects. He was witty, certainly not stupid, and had even read a little, although he liked to pretend to be a rustic. In fact, as he told me later, he had taken a course at a mining college and had worked in the mines of the Donbass. After the war with Germany, he had taken a most active part in the civil war, having become a fanatical communist. He had travelled almost the length and breadth of Russia, had twice been seriously wounded, and had only by a miracle escaped from prison and avoided execution. He had within him a strange mixture of unusually attractive geniality, endearingly childlike cheerfulness, Asiatic cunning and bestial cruelty.

Without batting an eyelid, he told me that he had drowned fifty captured white officers in a river, throwing them off a bridge one after the other.

'Why did you do something so appalling?' I asked.

'What do you mean, appalling? We couldn't take them with us – we were afraid of being captured ourselves – and we didn't want to waste bullets, because we were short of them.'

On another occasion he told me – with a laugh – how he 'had a little joke' with some Jewish trader they had arrested on suspicion that the leather he was carrying in his cart had concealed weapons under it. There were no weapons, but before letting the trader go, he wanted to have his 'little joke' at the expense of the 'bourgeois', so he stood him against a wall and ordered that he be shot – but they fired blanks. They did this three times – just so they could bring a little happiness to their prisoner when they told him he was free to go – although he could easily have died of heart failure …

He was unusually solicitous towards the soldiers under his command, even calling his Red Army men 'sons', and his soldiers liked him a lot. And he also treated us with great consideration and even tenderness. He pulled strings to ensure that we were given mattresses, books, newspapers and tobacco. He ensured that the food was improved, and increased the frequency with which we were given hot water for making tea. He would stand by my cell for hours and several times said how glad he was to have made my acquaintance and to have found out what Mensheviks really think. He treated the other prisoners with the same attention and interest.

'You can see now,' I remarked to him once, 'that we are not as terrible as we are made out to be. And when we were brought in you were scowling at us as if you were ready to kill us all there and then.'

'Believe me comrade Dan,' he replied, 'I greatly respect you, and wish you all the best with all my heart. But if they were to order me to shoot you, I'd do it straight away!'

Very soon all the Red Army men guarding us were brought into the discussions. Whatever started the conversation off, it would inevitably get round to the workers' strikes and the Kronstadt rising, of which we were reminded more and more often by the roar of cannon, which we could hear clearly. And from here we can move directly to the Bolsheviks' policies on food and the peasants. The papers continued, day in and day out, to denounce us for our demand that requisitioning be abolished, which was now supported by the Kronstadt rebels. 'Lackeys of the bourgeoisie!' 'Servants of the Entente!' 'Traitors!' But when we explained to the Red Army men that requisitioning, by leaving the peasants nothing more than the bare minimum for feeding themselves, and often even less, deprives the peasants of any desire to extend their sowing, thereby condemning the country to famine and pushing the countryside to rebellion, they had no argument and agreed with us. Most of them were themselves from the countryside. Only one of them – a worker by origin, intelligent and politically developed – stood firmly for the line of the Bolsheviks, and even he agreed that in many respects the Bolsheviks' policies were damaging. But all the same, it was necessary to stand up for them and crush all malcontents without mercy. This Red Army man also related to us very well on a personal level, and tried to explain in a friendly conversation how he had arrived at this attitude. He told me he had been living in Crimea, and had been mobilised by Wrangel. Life there was much better and they were better fed than in Soviet Russia. But he could not tolerate the lordly attitude of the officers to the workers and soldiers, and for that reason he was prepared to forgive the Bolsheviks everything – there were no 'lords' here!

I had another opportunity to observe a very sharp expression of this aspect of the people's revolutionary psychology, which many people somehow fail to appreciate fully.

We had already long enjoyed complete freedom of association with one another, and were even able to go from cell to cell – of which more below. One of the SR prisoners called to his comrades: 'Gentlemen! Come over to our cell, we're having a sing-song!' A Red Army man, who had just then been lounging on a bench and cheerfully chatting to one or another of the prisoners, jumped up as if he had been stung, red in the face with his eyes glaring, and bellowed: 'Don't you dare say "gentlemen"! I can't stand that word! If you say it again, I'll lock you all back up in your cells!'

Gradually our debates became more lively, and the guardroom became a kind of Red Army club. On one occasion I was standing around with S. As usual we were talking about the peasant question, requisitioning and the grain monopoly. Red Army men were crowding round us, taking part in the conversation and saying their pieces. The newspapers were brought in. I opened them and saw Lenin's notorious speech to the Tenth Congress of the Bolshevik Party. Lenin was setting out a complete turn in the policy towards the peasants: a renunciation of requisitioning, the introduction of a tax in kind, and freedom to trade. The papers immediately changed their line: all the articles were arguing, following Lenin, that requisitioning had just been an unfortunate necessity of 'war communism', that the Bolsheviks had always stood for a tax and freedom to trade and now that the civil war had finished, they were bringing those policies in. Now the Mensheviks were 'traitors' for slandering the Bolsheviks, for maliciously accusing them of favouring policies which had been forced upon them by the circumstances of war.

There and then I read out loud Lenin's speech and the newspaper articles. Their effect on S. and the Red Army men was like thunder in a clear sky. When I read out the concluding remarks of Lenin's speech, in which he said that the Mensheviks and SRs still needed to be kept in prison, there was embarrassed silence and indignation. S. made some kind of weak joke and hurried off to do some urgent task. The Red Army men just shrugged their shoulders in silence when I asked them what was the purpose of holding socialists in prison, and why it had been necessary to bombard the Kronstadters with artillery. Their main demand had been the abolition of requisitioning. Apart from that they had only called for free elections to the soviets (not 'soviets without communists', as the Bolshevik press had dishonestly claimed) and the removal of policing functions from communist party cells.

After that, S. began to avoid political discussions, and the conversations with the Red Army soldiers moved on to other themes, above all, the question of the meaning of terror and the anti-democratic policies of the Bolsheviks.

On the basis of these discussions, we became very close to our guards. Before a week had passed, the conditions of our incarceration had changed radically. Of course it remained unbearably cramped and stuffy. But the little windows in our doors, and soon the doors themselves, were open, we could speak freely with one another and visit one another, and in the evenings those who liked that sort of thing would gather in the largest cell, which held seven people, and sing in a choir. Some of the Red Army men would join in, and those who were standing guard would warn if the commandant was coming. S. got us the right to take exercise – half an hour per day. The Red Army men would do all sorts of favours for us, and through them we were able to send a letter to our families informing them of our whereabouts.

Our families had spent ten whole days chasing round the city looking for us. At the remand prison they were told that we had been taken to the Cheka. At the Cheka HQ on Gorokhovaya Street they were assured that this was a misunderstanding, and that we were still at the remand prison. Enquiries were made at all the other Petrograd prisons, but in vain. To be sure we had been allowed to send two postcards a week from the fortress. We all wrote them punctiliously, but the Cheka no less punctiliously filed them away in its offices, and not one of them reached its intended destination. Finally a letter, sent on by one of the Red Army men, revealed the secret to our relatives, and they started to besiege the Cheka, demanding visits and the right to send us parcels. Nobody got any visits, but eventually the Cheka agreed to the parcels. This opened a line of communication between us and our relatives, who had until then been desperately worried, as there had been clear hints given at the remand prison that in all probability we were no longer alive. Incidentally, those same Red Army men helped some family members visit and speak with their imprisoned relatives, on more than one occasion. But for obvious reasons I am not going to disclose how.

Certain young workers in our organisation showed remarkable courage and resourcefulness. Not only did they manage to make contact with us (again, I will not say exactly how), but also passed us letters from comrades and family, proclamations of our Petrograd committee and the *Izvestiya* of the Kronstadt rebels,[1] as well as taking messages from us to be sent on. Thus the attempt to isolate us behind a wall of silence was a definite failure, and within two weeks we had quite lively communications with the outside world.

Finally, even the authorities could not fail to notice that as far as strict isolation and discipline were concerned, the position in the 'food store' was not ideal. Maybe even S. himself had reported that his guard was 'disintegrating'. Some of the fortress staff even came and told us that according to their information we had been brought here on the night of 1-2 March to be shot. By this time our 'connections' even extended into the fortress commandant's office, which gave us some opportunity to keep abreast of the authorities' intentions for us, the conversations of the Chekists who came in to inspect our parcels and so on.

On 20 March our guard was changed suddenly. S. and the Red Army men from the armoured train left, to be replaced by guards from the Finnish battalion billeted in the fortress barracks.

Most of our new guards could not speak a word of Russian. And only one of us knew enough Finnish to ask for bread, water, a knife, or what the time was. Any political discussions became impossible. But if the authorities imagined that they could ensure a strict regime that way, they were sadly mistaken. There were almost no communists among the Finns, and they were all most unenthusiastic about their duties. The few chances we got to converse with them were enough to reach an understanding. On our first day with them there was also a lot of trouble when one guard grabbed the arm of L., one of the SRs, who had just come back from the toilets, to get him to return to his cell more quickly. The adjutant of the battalion came running, but it soon became clear that it was all a misunderstanding. The Finn had only grabbed the prisoner by the arm because, not knowing Russian, he could not explain what he wanted him to do, and so on. Exactly one day later all the cells were open again, and all our 'liberties' were restored in even greater measure than before. When the commandant unexpectedly turned up with some Chekists on the night of 1-2 April to take us to another prison he was dumbstruck: the guard on the door was soundly asleep in his chair, there were no other guards to be seen, there were twelve loaded rifles just standing against trestles in the middle of the guard room, and we were all visiting one another in different cells. I should mention, so that there remains no doubt on this, that all the 'privileges' and services we got from the Red Army men of the armoured train and from the Finns were provided without thought of reward. If we leave aside the bits of bread and other foodstuffs which we occasionally shared with them, neither we nor our relatives ever gave any of them anything.

I should say something about the make-up of the prisoners. I have already listed the party comrades who were brought to the fortress with me. Apart from the nineteen-year-old Malakhovsky, a talented lad who had just been released from nine months imprisonment only to be thrown into a dungeon again (he was not released until May 1922, in order to be sent into exile) all the others were experienced and active party members. This was not the case with the SRs. Of the seventeen SR prisoners, no more than four or five had maintained any connection with the party. When I showed them the proclamations of our committee, they said: 'We envy you. At least your organisation was and is still working, and you are not inside here for nothing. But us? We have not done anything in Petersburg for two years now.' Despite that, one of them had already been arrested seven times under the Bolshevik regime. Most of the 'SR' prisoners had been taken on the basis of old lists, and had long severed their connections with the party, and even abandoned politics altogether. This led to many 'letters to the editor' appearing in the Bolshevik papers with 'honest' repentance and even direct attacks on the SR party. Among the women detainees was T., who had only got on to the list of 'SRs' because on one occasion she had taken a parcel to an SR in prison. Another, a young girl, L., was guilty of nothing more than living in T.'s apartment! And, if Grigoriy Zinoviev had had his way, these people would have been among the 'hostages' taken for Kronstadt! At any rate, even those who 'repented' remained in prison for at least one-and-a-half to two months, others were inside for five, six or seven months, and some are still in prison – a year and a half later!

We spent exactly one month in the fortress. On the night of 1-2 April, accompanied by the Chekist Stepanov, we were driven out of the gates of the fortress in lorries and set off for the Vyborg side and 'Petrozhid'. We stopped on the street outside while the Chekist went into the prison office. A quarter of an hour later he emerged to declare that 'they won't take you'. This was a case of interdepartmental struggle: 'Petrozhid' was run by the Commissariat of Justice, which did not want the Cheka to be in charge of its prisons. We were taken along Shaplernaya Street, and at two in the morning we were once again at the hospitable building we had left in such dramatic circumstances a month previously.

NOTES

1. An English translation of all fourteen issues of this paper, *Izvestiya vremennogo revolyutsionnogo komiteta matrosov, Krasnoarmeytsev i rabochikh gor. Kronshtadta* [News of the provisional revolutionary committee of sailors, Red Army men and workers of Kronstadt] is available on: http://libcom.org/library/kronstadt-izvestia.

7

In the Remand Prison

The duty assistant and the girls in the office at the remand prison were very surprised to see us when we walked in, and not only because they had not been warned that we were coming. One of the girls asked me directly: 'How come you are still alive? We were convinced you had been shot!'

'Why?'

'Because they took you all away in the way they always take people away to be shot, "into the care of the Cheka commandant".'

We had to wait a long time in the office – there were no spare places in the prison! The remand prison, built for 700, was at that time holding 2000! Quite some time passed while they 'cleared out' our accommodation. This turned out to be a cell in the general section of the women's wing, which had been reassigned to men in view of the overcrowding in the prison. The women who had been brought in with us were taken to single cells upstairs and the rest of us, twenty-two people, were led into a cell which contained only thirteen beds. The general section was laid out as follows: three cells opened out on to a corridor, connected with the stairway through a heavy lattice door, and the duty warder sat on the landing.

When we went through the corridor, it was full of people sleeping just on the floor. Many were walking about carrying their things, looking for somewhere to settle down. These were the unfortunate inhabitants of the cell which had been 'cleared out' for us. It is not hard to imagine that they were far from delighted at our arrival, and they used some quite choice epithets towards the sort of people who enjoyed such privileges, for whom other prisoners could be turfed out of their beds. We all felt very bad about this and would have been prepared to spend the night in the corridor ourselves, but there was no use in causing trouble and we had no power to return the expellees to their places.

Somehow we all found places on the beds and the floor. I personally preferred to lie down on the floor, because more than anything I was afraid of catching lice which, as we discovered in the morning, were not in short supply.

In the morning we started to get to know the many and varied people who were crammed into the other two cells and the corridor. The most interesting of them were two groups: some engineers who had been working on building a power station on one of the rivers; and the Kronstadters. According to the engineers, they had been arrested as the result of a clash with a communist political commissar. They said that this commissar had been embezzling on a grand scale. When they tried to oppose him, he denounced them as counterrevolutionaries and saboteurs. Among the charges they faced was one of buying food for their workers on the free market in contravention of the rules laid down by decree. According to these rules they should first have applied for foodstuffs to all the various official bodies, and then have waited for these bodies either to fulfil their request or refuse to do so. On paper this was all very well, but in reality the workers would not have waited for the results of all this red tape; they would simply all have left. Now, according to the engineers, the commissar's dealings have all been exposed, and he had been arrested along with the rest of the party cell. So far as I can remember, all those engineers went to court and were found not guilty. I do not know what happened to the commissar. The engineers were interested to ask me about the positions of social democracy, but the question which concerned them most of all was whether social democracy stood for freedom of the press and for dissenters, including for 'bourgeois'. When I gave them the answer in the affirmative, they calmed down. 'Otherwise,' they said, 'from our point of view there would be no difference between you and the Bolsheviks. You are both socialists and, as the Russian revolution has shown, socialism is a utopia which does a lot of damage.' I was very interested to observe this new psychology among the intelligentsia in Russia, where traditionally any intelligentsia movement had, since time immemorial, had a more or less socialist colouration.

The other group, the Kronstadters, consisted of workers and sailors. The sailors were very embittered. They were outraged at the Petrograd workers who 'for a pound of flesh' had not supported them but 'sold them out'. Disillusioned in the Communist Party, to which many of them had formerly belonged, they spoke with loathing of all parties in general. To them, the Mensheviks and SRs were no better than the Bolsheviks: all parties were just striving to seize power, and, having seized it, to swindle those who had trusted them. 'You're all in it together! Look, when they brought you in, the Bolsheviks just chucked us out of our beds on to the floor, but for you, there's every comfort!', said one sailor angrily. We don't need any parties, we need anarchism – this was the conclusion drawn by most of the sailors from their disillusionment in the workers' movement and parties.

The workers' attitude was a bit different. I particularly remember one tall, strong, handsome young electrician. He described to me in detail how he and about ten other comrades were taken prisoner and brought round the coast of the Gulf of Finland to Petrograd. They were given nothing to eat for three days, and more than once their guards had tried to shoot them; only the intervention of the leader of the convoy had prevented this retribution. But, he said, after Kronstadt had been retaken, up to 600 prisoners were shot.

The rising, he told me, had not been expected even by the insurgents themselves. Nobody had expected that their modest demands,[1] for which virtually all the Kronstadt communists had also voted, would not only be rudely and decisively rebuffed, but would also bring about Trotsky's ferocious order for merciless retribution against the Kronstadters.[2] Moreover, once the rising had become a fact, absolutely everybody had joined it. It was also quite clear why the rising had failed: in order to succeed militarily, it would have been necessary to entrust the organisation to the officers, but the insurgents had feared the political consequences of doing that and therefore the rising had been defeated. The Bolsheviks had depicted General Kozlovsky as the leader of the rising. In fact, the sailors had simply obliged him to continue in the same post as commander of artillery that he had occupied under the Bolsheviks, and had not given him any power at all. But despite all this, it had only been possible to retake Kronstadt thanks to trainee officers who had had to be brought from as far away as Moscow, and Chinese troops. Kronstadt's warships had been unable to move for ice. There were even cases when the trainees refused to attack.

What struck me about what he was saying was the genuine tenderness with which he spoke of the atmosphere in Kronstadt during the rising. Everyone had been keen to share whatever he or she had, everybody willingly set about their allotted tasks, it was a time when 'everyone could speak freely', even the communists. Only ten of the communists had been arrested in the final days of the rising. But they had been held in good accommodation, had been fed the same as the insurgents themselves, and not a hair on their heads had been touched, even though one of them had been the Baltic Fleet Commissar Kuz'min, the editor of the Petrograd *Krasnaya gazeta*, which every day had been threatening the Kronstadters with the most terrible punishments.

The same joyful tenderness permeated what one of the leaders of the insurgency, Perepelkin, a member of the Kronstadt Revkom, told me. I got to know him later, when we were exercising in the prison yard. He had written a detailed description of everything he had experienced at Kronstadt, and this manuscript, so far as I am aware, was passed to someone outside the prison to be sent abroad. I do not know what happened to it. It will be a great pity if it turns out that this most interesting human document has been lost. I should say that Perepelkin's attitude also tended towards anarchism.

In his manuscript, Perepelkin told of the enthusiastic, 'springtime' atmosphere in Kronstadt, how the children were dancing in the streets with joy at being rid of the Bolsheviks and would take food supplies to the defensive positions, how there was fraternisation between the sailors, Red Army men and workers. All the naive political illusions of that movement and all its real tragedy were very vividly expressed in Perepelkin's story.

One further Kronstadt sailor left a lasting impression on me. Like Perepelkin, he was supposedly in 'strict' isolation, but I met him in the exercise yard. His surname was Savchenko, and he assured me that he had just been an ordinary participant. However, because of his surname he had been singled out by the Cheka as one of the 'ringleaders' of the rising. According to him, the papers had carried something about a former tsarist general Savchenko who had been involved in the rising, and they had mixed him up with this general. He was pale, with feverishly burning black eyes, and emaciated from living solely on prison rations, without receiving anything extra from outside. He was constantly haunted by the thought that he would be shot. I reassured him. I said that two months after the rising, after the Bolsheviks had fundamentally changed their economic policy in the spirit of that demanded by the Kronstadters, when they were worried about worker unrest and were trying to calm the workers down and to that end had even dreamt up the idea of a 'non-party conference', it was most unlikely that the Bolsheviks would think of starting to shoot people again now, when there was not the slightest need, simply for base revenge. That would simply be unjustified bestiality, and even without that, the Bolsheviks' position was hardly so brilliant that they could afford to stir people up against them with pointless, vicious, retribution. Savchenko would listen to me, half believing me, half not believing me. His hopes would rise, and then be dashed again. He was terribly tormented, sitting alone in his cell, without any books, constantly thinking about death. Alas! I proved to be a poor prophet. One cursed night two lorries came, took over forty of the Kronstadters from the remand prison, including Perepelkin, Savchenko and the cheerful young worker, and took them off to the Polygon to be shot. We found out about this only the next morning, and for a long time I kept seeing Savchenko's tormented eyes before me, and I could not come to terms with this senseless, unnecessary murder. According to the warder, as the doomed men walked out into the yard towards the trucks that would take them to their deaths, they sang 'Vy zhertvoyu pali',[3] while their drunken Cheka guards cursed them.

I should say here that there were some other prisoners connected in one way or another with the Kronstadt case who I met in the remand prison. First and foremost, the whole family of General Kozlovsky was held here: his wife, her eleven-year-old daughter and two sons, who were sailors. None of them had been in Kronstadt. Their sole crime consisted in their ill-starred 'choice' of parents. Nonetheless, all of them, apart from the little girl, after spending several months in the remand prison, were sentenced to several years in concentration camps. And before they had been transferred to the remand prison, Kozlovsky's wife and daughter had already spent one and a half months in one of the dark cells of the Petrograd Cheka, of which I shall say more below.

I also remember one young man of about twenty, a cadet at the Orianienbaum flying school and a member of the Communist Party. He showed me the written 'sentence' he had received from the Cheka, which read quite literally: 'Heard: case of X., member of the RKP, party card No. X, accused of abstention in a vote on a resolution. Resolved: one year's detention in a concentration camp.' (sic!) The young man explained to me what this startling piece of paper meant. There had been a resolution moved by the political commissar at a general meeting of the air cadets, demanding merciless retribution against the Kronstadters. My interlocutor did not feel able to put his hand up for it, and was immediately arrested. From other conversations I learned that the events in Kronstadt had in general had a very strong effect on the mood of the Petrograd communists, especially the youth, and many had been obliged to leave the ranks of the Bolshevik Party.

In May and June, a new category of Kronstadters began to appear in the remand prison – those who had returned voluntarily from Finland, where they had been made to live in concentration camps in the most difficult conditions. The newspapers sang their praises. They had made declarations about their repentance of their own accord, and some of them had even thrown dirt at their own former comrades. For all that, they, or at least most of them, were not set free, but were again put into various concentration camps. The ones I spoke to were lamenting their cruel fates and betrayed hopes.

In the common corridor, where it was difficult to move with all the people there, it was noisy and even cheerful. As I subsequently observed more than once, the prison administration and the prisoners themselves had developed a strange sort of indifference to the prison, as almost a kind of inevitable and normal stage in everyday life through which everyone must pass. 'You can't say no to prison or poverty' – in Soviet Russia that old Russian saying fitted the general attitude better than ever before. The mysteries of prison had ceased to terrify people. Over the last few years, virtually everybody had been there – if not as an inmate, then as a relative visiting and bringing parcels.

Each morning, the senior warder would change the duty guards. 'Look what a beauty I've brought you today!', she joked, addressing the prisoners crowded at the grated door. 'I chose you the prettiest one specially!' The sailors immediately set about trying to flirt with the 'beauty' – a healthy, good-looking girl – calling her 'little sister' and in return getting called 'little brothers'. And the warder, with her heavy bunch of keys hanging from her belt, would engage in cheery banter with the inmates, over whose heads death's scythe was swinging …

Around two o'clock we were brought our parcels. It turned out that our relatives, on arrival at the fortress, had learned that we were not there, but they were not told where we had been taken. They had lugged their heavy packages round various prisons before locating us. But no sooner had we started on this pleasant addition to the very meagre prison rations, when they came to take us off to the men's isolation wing. Here we were put two to a cell, but all exercised together in the small and stuffy prison yard, in a circle surrounded by a grille. On the other side of the grille, around the four sides of the yard, the prisoners on 'strict' isolation would exercise, and in this way we could talk to them: the extreme overcrowding in the prison would have made really strict isolation impossible, even if the ordinary prison staff had wanted to fulfil to the letter the 'regulations' which hung on the walls.

A few days later we were visited by the new head of the Petrograd Cheka, one Semenov who, like Komarov, had been a worker. He gave the impression of being a modest man of little learning. I asked him, among other things, what the change in the leading personnel of the Cheka meant – would it mean a change of course? He answered without any pretence: 'I don't know either. Wait and see!'

He told me about the 'elections' then taking place in the factories for the non-party conference, and proudly declared that there would be no more than ten or fifteen Mensheviks at the conference. I remarked to him that if the elections had been genuinely free, our party would have got at least half the delegates. He started to argue heatedly, but when I asked him, mockingly, 'Well, why not give it a go then?', he smiled and changed the subject.

This new theme was the conditions in which we would continue to be held in prison. Semenov declared that he understood very well that we should not be held in normal prison conditions, because we had not been charged with anything, but 'in view of the difficult period that Soviet power is going through at the moment', it was deemed essential to 'isolate' us from contact with the outside world and, in particular, workers. Consequently, everything possible would be done to alleviate our situation.

And, indeed, the next day we were transferred to new accommodation. The galleries of the fourth and fifth floors of one of the wings of the remand prison were separated off by a wooden partition, and were made available for our sole use. First all the males who had been held at the fortress were transferred here, and then this section, the 'socialist corridor', was filled at our request with imprisoned socialists and anarchists. In most cases we were one to a cell; only a few had to share as the number of prisoners grew. Our cells were open from morning until eleven or twelve at night, and we could have electricity all night. Instead of the usual quarter hour we got a full hour for exercise. In one of the cells on the upper floor an iron stove was installed, on which we could heat up food brought from home, boil potatoes and kasha, and get boiling water. This was an important gain, because the food in the remand prison at that time was not only very meagre, but also repugnant. Each day we got half a pound of bread, a teaspoon of sugar, and soup twice a day. At first, that soup was made from hares, although God knows where the Petrograd food supply organs got them from. I have rarely had to eat anything more revolting, and within a few days I had such heartburn and nausea that I completely lost my appetite for a week or two, and after that did not touch the official rations. When the hares had all been used up, they started making soup out of herrings, to which they added frost-damaged fodder-beet and then, once the port at Petrograd was back in operation, American beans, which for some reason tasted bitter, but were at least more nourishing than the infamous beet. But all this was given out in such insignificant amounts that those prisoners who did not receive anything from home starved terribly. The Kronstadt sailors who had returned from Finland suffered particularly badly. But worst of all was that in order to economise on fuel, the water boilers were not in use. So tea was boiled up in the same pots which had just been used for making hare or herring soup! It tasted and smelled disgusting. The 'coffee-style' drink, made with that water and the burnt sunflower seeds that they gave to prisoners instead of tea, could only be swallowed with difficulty.

In the evenings we would hold lectures in the corridor, and sometimes 'clubs' would meet in individual cells – social democratic, SR and anarchist. Women socialists would come over to the lectures and club meetings from the women's corpus. Once a week we would attend the theatre, set up in the opposite wing of the building. Imprisoned artistes would perform here – there were always a few of them – together with people invited from outside. Recitals, singing and balalaika orchestras were staples. There were often ballet demonstrations, for which they invited in second-rank dancers from the state theatres. Sometimes they even put on entire plays, particularly by Molière and Scribe, in revised and abridged versions. Once, they put on a revolutionary play, but it dated from the time of the February revolution of 1917 and therefore sounded rather strange under conditions of Bolshevik rule. Its subject matter concerned three soldiers who had been sentenced to death for propaganda among their comrades and insubordination to the authorities. The condemned men make a speech against the death penalty and in praise of freedom.

They are being taken out to be shot when another officer, also devoted to the cause of freedom, comes running up with the news that there is a revolution in Petrograd, the Tsar has been overthrown, etc. Of course, the condemned men are immediately freed, and their comrades organise a celebration for them. But this celebration also appealed to the prison audience with its denunciations of the death penalty, its speeches about freedom, and the character of the revolutionary tsarist officer. The communist in charge of prison 'cultural education' came to realise that, from his own point of view, he had not made the best choice of play for propaganda purposes. Attempts to use cinema for propaganda were no more successful. They showed some old German 'social' drama. Its story was as follows: the workers in some massive factory declare a strike, even though their young leader warns against it. The strike ends in failure, and the embittered workers try to blow up the factory and get even with the boss. But their virtuous leader saves the factory from being blown up and protects the boss against retribution. As a result, some of the strikers end up in jail, and the virtuous workers' leader is rewarded with a place on the board and the owner's daughter's hand in marriage.

We were allowed to receive parcels from home twice a week, and visits took place once a week, on any day. In addition, parcels could be also handed over during visits. Of course, we were able to establish better communications with the outside world than when we were in the fortress. Not only did we regularly get letters and information about the activities of our organisation, etc., but also *Sotsialisticheskiy vestnik*, which had begun to be published in Berlin. On one occasion the administration descended on us to carry out a night search, but we had been warned in advance and the search found nothing. On another occasion the Cheka tried to place their agent with us in the guise of an arrested Menshevik. But he behaved so awkwardly that we rumbled him straight away. The next day he was 'released'.

The number and variety of people held in our 'socialist corridor' continued to increase. Some new members of our organisation turned up. They had been arrested in March and April, and we learned some interesting facts from them about the worker disturbances and the Kronstadt rising. After my arrest, our organisation had received an invitation to send representatives to an 'Assembly of Plenipotentiaries of Petrograd Factories'. It was agreed to send one comrade to find out what this was about. It turned out the 'assembly' was pure fiction.

There were no 'plenipotentiaries', there were just some individuals calling themselves Plekhanovists, Left SRs, anarchists etc., none of them elected by anyone. Moreover, a leaflet had been issued under the name of this 'assembly', calling on the workers to rise up in the name of the Constituent Assembly, in complete opposition to our organisation's policy. Naturally, our comrade refused to have anything more to do with this unserious group of adventurists.

Another case I was told about showed how all sorts of dubious elements were trying to take advantage of the confused situation. One of our comrades was visited in March by a well-dressed young man with expensive rings on his fingers. He declared that he sympathised with the Mensheviks and, knowing that our organisation was short of resources, offered to help us financially. As a first instalment he was offering 300,000 rubles, which at that time was a very large amount. This generous offer, and the circumstances in which it was made, aroused understandable suspicions. The young man was told that at present the organisation did not need any extra funds, and he went away, leaving instructions on how to find him should the need arise. It was not possible to establish on the basis of these instructions where this offer had come from, in view of the arrest shortly thereafter of certain comrades and the enforced departure of others from Petrograd. But on the basis of the information we had, all the comrades who had had anything to do with that business formed a definite impression that this naive attempt to make use of our organisation had come from white guard circles, which had been beginning to stir quite strongly at that time.

Apart from members of our organisation, there were some non-party workers who joined our prison group. The discussions in our club and reading *Sotsialisticheskiy vestnik* brought them very close to us. The Socialist-Revolutionary group was also supplemented with some new members, mainly from those who had already been held for more than a year in Petrozhid and were now being transferred to us. Many of those who had been counted among the SRs when we were in the fortress, as I have already mentioned, managed to write letters of recantation and were released. Unexpectedly, such a letter was also written by a member of our group, Skvortsov, a young worker with the state document dispatch office who had always come over as one of the most right wing members in our club, accusing the party of 'conciliationism' towards the Bolsheviks. Cunningly, he had written an ambiguous letter to the Cheka, declaring that he did not support and never had supported party positions, leaving the Cheka to work out for itself in what sense he 'did not support' them. He was immediately excluded from the club, but had the cheek to demand that this decision be rescinded, threatening that otherwise on his release he would 'expose' the Mensheviks. Unfortunately, his example proved tempting to one of his colleagues from the dispatch office, a man with a family which could not be saved from hunger by the little help that the other workers could give them.

The 'SR Minority' group (the 'Narod' group) also had two representatives on our corridor, while the Left SRs had four or five people. Finally, there were lots of anarchists of all possible varieties. Among the anarchists one especially interesting group was the 'Americans' – Russian workers who had been living in America but had been tempted back by stories about the communist El Dorado in Russia. The reality had proved to be the most bitter disillusionment for them, and masses of them had ended up in Soviet prisons. Their experiences had had a strong effect on their attitudes, causing them to change their views on political freedom and to develop a burning hatred of the Bolsheviks. I was to meet one of my fellow prisoners, the worker R., again in Riga; he had been released but had then been threatened with re-arrest and he had preferred to go into hiding. He had managed to get to Riga with enormous difficulties and, having learned from the papers of my arrival there, sought me out to ask for help in returning to America. He told me he would now devote all his efforts to opening the eyes of American workers to the true nature of the Bolshevik regime. The extent of the surveillance of the 'Americans' who had returned to Russia was revealed by the following small but typical fact: one of the people on our corridor had been arrested by the Cheka in the street for talking too openly to a pair of 'Americans' who had asked him for directions.

Masses of prisoners were constantly passing through the prison – workers, minor civil servants, sailors and Red Army men. Compared to what I had seen in Butyrki prison two years previously, the make up of the prisoners had changed sharply. Looking into the exercise yard, I could see hardly any well-dressed 'speculators', top civil servants or white guard officers. They turned up in prison, but were lost in the grey mass of 'ordinary' people. The constant influx of wave after wave of new prisoners reflected the entire life of the city as if in a movie. When the Petrograd port reopened, ships began to arrive with goods from abroad. Before long you could gauge with mathematical accuracy how intensively the port was operating and the sort of cargoes that were being brought in just by looking at the make up of the prisoners. You would come across a new group of prisoners in the exercise yard, and in reply to the question: 'What are you in for?' you would get: 'For flour', 'For beans', 'For herring' and so on. The abnormal conditions of life were driving people to resort to embezzlement. En route to the government body to which they belonged, these cargoes were leaking out on to the free market through dozens of channels. Hundreds of people involved in unloading, transporting, storing and distributing the goods got away with it, but a few dozen would end up in prison.

This was the criminal section of the prison. But in the political section the life of the city was reflected even more starkly and obviously. There was unrest throughout the summer in the working-class districts of Petersburg. The factories, at a standstill because of the lack of fuel and raw materials, would reopen and then close again. Every time they opened, the starving workers would present certain demands, and when these demands were not met, there would be disturbances, strikes and even, here and there (the other side of Moskovskaya Zastava), attempts at mass street demonstrations. The beginning of the months of April, May and June were marked by such disorders. And on each occasion, a few intellectuals and party workers, together with hundreds of grey, non-party workers, would pass through the prison. There were tramway workers, workers from the Skorokhod, Obukhov, Putilov and Rechkin factories – all of working-class Petersburg. And each time the Cheka would start its repugnant work of intimidating the agitators, separating out the ringleaders, stirring people up against the 'intellectuals'. In the end most of those arrested would be let out after four to six weeks, but certain groups from each new haul would accumulate in prison or end up in concentration camps.

In order to deal with the workers' discontent, the Bolsheviks decided to make a show of rapprochement with non-party people. It was declared that Bolshevik power wanted to base itself on the non-party masses and bring representatives of those masses into leading Soviet positions. In that spirit, an agitational campaign was initiated in the factories and plants to prepare for elections for a conference of non-party workers in Petrograd. A mandate was drawn up, dealing with the workers' material needs, and this mandate was heavily pushed by the Bolsheviks during the elections of delegates. But no matter how far our organisation had been weakened by continual Cheka raids, it decided nonetheless to take an active part in that campaign, explaining to the working masses that any attempts at secure improvements in their situation without fundamental changes in overall policy were doomed to failure. Therefore our organisation insisted that delegates be given a political mandate, demanding democratic freedom, and that as a first step in that direction, elections to the soviets and to that conference should be free. Our agitation was fairly successful, although it was carried out by just two or three workers, unaided. Nobody from outside could show up at a meeting without being immediately arrested. Then the Bolshevik papers started to say that Soviet power, in fact, only wanted to develop closer ties with 'honest' non-party people. The only people declared to be 'honest' were those who were prepared to be content with the sops promised in the Bolshevik mandate and the dozen or so jobs in Soviet institutions, and would agreed not to poke their noses into politics. All the others were classified as 'dishonest', 'Menshevik stooges' and so on, and a merciless struggle against them was declared. After this the whole Soviet police apparatus was brought into play to ensure that, alongside the communists, only 'honest' non-party people, tempted by the prospect of becoming important bureaucrats, got through into the conference. Of the Mensheviks, only the three workers who had led the campaign got through to the conference.

Understandably, under such conditions there could be no real 'rapprochement' with non-party people, and the conference played no part in calming the agitated state of the workers. Ten or so 'honest' non-party people got more or less cushy posts and sank without trace into the mass of Soviet bureaucrats, while several dozen delegates found themselves immediately behind bars. The workers' disturbances followed their course, continually increasing the prison population and obliging the postponement of the promised elections to the Petrograd Soviet. The idea of 'non-party' conferences was abandoned once and for all.

This decision was also a consequence of the course of the conference itself, which was in no way to the Bolsheviks' liking, for all their careful screening of the delegates. The mass of non-party people, not united around any firm programme and without the opportunity for meeting with our couple of delegates in any organised way, could not, of course, take the conference into their own hands and conduct it according to their own wishes. The Bolsheviks were able to impose their own presidium and agenda without any difficulty. But the mood of the masses was such that our tiny faction found wide sympathy and active support. Thanks to this, the Menshevik speakers, the workers Zimnitsky and Baklenkov, were able to get up and speak, and their speeches received loud applause. Moreover, they were able to ensure that our party declaration was read out at the conference. Zinoviev read it out in his speech, of course, lacing his reading with polemical attacks on the Mensheviks. The danger seemed so great to the Bolsheviks that – in keeping with their well-known practice – there suddenly appeared at the conference a mass of new 'delegates', from the communist cells and the leadership of the trade unions. Nobody knew who had elected them.

The mood of the conference revealed itself sharply when my name came up. One of the Bolshevik leaders, replying to Baklenkov, reproached him for not thinking like a Marxist. Thinking on his feet, Baklenkov came up with this proposal: 'You may well be right that I, a mere worker, who had just pennies spent on his education, do not know my Marx well. But why have you Bolsheviks brought all your leaders here to argue in this learned way with us workers? If you want the Mensheviks to argue their case in a Marxist way, you can do that very easily: Zinoviev can get in his car and go to the remand prison and fetch Dan from there. Then we can have our argument.' This unexpected proposal was taken up by the audience, which did not quieten down for a long time, demanding that I be brought from the prison. They had to call an interval. The presidium, not knowing what to do, met to decide whether to bring me there or not. As a non-party worker who had been on the presidium told me later, even some Bolsheviks were wavering on the question, and Zinoviev had to be as forceful and unceremonious as he could to ensure obedience. The interval lasted several hours, during which time the delegates were given lunch and a Bolshevik working-over. When the session reconvened towards the evening, the chair, ignoring the shouts from delegates demanding to know what the presidium had decided about me, immediately gave the final word to Zinoviev. Then the resolution was voted through, although, in view of the mood of the meeting, compared to the initial draft it contained significantly fewer polemical attacks on the Mensheviks.

In his closing speech, Zinoviev spoke of his 'profound respect' for those old social democratic workers like Zimnitsky, who remain with the Mensheviks only through some misunderstanding. But within a few days I found myself talking to that same 'profoundly respected' Zimnitsky in the yard of the remand prison, from which he has only just now been released – more than a year after the conference! According to Zimnitsky, the representatives of the non-party workers on the presidium had complained bitterly to him that they had not known how to stand up for themselves and had let the Bolsheviks make fools of them. But the conclusion they, and by extension all the non-party masses, had drawn from this was not comforting. Yet another door, through which they had hoped to escape from their dead end, had slammed shut on them. They left the conference feeling aggrieved, but ever more apathetic and hopeless – after all, what can you do about it? They could only shrug and passively await the further course of events. The episode with the conference brought home to me particularly strongly just how criminally the Bolsheviks, with their dishonest tricks, were squandering that revolutionary capital which the workers had accumulated in decades of struggle!

Anyway, as imprisonment goes, the conditions of our incarceration were quite tolerable. But only people who have not had to spend months locked up could imagine that this would make prison any more bearable. However paradoxical it may sound, I would say from my observations and experience that the better the external conditions of one's confinement, the more sharply one feels the purely psychological oppression of being in prison. People – particularly political people – have an uncontrollable urge to be active. And the less effort and attention you have to devote to overcoming minor external inconveniences, the more your thoughts and feelings will focus on what is most unbearable in prison – the deprivation of freedom, being under constant supervision and observation, and the right of some hostile third party to regulate how you live, your contacts with the surrounding world, and your urge to be active. This psychology does not mean that the prisoner cannot appreciate the real humaneness of any improvements in prison conditions, but it explains why even in the most ideal prison the prisoners' struggle for greater and greater rights does not and cannot stop.

On entering a Soviet prison, nobody can know even approximately how long he will be in there and how the imprisonment will end. There is no firm code establishing any definite relationship between crime and punishment. There is no firm procedure for conducting trials, or any unshakeable guarantees for the accused. The case may be decided by the Cheka, or it may be handed over to a revolutionary tribunal which, in its turn, is also not constrained by any norms in the punishments it can hand out. In prison, a person, whether guilty of the crime of which he is accused or not, has an equal chance of being unexpectedly released or just as unexpectedly being dragged off to be shot on the basis of a decision the Cheka Presidium has taken behind his back, without his knowledge, sometimes without even a formal interrogation! And the charges themselves are formulated in such imprecise, elastic terms that the prosecution has no need to produce concrete proof that any concrete actions have been committed which incriminate the prisoner. Then, of course, anybody can suddenly be taken as a 'hostage' at any time. This is because, according to the doctrines of Bolshevik justice, it is not a matter of trying, but of *retribution* against elements who, for some reason, are regarded *at that time* as dangerous to the communist dictatorship. This was literally how the 'state prosecutor' Krylenko formulated the tasks of the tribunal I faced four years ago on a charge of 'slandering Soviet power'. In an issue of the paper we produced at that time I had written that the Bolsheviks were 'shooting workers with and without trial'. (The case was stopped by the tribunal.) In effect, anyone held in a Bolshevik prison is taking part in a kind of lottery, in which the stake is his life. It is not hard to imagine what sort of nervous atmosphere that creates in prison and how heavily it weighs on the minds of the prisoners!

For us socialist prisoners, there were further complications to this uncertain legal situation. In the previous chapter we saw the response to the unexpected rising of the Kronstadt sailors. People who were often guilty only of having fought at one time against tsarism under the banner of one of the socialist parties, or even people who simply had some personal connection with socialists and had been unlucky enough to get caught in one of the Cheka round-ups, suddenly found themselves in danger of being shot. This was in March 1921. At the same time Lenin, speaking at the RKP congress, had no qualms about accusing Professor Rozhkov and myself – without the slightest evidence – of supposedly being organisers of the Kronstadt rising.

And then in April Semenov, the chairman of the Petrograd Cheka, officially told us all that we were not accused of anything but were just being held in isolation. I should add that within two months Professor Rozhkov was freed on the orders of that same Lenin who had only recently been willing to have him shot!

But what does 'isolation' actually mean? It is no guarantee against unexpectedly having to face entirely new or, conversely, entirely old charges. The best illustration of that is the trial of the SR leaders. After two and a half years of isolation, at the whim of the Bolshevik government's political calculations, they were handed over to a revolutionary tribunal and their lives were once more at stake. In the final analysis, isolation simply means that one's term of imprisonment is completely indefinite, release becomes problematic, and it is quite obvious that all the interests of a living person are completely subordinate to the arbitrariness of the Cheka. All this brings about extreme nervous tension. More excitable people become jittery, feeling that there will be some kind of unexpected turn of events which will cut the Gordian knot, and start directly pushing for sharp and decisive forms of struggle in order somehow to break the chains of this arbitrary power. One needs a lot of *sang froid* to remain calm in such circumstances, and we should not forget that we are talking about people whose nerves have been stretched by long years of hard labour, prison, internal exile and emigration. It is hardly surprising that from time to time people start proposing hunger strikes, suicide and various forms of violent protest. And once the strings have been overstretched, this internal turmoil finds expression in one form of prison drama or another: hunger strikes, self-immolation and refusal to obey orders became common occurrences in the 'socialist' cells and corridors of the Bolshevik prisons. The question of a hunger strike was raised more than once in our group in the remand prison, but each time we were able to persuade our comrades not to hurry to put their lives and health on the line. Various anarchists did declare hunger strikes from time to time, and not without success, now and then, someone was released.

The atmosphere of nervous tension in Bolshevik prisons is intensified by another factor – the extreme instability of the prison regime itself. Leaving aside the significant differences of regime in different prisons, even in one and the same prison the regime is constantly changing, whether at the whim of the administration and the Cheka, or in line with the prevailing political winds, or depending on the intensity of the struggle carried out by the prisoners themselves and the response that struggle may get outside the prison and so on.

Our 'ideal' regime in the remand prison did not last long. Within a month they began gradually to take away the benefits we enjoyed – moreover, without any provocation from our side. It started with an unexpected ban on women coming to our wing to attend lectures. Then they told us that the cells would be locked at 7pm. At the beginning of June we were suddenly prevented from receiving visitors for two weeks without explanation. It later transpired that this was in connection with the workers' disturbances which had been going on in Petrograd at that time. On one occasion, while we were asleep at night, our iron stove was removed. This was a serious blow, given the disgusting nature of the boiling water supplied by the prison kitchen. Our workers immediately found a way around this, making miniature stoves out of bits of iron which were lying around the yard, which we put in the window space and heated with slivers of wood. But a short time later these little stoves were found in a night search and removed. After a long series of different petty restrictions, finally a stop was put to our major freedom; at the beginning of July they stopped opening our cells in the mornings and we found ourselves in the same position as other prisoners, only meeting during exercise and visiting each other only secretly, with the connivance of the warders, but hidden from the administration.

Naturally enough, this unprovoked worsening of our conditions unnerved our comrades. Appeals to the Cheka and personal talks with Semenov and other Chekists who visited were fruitless; they brushed us off with vague promises. A hunger strike looked as if it would break out any day, and only our appreciation of our extremely unfavourable position held us back from it. The events in Butyrki prison at the end of April eloquently testified to that position. The regime there had also been 'ideal', and the glories of the specially designated 'socialist corridor' had been trumpeted in Bolshevik papers both in Russia and abroad. But this had not prevented several hundred Chekists and Red Army men descending on the corridor one fine night, getting the prisoners out of bed and sending them off to different prisons in the provinces, where most of them were incarcerated in the most harsh conditions. Those who resisted were beaten up. The Petrograd Chekists also threatened that we would be sent off to different prisons in the provinces if we made any attempt to protest against the worsening of our conditions, and unfortunately the general situation at that time was such that they could probably have carried out their threat.

There is one further peculiarity of Bolshevik prisons which makes being in them unbearably harsh. This is the fact that you are always seeing a few people who are marked for death. You live with, and meet in the corridors with, people who are to be shot today or tomorrow. You see and hear these unfortunates being taken away, you can read the insane fear and terror in their eyes, and all the time you know that you are powerless, unable to avert the impending horror – cold, measured and implacable like a machine.

And maybe the most dreadful aspect of it is the ordinariness of the circumstances in which this mass slaughter of people is taking place, where it has become an everyday occurrence. All the attempts to depict the Bolshevik terror in its most extreme, outrageous forms, in its chilling and repulsive excesses, in its monstrosity, simply detract from the numbing feeling it creates in its 'normal' form, as its callous mechanism crushes hundreds of people in its path.

Here are a few impressions seared into my memory from the time I was in Butyrki in 1919.

A young man, a Latvian, is walking in the prison yard. He has a cocky expression and a shock of long, shoulder-length, brown hair. He talks to everyone, laughs and jokes – and everyone answers him. Nobody dares to not answer him. Every day he is in a new outfit; today it may be a sailor's outfit, tomorrow it may be court attire, and the next day, an engineer's double-breasted jacket. Where does he get all these outfits from? He readily explains – he has taken them from people who have been executed. He was a Chekist, temporarily resident in Butyrki, where he acted as a spy and snitch. His surname was Lejta, at least, that was what he was called in prison. After I had been freed, I met him by chance in the street, on Kuznetsky Bridge, in the company of a group of young men and girls, even though he was still 'in prison'. The Chekists who visited the prison had no qualms about talking with him in the yard and giving him money etc. Officially Lejta himself had been sentenced to be shot for some abuse or other. When I saw him in prison, a year had already passed since he was sentenced.

Here is another image. At five in the afternoon the notorious 'commissar of death' Ivanov arrives. As the familiar car drives into the prison yard, there is agitation among those who have been sentenced to death. Who has he come for? Whose turn is it now? It turns out that he has come for the large-scale 'speculator' V. But he throws himself on to his bed, saying that he is ill and cannot walk. He wants a stay of execution for just another day in the vague hope that maybe he can find a way out. But the Red Army Chekist cannot be bothered to wait. He slaps the man twice round the face, and the doomed man stands up, dresses and goes with his executioners.

Here is yet another. A tall, healthy, good-looking young man, a highways inspector, who has been sentenced to death and has spent the past month wondering every day whether the Central Executive Committee will pardon him or not, leans out of the window and shouts to his friend in another cell: 'Mitya, they've come for me! I'm sending you my boots, I'll go there barefoot. I don't want these b____s to get my boots as well. Goodbye!' And he disappears from the window, and his steps can be heard in the corridor for the last time. How simple! How ordinary! Even without any dramatic effects, it is unbearable, suffocating!

The final impression, which I took away with me from the remand prison, was another of those unforgettable experiences. One morning towards mid-July the workers who had brought us bread told us that during the night thirty cells had been cleared out on the ground and first floors of the men's block, and that many men and women had been placed in there, two or three to a cell. The entire wing which contained those cells had been isolated from the rest of the block; even the prison administration was not being allowed in there, and guard duties were being carried out by Chekists. Subsequently we received additional information that everybody being held in those cells had no right to exercise, visitors or parcels.

Out on exercise, we did indeed see armed Chekists, who would not let anyone into one part of the corridor. We could see from the yard that the windows of all the cells set aside for the new arrivals had been fitted with double frames, and despite the terrible heat and stuffiness, they were tightly closed. But there were two windows on the ground floor without the extra frames – there had evidently not been time to prepare and fit them yet. At each of these windows we could see the faces of three young women pressed up against the bars. I asked one of these groups what they had been brought in for. 'It seems we are very dangerous criminals, we're accused of conspiracy', they replied with a cheery laugh. But a Chekist entered their cell and interrupted our conversation, rudely shouting and making them get away from the window. Thereafter a guard was specially posted in the yard by those windows to make sure that prisoners did not try to look in.

It was clear to me that some new large-scale slaughter was being prepared. The smell of human blood was in the air. My suspicions turned to certainty when I saw the smooth, self-satisfied figure of Agranov, the Cheka investigator for special cases, in the corridor. And when I left the remand prison a few days later, I took with me the heavy foreboding of what was to come, and the image of those young faces, happily laughing behind prison bars, while death was already just around the corner.

In Moscow I was to read of the outcome of that 'conspiracy', which was connected with the name of Tagantsev. Sixty-one people had been shot, including the poet Gumilev, and Professor Tikhvinsky (who in the past had done much for the Bolsheviks in the 1905 revolution by concealing the bombs and weapons of their fighting organisation), old women, young women and girls. They probably included my three young interlocutors with their carefree laughter ...

The monotony of our confinement was sometimes broken by the release of individual comrades. But their places were quickly taken by new arrestees. From time to time the Chekists spread rumours that we Mensheviks were all going to be released soon. In particular, various prisoners were told during interrogations that I was going to be released. I do not know why they did that, but at least once a week I heard 'reliable' information that I was due for release the next day. Semenov came to visit us again and on that occasion told us openly that we Mensheviks were under the authority of the CC of the Communist Party, and that he could not therefore tell us anything about our case.

We were told the same thing by Agranov, who unexpectedly called Rozhkov and me in for questioning. I was asked about my attitude to the Constituent Assembly, the New Economic Policy, the peasant movement and the Kronstadt rising. In the interests of countering deliberate falsification of our party's position I wrote fairly detailed answers to these questions. My depositions were later included in one of the secret bulletins published by the Cheka for its local bodies and high officials.[4]

After questioning me, Agranov began a fairly lengthy conversation with me, during which he expressed regret that Soviet power was not able to keep people like us, who had not been charged with anything but were just being isolated, in 'palaces'. But for the moment, instead of 'palaces', the conditions of our imprisonment continued to deteriorate ...

NOTES

1. These demands, and an English translation of all fourteen issues of the Kronstadt *Izvestiya*, can be found on http://libcom.org/library/kronstadt-izvestia
2. It is not clear which of Trotsky's orders Dan has in mind here, but he may be referring to Trotsky's 'final warning' to the Kronstadt rebels, issued on 5 March 1921, in which he stressed that 'only those who surrender unconditionally can count on the mercy of the Soviet Republic'. See V. P. Naumov, A. A. Kosakovsky, compilers, *Kronshtadt 1921*, Mezhdunarodnyy fond 'Demokratiya', Moscow, 1997, p. 70.
3. 'Vy zhertvoyu pali' was a traditional funeral anthem for the Russian revolutionary movement. The lyrics were written in 1878 by Anton Arkhangel'sky. A free translation of the first stanza:

   You fell a victim in the fateful struggle
   With selfless love for the people
   You gave all you could for it
   For its life, honour and freedom.

4. See appendix IV for the text of Dan's deposition.

8

The Petrograd and All-Russia Chekas

On 20 July, immediately after lunch, the chief warder came to me: 'Get your things and come to the office!'
'Where am I going?'
'I don't know.'
I guessed, however, that I was being taken to Moscow. This had been on the cards for a long time: all the other arrested members of our Central Committee were being held in Moscow, and my family were living there. There were absolutely no good reasons for keeping me in Petrograd other than to cause me personal inconvenience, but more than six months had passed before they decided to transfer me to Moscow.

A Chekist was waiting for me in the office. We got into a car and drove out onto Gorokhovaya Street.

At the Cheka office the young man sitting behind the desk who took my forename, surname and all that turned to me and asked: 'Are you Menshikov?'

I looked at him with amazement. 'I'm Dan.'
'Yes, but that's your party name; is your real name Menshikov?'
'No.'
'Strange. So you're not Menshikov, then?'
'No.'
Giving me a disbelieving sideways look, the bureaucrat called the guard and whispered something to him. I was taken to the reception area, where I had begun my prison ordeals on the night of 26-27 February. Again I underwent the most thorough search here, and then I was taken up the stairs to a door marked 'Solitary Block'.

At a knock from the guard the warder opened the door and, passing through a passageway with a long bench, we entered a fairly large room. What I saw here made me freeze on the spot. Along three walls of the room a sort of wooden barracks had been built, divided into tiny cells, each of which had a door opening on to the room with a little window that could be opened and closed. The same sort of barracks had been constructed in the middle of the room, with two rows of cells opening in opposite directions. By the only window in the room, which opened on to the yard, there was a desk for the warder. A guard sat on a chair by the door. Faces looked out with curiosity at me from all the little windows in the cell doors – male and female faces, old and very young.

Having recorded my name in a book lying on the desk, the warder opened the door of one of the cages and invited me to enter. I found myself in a cupboard about the size of a changing cubicle. Along one wall there was a bench less than two feet wide, on which a crumpled mattress had been thrown, stuffed with a little straw which had disintegrated into dust. There was no way in which a person of average build could lie down and stretch out on that bench. Of the remaining space, also less than two feet wide, a third was taken up by a little wooden table affixed to the wall. There was just enough space for someone to stand and move from one leg to the other – the only form of movement available to someone imprisoned in that wooden cell, where you had to pass the time without fresh air, without daylight (an electric bulb was on day and night), without exercise, without books or newspapers.

The wife of General Kozlovsky spent a month and a half with her underage daughter in such a cell. Next to me there was a tall young woman who had been arrested three weeks previously, and next to her was a Left SR who had been arrested in the wake of Kronstadt and had spent more than two months there with no prospect of release.

Nonetheless, there was cheerful chatter from all the cells and sometimes even the laughter of young women. The warder did not try to stop people from talking to one another, willingly went round all the cells giving out cigarettes and things to eat, brought boiling water and let people out to visit the toilet at the first request.

The other prisoners told me that the warders were far from all like that, and moreover, a prisoner is entirely dependent upon them. They could refuse boiling water, they could keep people waiting for hours before letting them out to the toilet, and there was nobody to hear complaints. They could allow themselves all sorts of things. There were two inscriptions scrawled on the wall of my cell, both in the same hand: 'Why should I, so young, and, they say, beautiful, have to die? I want to live. Lord, let me live, save me!' And below that: 'To any women held here after me. Be on your guard. Don't sleep too deeply at night. I only managed to fend off the warder tonight by throwing a glass of cold water in his face.'

But that day the warder was very good. Both he and the guard were constantly going round the cells, carrying out various little errands for the prisoners, were not preventing them from stopping by other cells and chatting on the way to and from the toilet, and were offering boiling water on their own initiative. But, having sat down on the bench and looked around, I definitely decided against drinking any tea or eating anything here; there were bugs crawling out of every crack and mice running along the floor. It was repugnant. I stood up and avoided sitting down, having decided to remain standing until such time as tiredness obliged me to overcome my aversion.

I should add that according to other prisoners, the Cheka had another room with the same sort of cubicles, padded with cork and completely sealed (our cells had no ceilings). They would seem to be for especially strict isolation, and the cork is there to prevent communication by tapping. Some prisoners told me that they had themselves spent time in those cork-lined boxes and considered that they had been specially made for torture. It is so hot and stuffy in them that people would just pass out. I personally did not see any such cells, and am merely stating what I was told, without vouching for its accuracy.

I had spent about two hours in that cubicle when suddenly I heard the noise of the door opening, and the warder told me the commandant was coming. A fat unshaven face with a black moustache appeared at the window of my door, and asked me in a thick bass: 'So you're not Menshikov, then?'

'No, but what's all this about?'

But the commandant, without answering, turned away from my cell and left the room, leaving me completely bewildered. And suddenly it dawned on me – these good people had presumably been told that they should fetch the *Menshevik* Dan and they, through their political ignorance, did not understand what a Menshevik was, and turned the word into the surname Menshikov! I immediately asked the warder for a piece of paper and wrote a note to the commandant roughly as follows: 'I am constantly being asked whether I am Menshikov. I suggest there may be a misunderstanding here and you really want to know whether I am a Menshevik. In that case I can affirm that yes, I am the Menshevik Dan.'

The warder ran with my piece of paper to the commandant. It worked like lightning. Within fifteen minutes I had been asked to gather my things, and a Red Army man brought them for me to the commandant's office. The commandant sat behind his desk and laughed: 'There's been a misunderstanding. Soon you'll be going off to the station, to Moscow. You can wait here.' I thanked fate for having saved me from that terrible bug-infested place, but also for having allowed me, thanks to a misunderstanding, to see with my own eyes how people could be held in Petrograd, a capital city, in the year 1921 of Our Lord and year five of the Russian Revolution! I was later told that the Moscow Cheka had the same sort of solitary cells.

I was in the commandant's office for over an hour. A tall man came in, in a new leather suit, with an unpleasant, haggard face and a deformed right hand, missing a few fingers. This was commissar Borisov. I climbed into a car with him and two Red Army men and we drove along the Nevsky Prospekt to the Nikolaevsky Station. Nevsky still had its previous dismal, deserted and run-down appearance. But there were also some symptoms of the New Economic Policy to be seen: here and there linen signs had appeared bearing words like 'Groceries', 'Women's Fashions' 'Cafe' etc. It was all pretty wretched.

At the station we went to the office of the regional transport Cheka. I remained with the Red Army men in the reception area, while Borisov went into the boss's office. He came back out again looking crestfallen; thanks to some misunderstanding no places had been set aside for us on the train. We had to go back to Gorokhovaya Street and come back the next day.

The commandant was already gone, and we were received by the official at the reception – not the same one as that morning. I was taken from the office back to the infamous solitary block. Its inmates and the warder began asking me why I was back. But before I had even had time to answer and go through the cell door which had been opened for me, a Red Army man came running up: 'Come along with your things. You are being put somewhere else.' I felt somewhat awkward and embarrassed to be leaving that den, where so much human suffering was concentrated in such a small space ...

We went downstairs. I was met there by the commandant's young assistant, who ordered the soldier to take me to the Isolation-Transfer Unit. This unit consisted of three rooms, one for women and two for men. The men's section contained thirty beds with straw mattresses, covered with clean bed linen. Overall it was very clean and tidy. There was nobody else in the men's or the women's sections. The unit was intended for transferring and quarantining groups brought in from the provinces. Those who come in undress in the anteroom, get a warm shower, and then get dressed in prison clothes while their own clothes are disinfected. The warder on duty suggested that I took a shower, an offer I willingly accepted. Whether all groups who are brought in pass through this unit, I was unable to ascertain.

Besides the duty warder, the commandant's assistant arranged that the senior warder be posted in one of the rooms. This was the same elderly man who had already searched me thoroughly twice, after my first arrest and now this afternoon. From talking to him I was convinced that he was basically a very good-natured man, but he was terrified and therefore carried out everything that was asked of him in the most fervent way. He had worked in that building (formerly the Petersburg city hall) and even in that same part of the building, for more than thirty years. Where we were now sitting had previously been the department for issuing foreign passports. He had been a courier. After the Bolsheviks had taken power he had nowhere else to go, and he was old, so he decided to remain and enter the service of the Cheka. He was telling me about how things had been. He praised Uritsky highly for his attentiveness to the needs of his staff and his kindness. Incidentally, during my conversation with the Cheka Presidium on the day of my arrest, Komarov, among other things, told me that Uritsky had always voted against shooting people and had refused to sign death sentences. Whether that was true or not, I do not know, but Komarov told me this with a slight tone of mockery towards Uritsky's fastidiousness, given that 'after all, he bore responsibility for everything that happened when he was in charge'.

I spent a whole day in that unit, and slept very well. The lunch and dinner they gave me came not from the inmates' kitchen but from the staff kitchen, and I must say that by Petrograd standards the meal was very plentiful and tasty: meat soup, macaroni, and kasha with butter. But the commandant's assistant complained that things were not like they used to be: 'Can you believe it? My wife asks me to get her five pounds of beans, and I can't get them. Was it like that under Uritsky? No, at the very mention of the name "Cheka" everyone took fright and things happened straight away!' In general, in all sorts of strange and unexpected ways, the Chekists represented Uritsky's time as a sort of heroic epoch, about which legends were already beginning to form ...

Towards the evening I was again taken to the station in a car. This time, everything was in order. We were allocated two adjoining, connecting, second-class compartments with couchettes. In one of them I travelled with two guards, and in the other, Borisov travelled with some girl, who had been waiting for him at the station and seemed to be a relative taking advantage of the opportunity to travel to Moscow.

We reached Moscow on 22 July at one o'clock in the afternoon, without any mishaps. As in Petrograd, we went to the offices of the transport Cheka. Borisov went off to telephone the All-Russia Cheka for a car, and I stayed in the office with the guards. There were two railway workers in here, newly arrested for 'speculation'. The Chekists were tipping hundreds of packs of cigarettes from a big canvas bag the workers had had with them, counting the packs and drawing up a report. The arrestees looked on with sad but submissive faces as their goods were confiscated, without attempting to object. At the same time, one of the functionaries sitting behind the desk called to a boy on the platform and started buying cigarettes from him at 100 rubles apiece. From the sidelines it was hard to tell where the freedom of trade permitted by the New Economic Policy ended and criminality began. I could only establish that at that time there was a state monopoly in tobacco products, which were officially distributed only on ration cards and only to smokers. They could only have been on free sale through unauthorised means. But that did not stop there being a lively trade in cigarettes and tobacco on all Moscow streets.

The car promised by the All-Russia Cheka never arrived, and after waiting for almost two hours, we decided to walk. It was very pleasant to walk the city streets after so many months under lock and key.

It was about four o'clock in the afternoon when we arrived at the former building of the 'Rossiya' insurance society on Lubyanka Square, where the Cheka (now the GPU) has its headquarters. After the usual booking-in procedures and a search of our outer clothes in the commandant's office, I was taken into a fairly large room, also on the ground floor. This was known as 'Avanesov's office': at one time it was where the counting-house was located, and it got its name from the gold letters which had survived on the large mirrored window in that room. It was mainly arrestees from other cities who were put in this room. Occasionally people arrested in Moscow were also put there, although mostly they got put in another, adjacent room, known as the 'manager's office', also from the sign on the door left over from former times. Men and women were held in there together and could spend several days there before being sent on to better-appointed prison accommodation. There were no toilets; they were out in the yard, and arrestees had to be taken out to use them under guard.

When I entered 'Avanesov's office', there were no women there. Prisoners were sitting and lying on trestles, which almost filled the whole office. Some, who could not find a space, were just lying on the floor, along with their things. With its stuffiness, filth, and the abundance of bugs and lice, this notorious 'office' was more like the worst sort of doss-house.

From one of the plank beds I heard a familiar voice: it was my party comrade G. Binshtok, who had been brought in from Ryazan' two days before. But I had hardly started talking to him when my attention was drawn to a tall, lean man with a black but greying moustache, dressed in a neat jacket. In his buttonhole there was a red ribbon with some kind of symbol and next to it, on his lapel, was a miniature portrait of Lenin. This stranger was sitting on the edge of a bench, sobbing quietly. It turned out that he was an American, K., a delegate to the Third Congress of the Communist International which was taking place at the same time. He had been called out of a session of the congress, immediately seized by Chekists and brought to 'Avanesov's office' in the very clothes he had been wearing at the congress. He could speak a little German, and I got talking to him. According to him, he had been arrested on the strength of a denunciation by another American delegate, Haywood, in revenge for a polemical pamphlet K. had published against him in America. K. was obviously very frightened and repeatedly stressed his devotion to everything the Bolshevik government did, including the practices of the Cheka.[1]

I spent no more than half an hour in 'Avanesov's office'. I was taken through the yard, then up the stairs to the third floor and into the hallway of an apartment, with a sign on the doors saying 'office of the Cheka internal prison'. This prison took up several floors of the building, where there had previously been furnished rooms.

After another search, in the course of which all paper was taken off me, I was taken down a long winding corridor. It was lined with doors, into which spyholes, closed with little moveable boards, had been cut. I was put into one of the rooms.

This was a fairly large room with two windows, blanked out with white paint and covered with an iron grille fitted internally. It contained eight trestle beds, seven of which were occupied. The eighth, unoccupied one was for me. The warder closed the door with a snap. The other prisoners started to ask me in a whisper who I was and where I had come from, warning me not to speak out loud. When I asked them in astonishment why not, they pointed to the regulations, hanging on the door.

I have seen many prisons in my time, and have read several sets of prison regulations. But I had never before seen anything like what was hanging on the door. Prisoners were forbidden from reading, writing, playing cards, chess or draughts, singing, talking loudly or making any kind of noise. There was no provision for exercise or visits from relatives. Prisoners would be taken out to use the toilets in the corridor twice a day. In order to get the right to books, newspapers, visits from relatives and a half-hour exercise period between 1 and 2am, members of our Central Committee, who were being held for a time in the 'internal prison' after the Butyrki killings mentioned above, had to declare a hunger strike. For breaking any rule, the regulations threatened the severest punishments. In the toilets there was a sign with a reminder of the ban on talking loudly, which declared succinctly and expressively: 'For everything you will be putt in a punnishment cell' [sic]. I have reproduced this dictum word for word, with the original spelling.

Thus, the inmates of this prison were deliberately condemned to 'doing nothing at all'. The prison also has individual cells, where people would spend months on end! The regime had been especially designed to drive people to stupefaction, weaken their nervous systems and thereby 'prepare' them for interrogations, which were often carried out at night!

In the cell I had been put into, the prisoners kept a 'diary' with a pencil stub and a little piece of paper they had managed to conceal. They noted all the 'events', by which they meant any occasion when the doors were opened: for visits to the toilet, receiving meals and hot water etc. The arrival of a new prisoner, someone being taken away, or an interrogation – those were 'events' of enormous importance. For the month they had been keeping that diary, the greatest number of 'events' in one day had been eighteen, but that had been a rare exception. Usually the number of 'events' did not exceed ten or twelve, and sometimes the number, especially on Sundays, when no dinner was served in the 'internal prison', could be as low as five or six.

As you can imagine, the arrival of someone who had just had contact with the outside world, and had even managed to smuggle two fresh copies of a newspaper into that hell-hole of enforced idleness, was a big event for the prisoners. They surrounded me and tirelessly questioned me about the most varied things, jumping from subject to subject. Our cell was at the very end of a long corridor, and the warder could not be bothered to walk all the way up to it. Nonetheless, we continued to try to talk in whispers and, when reading the papers I had brought in, we sat in such a way as to hide them from the gaze of the warder or commandant if they were to decide to look through the spyhole.

I gradually began to get to know my room-mates. Our cell was a 'spies'' cell, in that all the people held there were accused in cases connected in one way or another with foreign states or 'white' governments and armies.

The most notable of the prisoners was Shch., an artiste at the Warsaw Theatre who had been appearing at the Moscow Arts Theatre. Six months before I had seen him in the role of Pomponnet in *La Fille de Madame Angot*. And now he was my cellmate in prison. As he explained, his case was as follows: preparing to return to Poland, he handed a certain sum of money and some valuables to an acquaintance, who promised to get it sent on to Warsaw via one of the foreign missions. The acquaintance was arrested, and through him they caught Shch., who was later convicted and sentenced to several years in a concentration camp. Finally, he was used in exchange for Russian citizens who had been convicted in Poland.

Even in the miserable conditions of the 'internal prison', Shch. invariably retained, or, at least, kept up a show of, his cheerfulness. He was uncommonly attentive to his fellow prisoners, and did everything he could to keep their spirits up. And many of them needed that, especially one young Polish officer from the Polish reparations commission, which at that time was operating in Minsk alongside an analogous Russian commission. With a few days leave, this officer in Polish military uniform got it into his head, he said, to go and take a look at Moscow. He was still on his way there on the train when he was arrested, and now he did not even know how to let his superiors or his family know where he was. He had not had anything with him.

A third prisoner was an engineer. He had already spent time in the 'internal prison', had then been transferred to Butyrki, and had now been brought back here for 'interrogation', for which he had already been waiting three weeks. What he had been accused of, and what happened to him subsequently, I do not know.

Next to the engineer there was an interesting pair – the Croat M. and the Serb S. These were the chairman of the Slavic Council in Moscow and his deputy. Both of them were communists. They claimed they had been accused of sending former Kolchak officers to other Slavic countries under the guise of communist agitators, providing them with documents and money through the Executive Committee of the Communist International. They assured me that the accusations were false, and that this was the result of intrigues by Czechoslovak officers who had themselves been white guards and Kolchakists, but were now presenting themselves as communists and had taken their places on the Presidium of the Slavic Council. They had both been in prison for a month and had nothing with them, not even a change of underclothes, as they had been arrested at work. They had been writing fruitlessly to Milkić, the Serbian delegate to the CI congress, they did not even know whether their letters had been reaching him. I promised to try to inform Milkić of their plight, and did so, but I do not know what, if anything, came of it. They were both very despondent and even worried about the fate which awaited them. They assured me that their experiences had taught them a lot, and that although they remained communists, they would always fight against the terror and arbitrariness of the Cheka. Unfortunately, I know nothing about their subsequent fate.

The remaining two prisoners in our cell were an old man from Kuban' and a middle-aged Estonian. I did not get a chance to ask them about their cases, because the very next day I was taken off to Butyrki prison.

The lorry in which we drove out of the Cheka yard was packed with the most diverse people. I unexpectedly met my old party comrade, Garvi, from Odessa; he had been in prison in Vladimir and had now been transferred to Moscow. And here, too, squeezed into a corner of the lorry, was the unlucky Comintern delegate in his neat jacket with the red ribbon in the buttonhole.

NOTES

1. Dan is certainly referring here to Adolf S. Carm (1877-1958), a Swedish-American labour activist. At that time, Carm was a prominent member of the US Socialist Labor Party (SLP) and a leader of the Detroit-based Workers' International Industrial Union (WIIU), which originated in a local split in the Industrial Workers of the World (IWW) in 1908. Relations between the WIIU and SLP on the one hand, and the IWW on the other, had long been very poor. In 1918, over a hundred leaders and activists of the IWW had been tried in Chicago following police raids, and Carm had covered the trial as a journalist for the SLP's *Weekly People*.

    Carm had gone to Moscow in 1921 to try to represent the WIIU at the Third Congress of the Comintern and the First Congress of the Profintern (Red International of Labour Unions), but his mandate had been rejected. He had, however, been granted an observer's pass. On 17 June 1921, the veteran US syndicalist leader, William 'Big Bill' Haywood, who was in Moscow representing the IWW, sent a letter to the Cheka denouncing Carm. Haywood alleged that Carm had consorted with and assisted the prosecution in the trial, and was therefore a 'bourgeois informer' who should not be allowed to be present at the congresses. Carm was arrested by the Cheka, and was not released until early September. For further details of the case, see Eric Hass, *The Socialist Labor Party and the Internationals*, SLP, New York, 1949, pp. 153-170.

9

In Butyrki

When I arrived in Butyrki prison there were relatively few socialist and anarchist prisoners there, and almost all of them were kept in the solitary block. After the breakup of the socialist wing back in April, it was mainly members of the central committees who had been returned here. Most of the rest remained scattered around provincial prisons – in Yaroslavl', Vladimir, Ryazan' and Orel.

From our central committee I met Ezhov, Pleskov and Nikolaevsky here. From the SR CC there were Gots, Timofeev, Vedenyapin, Gendel'man, Artem'ev, Donskoy, Likhach, Tseytlin and others. Most had already been in prison for over a year, and some of them for over two years. Members of the Left SR CC Kamkov, Mayorov and Bogachev had also been inside for the same sort of time. They had all managed to survive all sorts of perturbations – sharp changes of prison regime, transfers from prison to prison. As I have already mentioned, members of our CC had gone on hunger strike for three days in the 'internal prison' in order to get the most elementary conditions for human existence. Overall, this 'internal prison' had not failed to leave its mark: two of them, Ezhov and Nikolaevsky, having spent about two months there, had returned to Butyrki with severe cases of scurvy. All of them had been held in complete ignorance about their further fate, being fed much the same contradictory rumours that had gone around our remand prison in Petrograd.

Apart from the members of the various central committees there were solitary units in both the men's and women's sections, with around fifteen or twenty socialist and anarchist prisoners. One particular group was the 'Panyushkinists' – Bolsheviks who had organised an opposition party under the name 'Hammer and Sickle'. The position of this party overall was fairly hazy, because the most diverse elements were involved in it. There were utopians who demanded a return to 'the politics of October 1917', workers who felt themselves bound hand and foot by bureaucracy and had begun vaguely to understand the damage that the communist dictatorship was causing, along with some dubious adventurists who were dissatisfied with the fact that the new course of the Bolshevik regime had squeezed them out from their previous posts or was hindering them from fishing in the muddy waters of a regime of terror. One of the leaders of this motley party was the sailor Panyushkin, who had distinguished himself by killing with impunity some students, the Ganglez brothers, in the very first days after the Bolshevik takeover. The new party from the outset made a big noise, and even called a public meeting at which the policy of the government was sharply criticised. But its leaders, including Panyushkin, were soon arrested and the party disintegrated. This group generally kept itself apart from us. Several times they declared a hunger strike, but were not at all serious about that form of protest and would call the strike off without having won anything. Finally they were sent off to Vologda gubernia. I do not know what happened to the rest of them, but Panyushkin himself very quickly 'repented', published a letter in the papers attacking the Mensheviks and SRs who had allegedly led him astray, and announced his return to the bosom of the Bolshevik party, which he promised to serve faithfully and truly.

One other prisoner stood out against the general background: a tall fleshy man with a long light-brown beard and blue eyes, quiet and retiring. This was the Finnish communist writer Eloranta. He only spoke a few words of Russian, and it was difficult to make oneself understood with him. He had already been in prison for about a year in connection with the murder of members of the CC of the Finnish Communist Party in Petrograd (in August 1920). The killing had taken place on the basis of a factional struggle, complicated by arguments about how to divide up money which the Finnish communist emigration had received from the Bolsheviks. The killers had been young party members who had burst into a meeting of the CC firing revolvers furiously, killing eight members of the CC and wounding eleven. They were now in common cells in Butyrki prison, but Eloranta was kept in solitary. In February 1922 – a year and a half after the killing! – the revolutionary tribunal sat on the case. The immediate participants in the murder were sentenced to various terms of imprisonment, but Eloranta, as the leader of the workers' opposition and the ideological inspiration for the killing, was sentenced to be shot. He, as a writer, had been found guilty of 'demagogic agitation', dragging the workers' opposition into 'quarrelsome struggle against the Finnish CC'. It would seem that the tribunal felt embarrassed at its own monstrous sentence, and, applying the amnesty decree of 7 November 1921, resolved that execution be commuted to five years' imprisonment. But the Presidium of the Central Executive Committee rescinded the granting of the amnesty, and in the night of 16-17 February 1922 the unfortunate Eloranta was executed.[1]

Apart from socialists and anarchists, there were few other political prisoners. Most of the cells were occupied by criminals, accused of theft or banditism. They filled the entire upper (second-floor) gallery of the men's solitary block (MOK, as the prisoners and administration both called it; the women's solitary block was ZhOK). Most of them were held under the 'strict' regime, and among them there were many who were awaiting a death sentence or had already been sentenced to be shot.

The head of this enormous prison, which held about 2500 prisoners, was a certain Popov, the author of the famous regulations for the 'Cheka internal prison', where he had been commandant before his transfer to Butyrki. A former NCO in a guards regiment, he was tall and thin like a rod, with a horse-like face and colourless, tin-grey eyes. Ignorant, dense and cruel, Popov was also appallingly stupid and stubborn. It was impossible to convince him of anything or demonstrate to him the stupidity of any instruction he had thought up. On one occasion he decided that all prisoners should be taken out to the toilet (which according to the regulations should happen twice a day) one by one. It was futile for the prisoners to try to show the pointlessness of that sort of isolation of people who were taking exercise together. It was futile for the warders to work out that with such a rule it would take all day to let the seventy to seventy-five people imprisoned in each gallery use the toilet twice a day. Popov would stubbornly assert, 'See, everybody wants to be cleverer than me. But I know how things should be done', and for a long time he never failed to repeat his instruction every time he entered the MOK to 'put things right' and noticed that it was not being obeyed. Of course, it had not been obeyed from day one. But most of all, he did not like people mocking him: 'They all laugh at me', he complained to the All-Russia Cheka chairman about the lack of respect from the socialists. He could not reconcile himself to our struggle for a freer regime, and every concession the authorities made clearly wounded him to the depths of his soul. Even once we had won the right to have our cells open and several other privileges, one fine day he hung up in all the cells a new set of regulations he had composed, which was a pale copy of the regulations in the 'internal prison'. When we immediately took these regulations down again, and the Cheka authorities confirmed all our rights, Popov could take no more and left Butyrki. Afterwards, when I was travelling through Riga, I learned that Popov was now in charge of a sanatorium for leading Russian communists on the Riga coast. It seemed that he was even annoying this set of inmates, by trying to introduce regulations banning conversation over dinner or receiving guests in the rooms, and otherwise trying to regulate their every step.

His assistant in MOK and ZhOK was Sokolov – a small, slippery man with darting eyes. He tried to present himself as being his own man, and had indeed himself spent time in prison on a charge of association with a Menshevik organisation (Sokolov was of worker origin), but at the same time he quietly made things unpleasant for the prisoners in many ways. Although he was a bit wary of provoking sharp confrontations in the MOK, he carried on however he liked in the ZhOK, and almost every time he appeared there, there were some new restrictions and new scandals. Sokolov was not around for long when I was there: he went off on leave and never returned to his place of work. He was replaced by new assistants for Popov – Knoppe, a Latvian Bolshevik who had been in internal exile, and Darin, a bright young man who had at one time been in trouble for printing Bebel's *Woman and Socialism* on a duplicating machine, without having realised that a Russian translation of it had been published legally long before. Our relations with both of them were quite satisfactory.

It is worth saying a few words in particular about one of Popov's assistants – Kachinsky. Some SRs, who had been serving hard labour in Butyrki back in tsarist times, recognised him as the former head of the hard labour section. He had been notorious for his coarse treatment of political prisoners and even for beating them up. Dzerzhinsky, now the head of the Cheka, had at one time been one of the hard labour prisoners who had had to put up with a lot from him. Kachinsky had made himself so reviled among the political prisoners that Dzerzhinsky would say of him: 'if ever the revolution puts power into our hands, I shall not fail to hang that butcher!' And now Kachinsky had rebranded himself as a communist, and was working as an assistant to the head of the prison. He was still working in the same cells where he had been tormenting Dzerzhinsky's fellow political prisoners under the tsarist regime. We decided to write a statement to Dzerzhinsky about Kachinsky, and made details of his biography known to Sol'ts, the chairman of the Communist Party's Control Commission, who had happened to visit the prison. A short while later Kachinsky was arrested and, they told us, sentenced to five years in a concentration camp. He disappeared from our horizons. But how many more Kachinskies are working, unexposed, behind communist masks in Soviet prisons? And can we be sure that Kachinsky himself, after serving a while and then being amnestied, will not turn up somewhere in the provinces and again get power over hundreds of prisoners?

The six months I spent in Butyrki were taken up with the struggle by the socialist and anarchist prisoners to improve their situation.

From the first we had to wage a struggle for the right to visits from our relatives in some kind of acceptable conditions. Visits took place in a few rooms by the prison offices. In each visiting room there were usually five or six prisoners at a time, being watched by two or three warders and Chekists. But suddenly the authorities decided it was dangerous to let prisoners sit next to their visiting relatives, because that way notes could be passed and so on. Therefore the administration decided that the prisoners and their relatives should be separated by a wide table, which made it impossible not only to embrace our loved ones but even to have any kind of private conversation. We had to talk so loudly across the table that our conversations were audible both to all our neighbours at the table and to the warders. Our protests were ignored, so we announced that we were going to refuse visits. Within two weeks the Cheka had relented and visits were taking place in the old way.

No sooner was the story of the visits over, than further disturbances among the prisoners were provoked by a Cheka search. About three in the morning I was woken by the noise of my door being opened. Kachinsky burst in and, turning on the light in the cell, shouted: 'Search!' Straight after him someone barged in, an ungainly being in a long coat which reached down almost to the soles of its feet, and with a wide, bony, rough-looking face. Two Red Army men also entered carrying rifles.

'Get up, comrade, and get dressed!' The voice which said this aroused a certain suspicion in me, and I turned to this indeterminate being, which had already launched itself at my books and started to rummage through them.

'Are you a woman?'

'Yes, I'm a woman, but that's got nothing to do with it. Get up and get dressed!' I flatly declined this kind suggestion. This Chekist, a Latvian woman, tried raising her voice, but I demanded that she speak politely to me and, most importantly, that she tell the person in charge of this search that I protest against this way of conducting searches and insist on the immediate removal of this delightful person from my cell. After a lot of wrangling the worthy woman nonetheless did go off to report to her superiors, leaving the Red Army men in my cell, and did not return and was replaced by a young man who, to be honest, showed no enthusiasm for conducting a search. Within five minutes I was left alone again.

I discovered later that, once I had been relieved of her presence, this androgynous Chekist found more to do in the prison. She not only had no qualms about ordering people to dress in front of her, having first felt along all the seams of their underwear and so on, but even put her own hands into the slop buckets to pull out and minutely examine all the little pieces of paper! Her dedication to her work was simply astounding!

Not everybody was as fortunate as me. In certain cells the search lasted for an hour. Sometimes the Chekists took away all pieces of paper with any writing on, and sometimes they took away all books. There were some strange anomalies – one person not only had two issues of the criminal *Sotsialisticheskiy vestnik* confiscated, but also a work by Jules Verne he happened to have. Strange anomalies are all very well, but the results of that search were keenly felt by the prisoners. Back in tsarist times, prison for many of us really served as a kind of school. Life in the illegal underground outside prison was exhausting and wearing, without any time for serious intellectual work. The lack of any space to call one's own, and the need to move around between safe houses, made it impossible to do any systematic studying. Prison could serve as a place of rest, where one could read, think, gather one's thoughts and try to set them down on paper. For revolutionaries, prison was a place for intense intellectual effort. But that is not the case in Soviet prisons.

It is very hard, if not impossible, to get hold of a book in a Soviet prison. There is even a massive shortage of paper and writing materials. Such conditions make systematic intellectual work extremely difficult, and in prison enforced idleness reigns. It becomes quite impossible to work, when all manuscripts without exception are confiscated during the periodic searches. It is true that the Cheka does return them after inspecting them, but the inspection process takes months, and moreover some part of the manuscript will invariably be lost. There were materials taken from certain comrades during August which they got back, after numerous requests and reminders, only in December. One can understand the indignation that this sort of thing causes among people who, in the most unfavourable circumstances and with great effort, are trying to use their spare time in prison to do some writing.

During my time in Butyrki, the socialist prisoners were held in single cells. They took exercise in groups of five, but immediately after the exercise period they were taken back to their cells and locked up. It was of course hard to come to terms with this. Almost all of us had, over many long months in prison, been able to associate freely with other prisoners. We could not understand why it was now necessary to keep us apart from one another. We had been told more than once that there were no proceedings against us; that we were, in Lenin's phrase, being 'carefully kept in prison' only in order to deprive us of contact with the outside world, not with each other. Popov, together with his underlings, displayed the most stupid formalism in this respect: people had just been exercising together, but if Popov caught them together by the cell doors, there was a huge fuss. This all annoyed us intensely. We decided to win the right to free association.

As always, there was an argument about tactics. There were those who advocated decisive actions: giving an ultimatum, a hunger strike, active resistance etc. But the 'moderate' tendency won out. It was decided that, while we would try as far as possible not to cause a massive fuss, we would try to eviscerate the established regime from within by stubbornly, systematically, extending the boundaries.

All these tactical discussions were held during exercise, through the trustees who gave out the rations, via little notes, which we had all sorts of ways of passing to one another, and finally, by just holding conversations at the windows.

These conversations also gave rise to several conflicts. In other prisons such as Lefortovo, also in Moscow, the guards simply shot through the windows at the prisoners, just like in tsarist times. In Orel in such a case one of our comrades was shot in the arm. Although Popov fumed and raged, in our prison he did not decide to resort to extreme measures. Once his assistant Sokolov decided to take energetic measures in the women's section and confiscated a stool from one of the woman prisoners. However, this prisoner happened to be pregnant and was unable to get down from the high window-sill without her stool. Within a few hours Sokolov was obliged to return the stool, with the embarrassed explanation that no punishment had been intended, but that the stool had simply been 'needed in the office'. After a few other attempts of that type the authorities just gave up and our positions at the windows were secure.

At the same time as our assault on the windows we advanced on the doors. More and more often, as we returned from exercise, trips to the toilets or meetings with visitors, we would take the opportunity to nip up to the doors of other cells, open the little window and talk with our comrades. The authorities tried to combat this by locking the cell door windows. But this was not easy. On most of the little windows the locks were broken. Moreover, the warders were none too happy at having to run from cell to cell all the time at the prisoners' call. In a Soviet prison, where everything is falling apart, where everything is in short supply, life cannot carry on with the monotonous regularity of well-organised 'normal' prisons. Finally, after a number of clashes, some of them quite heated, the little windows in the doors were also left under our control.

We then moved on to the next steps. We had a few locksmiths among us. They were able easily to make skeleton keys out of nails and bits of scrap iron from the yard. If one's door was only locked with one turn, it was easy to stick one's arm out of the door window and open it, and they only locked the doors with two turns at night. On one occasion, Popov was walking along the corridor when he encountered the spectacle of an arm surreptitiously opening a door. He was dumbstruck. After waiting for the prisoner to leave the cell, he came up and stuttered: 'How did you do that?'

'Like this', the prisoner replied, showing the 'cunning device' to the dumbfounded administrator. Popov stood there in silence and then, with a wave of his hand, walked away.

The result of all this was a visit from a team of 'specialists' headed by a prison architect. The 'specialists' examined the doors, but could not think of anything other than advising the staff to lock the doors with two turns during the day as well. But again this was fraught with great inconvenience for the warders. Most importantly, though, we found our own prison 'specialists'. Within two weeks all the internal springs had been removed from the locks, which meant that at any time they could be opened with the simplest of skeleton keys. The unsuspecting Popov had another serious shock when on one occasion during a night inspection he found four prisoners in one cell calmly playing cards. As usual he stood there without saying a word, gawping at the card players, who just carried on playing. He then left, profoundly upset, and did not reappear on our block for a long time, neither by day nor by night.

There was, however, nothing he could do. It is not so easy to get several dozen complex locks fixed in Soviet Russia. And there were no guarantees that the newly repaired locks would not be broken again immediately. One option would have been to make an open fight of it, but for various reasons the Cheka decided against that at this time. The memories of the Butyrki beatings of 27 April were still fresh, and that event had not enhanced the Bolsheviks' reputation among workers either in Russia or abroad. And once again the number of socialists and anarchists imprisoned in Butyrki was swelling to serious proportions. Gradually the people who had been dispersed to provincial prisons in April were returning. New people were also coming in as a result of arrests. Prisoners were being brought in from other cities, because the cases of all the socialists were being concentrated in the All-Russia Cheka, and the local Chekas were more than willing to be rid of these turbulent people, who were not so easy to deal with, and whose presence in prison not only served as a constant source of dissatisfaction among the local workers, but also embarrassed the rank-and-file communists. By December no fewer than 250 such prisoners had accumulated in Butyrki, and getting into a sharp conflict with them could have caused a further lot of trouble.

They washed their hands of us. At first they simply closed their eyes to the complete collapse of the strict prison regime, and the official line was that 'everything is fine' as far as obeying instructions was concerned. Then, as a result of several discussions with the Moscow Cheka, which was formally in charge of the Butyrki prison, and the All-Russia Cheka, which was in charge of our cases, all the freedoms we had won were formally recognised. From November-December within the prison we enjoyed completely free association with one another, could take exercise together, could hold lectures and discussions, organise clubs and so on. We had a council of elders, consisting of one delegate from each faction, to represent us in all our dealings and negotiations with the prison administration and the Cheka. The council determined which of the new arrivals would be put in our block.

There remained the old, but ever fresh, question of association with women prisoners. In the ZhOK the process of shaking the regime took place in parallel with that in the MOK, although a little later and with a great deal of conflict. The postal service between the women's and men's blocks was more regular than anywhere else in Soviet Russia, although I cannot reveal the methods we used to achieve this level of reliability, which still eludes the People's Commissariat of Posts and Telegraphs. Every day at eight in the evening the correspondence was delivered to the correct addressees. Those who wanted to could even talk via a special 'telephone', the construction of which had nothing in common with Edison's invention.

But this was not enough. There were relatively few women prisoners – about twenty-five. They wanted to take part in the lectures and discussions which we were organising, and which acquired particular importance given the lack of books available to us. Some of them had husbands or brothers in the MOK, and there were no good reasons why they should not see each other. The need to see each other was all the greater given the indeterminacy of the sense, purpose and timescale of the socialists' imprisonment. Finally, a considerable part was played by that aspect of the prisoner's psychology I discussed above, in which every new extension of their 'freedoms' within prison just intensifies the sense that this 'freedom' is a fake.

The authorities, however, resisted on that point for a long time. But eventually their resistance began to weaken, and they agreed at least that the elders on our block could visit the women's block every day. However, things did not stop there. At the beginning of December there was an incident which will go down in the history of the Butyrki prison when the men broke through into the ZhOK. Around ten to a dozen male prisoners were exercising in the yard, when they saw that the gates into the women's yard were open for a delivery of firewood. They burst through into the women's yard, and from there into the block, where they visited prisoners in their cells and drank tea. This did not result in any great conflict with the administration. But they refused to allow a return invitation to the women to visit the MOK. Conversations began about forcing the issue. The incident was smoothed over only through the intervention of the elders, who thereby earned themselves an unenviable reputation for 'moderation' and 'pliability' from the more excitable section of the ZhOK inmates.

However, this incident of breaking into the women's yard meant that the question could not be dodged. Something had to be decided, and the authorities opted in the end to concede all along the line. The reason for this willingness to concede was mainly the situation of the criminal prisoners in our block and in general of everyone who the Cheka wanted to keep in 'strict' confinement. Naturally enough, the privileges we enjoyed had their influence on all the other prisoners in our block. The whole prison regime was shaking. The warders started to become more slapdash in their fulfilment of their duties. Then the Cheka came up with a plan – to turn the ZhOK over to criminals and 'strict' cases, and to concentrate all the socialists, male and female, in the MOK. In mid-December the final bastion of the old regime of isolation fell; the women prisoners were transferred into the cells vacated by the criminals, and the MOK became a solid socialist oasis within Butyrki prison, enjoying all the 'freedoms' which are possible in a prison.

Along with the improvements in our conditions there were improvements in our rations, since around January the socialist prisoners were put on to 'medical' rations. Supplies received from relatives were divided up evenly among the comrades in each particular faction. The Political Red Cross also provided some help. This organisation has operated for some years in Moscow. But in other cities, such as Petrograd, the Cheka stubbornly not only refused to allow that sort of organised assistance for political prisoners, but mercilessly arrested everyone suspected of 'illegally' attempting to collect funds for political prisoners. The Red Cross helps not only socialists but all political prisoners without distinction. In general, I should say, that one morally difficult aspect of the privileges we won in prison was that they only applied to us socialists. They were not extended to the 'counter-revolutionaries' who, although they were politically hostile to us, were nonetheless a group of people, many of whom had undoubtedly acted not from selfish, but from ideological motives. I have already explained the essential difference between our incarceration and that of the other inmates of the prison. But for all that there can be no doubt that the way the Soviet authorities treated their political prisoners in the so-called 'counter-revolutionary' category can only be described as completely shameful. Unfortunately, it was not within our power to change that situation.

I should add that, like everything else in the Bolshevik world, the prison 'paradise' which we won in Butyrki over six months of struggle did not last long. At the end of January 1922, shortly after I left the MOK, they began to empty it, sending prisoners under various pretexts to other, often appalling places of incarceration, and by the end of February the MOK had been completely emptied. The Socialist-Revolutionaries who had been in prison with me – Gots, Donskoy, Timofeev, Vedenyapin and others – who were already in their second and third years of imprisonment, and who had been repeatedly assured by the Chekists that they were just being held in isolation, were suddenly handed over to the courts to be tried for real or imaginary crimes committed in 1918. A stormy campaign of protest was needed, embracing the working-class parties and organisations of almost the entire world, in order to win guarantees that they at least would not be executed.[2] As we can see, the prison 'paradise' in Soviet Russia should not be praised too lavishly ...

Now, in April 1922, Butyrki prison is again beginning to fill up with socialist prisoners, and this time the pioneers are members of our social-democratic youth league – young people who had already passed through Butyrki during the time I was there. And now they themselves must fight again to win at least a part of those 'freedoms' which we won in our time and they were able to use. They have already had to wage a three-day hunger strike in order to get out of the foul sewer which is the 'internal prison'. And they will surely have to strain their nerves still further to win themselves more or less bearable conditions in a Soviet prison system which is constantly changing, always inclined towards crude violence, and forever making 180-degree turns.[3]

NOTES

1. Dan is mistaken here about the date of Voitto Eloranta's execution – the death sentence was not actually carried out until 1923. The case of the 'workers' opposition' (later dubbed the 'murder opposition') was one of the stranger episodes in the early history of the dysfunctional Communist Party of Finland (SKP), formed by Red Finnish émigrés in Russia fol-

lowing the defeat of the 1918 Finnish revolution. The SKP organisation in Petrograd was dominated by the brothers Eino and Jukka Rahja. The opposition, including Eloranta, accused the Rahjas (probably with justification) of gross corruption and abuse of power. By August 1920, having been excluded from participation in a secret SKP congress, the opposition decided to resort to armed force against the Rahja brothers and their supporters. A group of opposition supporters burst into a SKP CC meeting at the Kuusinen Club in Petrograd on 31 August 1920, shooting indiscriminately. They killed eight people, including Jukka Rahja. Although Eloranta took no part in the assault, the assassins had met at his flat beforehand, and the Cheka considered him to be their intellectual leader. Eloranta's subsequent fate was determined by political considerations; some in the Bolshevik hierarchy favoured leniency, while the surviving Rahja brother (Eino) and others pressed for the sentence to be carried out. See Jukka Paastela, *Finnish Communism under Soviet Totalitarianism*, Kikimora, Helsinki, 2003, pp. 139-187 for a detailed account of the 'murder opposition'.
2. Author's footnote in the original edition: At this very moment, as I am checking the proofs of this book (11 June 1922), the Bolsheviks have again cast doubt on these guarantees.
3. Author's footnote in the original edition: Now (June 1922) all these young people have been sent into administrative exile to remote uezd towns in the provinces.

10
Hunger Strike – and Leaving the Country

Our six-month struggle to improve our prison conditions was not as smooth as it might seem at first sight. It exhausted us, irritated us, frayed our nerves from day to day, and caused a series of clashes with Popov, his assistant and certain members of the lower administration. Although these clashes were petty, in prison such things are always worrying. Young people, and people whose nervous system has already been shaken by all they have experienced, can easily lose their sense of proportion, and sometimes the most radical measures of struggle were proposed. But the more balanced prison inmates always succeeded eventually in getting the upper hand and resolving the conflicts which had arisen peacefully, through discussion and compromises.

But from mid-November we began to see the signs that we would need to fight over something more than just prison conditions. When they visited the prison, the Cheka people would often say that the Menshevik cases would soon be ended and Mensheviks would no longer be held in prison. Through vague hints they gave us to understand that the conclusion of these cases would simply lead to the social democrats being freed. There was nothing inherently improbable in such an end to our nine- or ten-month isolation. Individual comrades really did start to be let out, sometimes on the pretext of an illness to which the Cheka had previously paid no attention, and sometimes without any pretext at all. But we nonetheless remained sceptical about the rumours of a general release of social-democrat prisoners: the overall policy of the Bolsheviks gave no grounds for imagining that they had finally concluded it was necessary to tolerate a social-democratic opposition.

Our scepticism proved to be well-founded: at the end of November about ten of our comrades in prison unexpectedly received sentences from the All-Russia Cheka, saying that they were to be sent to Turkestan into the care of the local Cheka. They were asked to prepare immediately for transfer to Taganskaya prison, from where they would be sent on. At the same time we learned that the same sentences had been sent out to another ten of our comrades, who were then being held in provincial prisons. By what criteria the All-Russia Cheka chose those particular twenty comrades it was impossible to understand. The lists included old experienced party members and inexperienced youths, members of leading party bodies and people who had not been very active politically.

Our faction gathered to discuss the position. This was something to think about. This was the first time that the Bolsheviks had used administrative exile against socialists on a mass basis. There had been individual cases previously, but they had been exceptional. The Bolsheviks had used mass exile mainly against workers guilty of participating in strikes. For example, hundreds of Khar'kov and Kiev railway workers had been sent to the Far North, to the Murmansk railway. But this had been done under the pretext and through the procedures of 'labour mobilisation', which supposedly required this method of 'distributing the labour force'.

We decided to send a declaration to the CEC Presidium, protesting sharply against the resurrection of one of the most shameful methods of the tsarist regime in its struggle against socialists – administrative exile. In addition, we categorically demanded that those sent away should be guaranteed, at a minimum: 1) that they would not be sent there under convoy; 2) that in Turkestan they would be at liberty and protected against arbitrary actions by the local Cheka; and 3) that they would be allowed to take their families along with them if they so wished and sort out their personal affairs, for which purpose they would need to be released for a certain time before their departure. We ended our declaration by saying that we were holding up this sort of behaviour on the Bolsheviks' part to be judged by the international proletariat.

It was decided that, until we received a reply from the CEC Presidium, comrades who had received one of these sentences should refuse to go anywhere at all.

There began endless discussions with the prison administration and Chekists who came to see us. The Chekists assured us that there would be no question of travelling under convoy; everyone would be travelling in special carriages without changing trains all the way to

Tashkent. They also said that people would be at liberty in Turkestan, and that everything is fine there – it is warm and well supplied. As for temporary release in Moscow to set their affairs in order, that would be unthinkable. The only option would be a certain delay in the departure so that the people being sent away could take care of their affairs without leaving the prison.

We stuck to our position: we were holding out for a reply from the CEC Presidium. But no reply came, and the Chekists decided against resorting to force, so the business dragged on for weeks.

At that time some fairly strange things began happening, which showed the completely thoughtless and arbitrary way that the Cheka decided the fate of the people who fell into its clutches. Some comrades who had been earmarked for sending to Turkestan were simply released. Others began to get new sentences, replacing exile to Turkestan ('to be kept under guard', it said in the official document, which went quite against what the Chekists had been promising us) with exile 'under open supervision while remaining at liberty' to other places. These included the remote Mezen' and Pechora uezds in Arkhangel'sk guberniya, and the starving Mari oblast', with a ban on living in the only little town in that oblast', etc. And a few days after that, some of those who had received these new sentences were also released without any further consequences. It became clear to us that around the question of winding up our cases there was some kind of intrigue and manoeuvring going on, some kind of internal struggle, in which we were being kicked about like footballs, and that the fate of each of us depended on pure chance. We were informed that even in the highest echelons of the Bolsheviks there was no unanimity about what to do with us.

But whatever was going on, we had to do some thinking so that we were not caught off guard by events. In a series of faction meetings we worked out a definite line of action. The majority did not think we should push for too much, and it was decided that we should limit our ultimatum demands to the bare essentials, but that we should not give way on that minimum and defend it with all means possible. Our minimum demands were that if we were to be exiled, we should be exiled to *towns*, even if they were only uezd towns, and that these towns should be *on railway lines*. In present conditions in Russia that is absolutely vital to avoid being completely cut off from one's relatives and the civilised world.

A few days before the New Year we were visited by Dzerzhinsky's deputy, the de facto chairman of the All-Russia Cheka Unshlikht. He assured us that all the Menshevik cases were finally going to be closed. Exile to Turkestan and anywhere else was being cancelled. Comrades who were found to be ill would be freed completely. The rest would be temporarily prohibited from living in Moscow or other industrial centres, but with those exceptions they would be free to settle where they wished and to travel to their chosen places entirely freely, without any convoy. Everyone would receive benefit payments at the minimum subsistence level until they found work. Given that the Bolsheviks had already started to follow the custom of the old regime by exiling people and expelling them from industrial regions etc., I asked whether they would also follow the tsarist government's practice of allowing people to be exiled abroad in place of these restrictions. Unshlikht did not give a definite answer. We parted with a promise from Unshlikht that the next day he would present us with a list of places where we were not allowed to settle, and we would consider this new situation.

However, the list Unshlikht had promised was not forthcoming, neither the next day nor the days after that, and the prison administration began to spread rumours that there had been another change of heart on our case, and that it had been decided to free us unconditionally.

So, with this uncertainty, and these rumours and preparations all around, the matter carried on into the New Year. Some SRs, who were already in their second or third years in prison, were allowed to see in the New Year in the office with their relatives. None of the Mensheviks got that privilege, and the administration again explained it by saying that the All-Russia Cheka had an order for our release, and it was purely for incidental reasons that it had not been delivered to the prison in good time.

We saw in the New Year in cheerful mood. At first we had an evening of music and literature in the corridor of the isolation block, which we organised ourselves. Then we divided off into our factional groups to see in the New Year, we had a meal, and had even managed to acquire a little wine. Speeches were made, there were readings from a comical paper devoted to prison life, and songs were sung. From one in the morning there was a dancing party for everyone, which continued until the morning. As it was underway the infamous

Samsonov appeared in the corridor. He was a member of the All-Russia Cheka Presidium, in charge of the secret operations department, a coarse, cruel man well known for his malice towards socialists. He walked round the galleries and left without saying a word.

On the third day of the New Year, a Chekist attached to our isolation block told us that an investigator, Ramishevsky, had arrived to deal with our Menshevik cases, and had brought a document which concerned us. I went to the office with comrade Nikolaevsky, where Ramishevsky told us that a resolution of the All-Russia Cheka Presidium had sentenced all Mensheviks to be exiled for one year, and members of our party CC for two years. He then showed us a list of places where we could choose to be sent. These were the most remote uezds in certain gubernias in European and Asiatic Russia. It was specifically spelled out that within these uezds we would not have the right to settle in towns, along railway lines, or anywhere where there were factories. Nobody was to be let out to settle his or her affairs, and we were all asked to prepare immediately to be transferred to Kisel'nyy pereulok, to the Moscow Cheka prison, where we could have daily visits from our relatives prior to our departure.

This was an open challenge. They obviously wanted to put us in a position where not only would any political activity be impossible, but any kind of cultured existence at all – moreover in conditions which would condemn us to starvation, disease and death.

We demanded that Unshlikht come to the prison immediately. We pointed out that this resolution contradicted in the starkest possible way the promises which he had made to us a few days previously in his official capacity. We were not going to submit to this resolution voluntarily.

We demanded that our declaration be telephoned through to the All-Russia Cheka. The Chekist attached to our prison replied rudely that it was not his job to carry out our requests and that there was no use in making any declarations because everything was now finally decided and nobody was going to come to see us. We should therefore immediately get ready to be shipped out to the Moscow Cheka prison tomorrow. We nonetheless managed to get the prison administration to telephone our declaration through, but neither Unshlikht nor any other member of the Cheka Presidium came to see us.

We immediately held a faction meeting. At that meeting I, who had always been very cautious and sceptical about sharp forms of prison struggle, was the first to propose calling a hunger strike. The situation was so clear that there was no need for lengthy discussions, and the hunger strike was agreed almost unanimously. A special committee was elected to lead the strike and carry out any discussions during its course. It was decided that all resolutions of that committee would be final, the strikers would be informed of them and they should be carried out unconditionally. The committee also had the right to call an end to the strike as it deemed necessary.

Prisoners from other factions immediately suggested joining our strike. Our committee asked them to hold off, considering it unnecessary to extend the parameters of the struggle. Above all, we did not want to involve the SRs, because their situation and prospects, according to the information we were getting, were considerably worse than our own. We had heard from an accurate and well-informed source that Kamenev had said: 'Let the SRs so much as lift a finger, and they'll see how we deal with them!' It is clear that the Bolsheviks already possessed Semenov's denunciation, which was to serve as the pretext for holding a trial of the SR leaders on accusations of preparing acts of terrorism, rebellion and robbery.[1] We feared that if we involved the SRs in our struggle, we would thereby greatly worsen their position and give the Bolsheviks a pretext for unleashing all their vindictive malice against them. But from feelings of comradely solidarity, the other prisoners were constantly keen to get involved in the struggle alongside us, and we had to expend a lot of effort dissuading them from such an ill-considered step. The committee resolved that the five members of the Don committee of our party who had been sentenced to five years in prison and were therefore not eligible for exile would not take part in the hunger strike.

The committee sent a declaration to the CEC Presidium which stated that, having become convinced that the Bolsheviks not only wanted to paralyse social democracy politically, but to destroy us physically, we were declaring a hunger strike with the demand that we be either released or tried in open court. That was, so to speak, our maximum programme. Subsequently the committee was given the right to reach a compromise agreement if a basis could be found for one.

The hunger strike began on the morning of 4 January, and proceeded with a degree of discipline rare in the annals of prison life. Only boiled water and tea without sugar were permitted. There were to be no exceptions; if people's strength gave out completely and their life was in danger, then the strikers should be sent to hospital, but on no account should the strict rules of the hunger strike be broken while in prison. Happily things did not get that far, although in the final days of the strike many people felt very unwell, and some did not recover from its consequences for a long time after their release from prison.

All the strikers were advised to remain in their cells as far as possible and to keep lying down. Members of the committee, who remained on their feet the whole time, would go round the cells several times a day, conveying news and carrying out errands. There was a health team, composed of imprisoned doctors not involved in the strike, who kept an eye on the health of the strikers. I should say right away that the majority, including women, survived the six and a half days of complete starvation very well. Personally, I only suffered from feelings of hunger for the first two days. My legs swelled up a bit, but overall to the very last day I did not lie down. I read, talked and even played cards.

The first day of the hunger strike was quiet. Neither the prison administration nor the Cheka seemed to pay us the slightest attention. But during that day we managed to do a lot for our cause: thanks to the general sympathy which surrounded us, we were unexpectedly able to establish regular contacts with the outside world. Every day, and sometimes twice a day, we received and sent letters: we wrote in detail about everything that was going on inside the prison, and in return we received detailed information on what was going on outside, particularly in Bolshevik circles, where the news that we had declared a hunger strike had caused some commotion. The other very important task was to ensure that our comrades outside were able that day to get the news that we had gone on hunger strike abroad by telegraph. They managed to circumvent the Bolshevik censorship by some very cunning method, of which I shall say nothing. We know that the protest campaign around our hunger strike, waged in the workers' parties and the working-class press of Europe, played a massive – possibly even decisive – role in our fate. Thanks to this same cunning method of communication, we were kept generally informed about the course of the campaign, and about the panic it caused among the Bolsheviks, who had not been expecting this turn of events. This, of course, did much to raise the spirits of the strikers.

On the second day of the hunger strike, after lunch the members of the committee were called into the office. There we were met by E. P. Peshkova, a member of the committee of the Political Red Cross. She told us she had met with Unshlikht and now wanted to talk with us to find out on what conditions we were prepared to end our strike, since it was impossible either to release us or hand us over to an open court. We talked for quite a long time, but without result. In this case we did not consider it possible to use the intercession of the Red Cross and reaffirmed that we had nothing to add to what we had written in our declaration to the CEC Presidium. Peshkova left upset. But we concluded from this episode that the Olympian calm which the Cheka had displayed up to now was beginning to be shaken.

And indeed, the next evening Unshlikht turned up. He was as sweet as honey, and expressed his chagrin: how could we have embarked on such a step without even having spoken with him? 'Well, your agent told us that there could be no discussions and that nobody from the All-Russia Cheka would come.'

'That was a misunderstanding, nobody instructed him to say that.' It also turned out to have been a 'misunderstanding' that nobody could be released from prison to sort their personal affairs out and that we had to be transferred immediately to the Moscow Cheka prison. Our transfer to Kisel'nyy pereulok had been proposed just for our 'convenience', but if we did not wish to avail ourselves of this 'offer', then that was up to us, nobody was going to force us.

But how to explain the crude discrepancy between what Unshlikht had told us before the New Year and the resolution which had been presented to us now? How was it that instead of a limited list of places where we were *forbidden* to live, and the right to a free *choice* of residence outside of these limitations, there was now a limited list of places where we were *permitted* to live? Unshlikht did not give a clear answer to that question, nor did he reply to the question of why we were not being brought before a court. He simply said: 'Unfortunately, I cannot talk openly with you, because my every word will then appear in the *Sotsialisticheskiy vestnik*.' As for the main issue, Unshlikht said that the resolution could be changed. And he proposed to us that: 1) we could settle in one of three uezd towns: Kashin in Tver' gubernia, Lyubim in Yaroslavl' gubernia, and Korotoyak in Voronezh gubernia; 2) we could travel there freely, without escort; 3) our families could move out there with us at state expense; 4) that until we found work we would receive a state benefit of 750,000 rubles a month; 5) we would be allowed to find work in government institutions, and the local Chekas would be informed of that; 6) those who wanted to would be allowed to emigrate abroad with their families at state expense; 7) the sick would be freed entirely; 8) everybody would be let out for three days to get their affairs in order.

Our discussion with Unshlikht convinced us that the Cheka's position was shaking. In order to clarify the extent of the concessions which could be won at that particular time, we stated that the committee could not give any reply without first discussing it with the comrades. But in any case we did not think that they would be satisfied with those uezd towns, one of which, Korotoyak, could not really be regarded as existing, since it had been thoroughly destroyed in the course of the civil war, and so had the 25-kilometre branch railway line on which it stood. To this Unshlikht replied that he could add one gubernia town to the three uezd towns – Vologda. 'How would you all like to be sent to Vologda?'

We laughed: 'What? The Cheka wants to create such a powerful social-democratic organisation in Vologda at one stroke? Anyway, we do not think that in present circumstances you could find accommodation for forty-five people and their families in Vologda!'

We ended by saying that in view of all the 'misunderstandings' that already seemed to have been discovered in what we had been told verbally, we would only take the proposals for the comrades' consideration and give our response if we had those proposals *in writing*. 'Fine, I shall go to the office and write down everything I have said to you now and send it to you', replied Unshlikht, and on that we parted.

This was visiting day, and all the free rooms by the office were filled with prisoners and their visiting relatives. We all still felt very uplifted, and therefore made use of our right to receive visitors. Someone overheard Unshlikht in the adjacent office talking on the telephone – we do not know with whom, but some individual words could be made out. Unshlikht was heard saying: 'They won't agree to that, evidently. We'll need to add some more towns.' The telephone conversation went on for quite some time, but we did not succeed in hearing anything else. Unshlikht soon left the office, but without having written out the paper he promised us.

The next evening we nonetheless received this piece of paper; it was brought to us by the prison governor. Everything in it was written as

Unshlikht had said, except the promise of Vologda had disappeared from the list of permitted towns.

Having considered the matter, we resolved to continue with the hunger strike. How right we were to do this, and how frivolous and completely arbitrary the All-Russia Cheka's attitude was towards the fates of those people who were in their hands can be seen from the fact that on the fourth day of the hunger strike there came an unexpected order for seven or eight comrades, who just four days previously had been sentenced to exile, to be freed completely. The freeing of comrade Binshtok was a particularly typical example of the way the Cheka carried on. Even before the Cheka had decided on all our fates, he had been given a Cheka decision that he would be sent to Mari oblast'. This was a completely undeveloped and starving region with an epidemic of typhus. He was banned from residing in the only town in that area, Krasnokokshaysk (formerly Tsarevokokshaysk). Within a week or two, he was included in the general sentence passed upon social democrats held in prison, and as a member of the Central Committee was among the particularly dangerous people to be exiled for not one but two years. And another four days later, after eleven months in prison, he was freed unconditionally. All this had more than a whiff of arbitrariness.

The committee resolved that everybody who received an order for release should immediately abandon the hunger strike and, having gathered a little strength, should leave prison the next day after lunch.

On the fifth day we were visited by a Cheka doctor, accompanied by Andreeva, a middle-aged woman who was Samsonov's assistant. I later learned that she had graduated from two faculties – in law and in medicine. Such immense intelligence, and she had ended up working under a coarse, illiterate Chekist! The doctor examined each of the hunger strikers and wrote something down. Andreeva sat silently, sullenly watching the doctor at work, and it was only when he said to me, 'You have swollen legs', she interjected hotly, 'But only a bit swollen!'

On 10 January, on the seventh day of our hunger strike, at around four in the afternoon Unshlikht appeared again, and again he was unusually gentle and pleasant. He said that he had come with the final concessions which the Bolshevik government considered it possible to make on top of the ones which had been set out in the paper given to us earlier: 1) in place of the three uezd towns, we were offered the choice of two gubernia towns, Vyatka and Severodvinsk (formerly Velikiy Ustyug); Vologda 'for various reasons' was not longer to be considered an option; 2) all those freed would have not three but seven days to sort their affairs out, and those from the provinces would have the same time again to travel to their homes. 'Since you do not trust verbal declarations, I shall write it all down for you', said Unshlikht and, taking a sheet of paper, really did write down all these concessions and signed them. He then added that in addition to those already freed, comrades Nikolaevsky, Dmitrieva and Naloev, on grounds of illness, and also some workers with large families (from among the Smolensk comrades) would be given the right to settle in the uezd towns and villages of Smolensk gubernia should they wish. We were careless enough not to insist that these additional concessions be immediately out in writing and, I should add here, we were shamefully deceived: neither of Unshlikht's promises was honoured.

Having handed us the piece of paper, Unshlikht said that he would be waiting for our response there in the office. We received information from outside that the Politburo of the Bolshevik CC, which all the time had been the decisive body in our case, accepted the concessions formulated by Unshlikht only by three votes to two, against the strong resistance of Trotsky, who was insisting on dealing with us as harshly as possible. It had resolved that these concessions were as far as it was possible to go.

It was clear that any further struggle would involve enormous sacrifice, and its outcome would be highly doubtful. On the other hand, we could say that we had already achieved very significant successes, and had to a considerable extent been able to use the political situation the Bolsheviks had created in order to open the eyes of both Russian and foreign workers. We were aware that in the night of 9-10 January our Moscow organisation had pasted up illegal leaflets on walls in the city about our hunger strike and calling for protests. One such leaflet was pasted to the walls of Butyrki prison; it was torn down around midday by the prison governor. In the factories there were lively discussions about the persecution of the social democrats and the hunger strike.

Having considered the situation and assessed what we had already achieved, the committee resolved to end the strike at six o'clock in the evening. The strikers were immediately informed by the committee, who set about taking food under the observation of our health team.

It was decided that, once they had recuperated some strength, the prisoners would begin to leave prison on 11 January. Many remained there for two or three more days, partly because they felt very weak, and partly at the request of other prisoners, who had planned celebrations for 12 January. It was painful and sad to leave my fellow prisoners, with whom for several months we had shared our joy and our pain, and everyone who did not have relatives waiting for them in Moscow decided to prolong their stay in prison in order to share the leaving party with those who were remaining inside.

I went to the office to inform Unshlikht of our decision. He offered, if I so wished, to sign an order for my release there and then and to send a car within an hour to take me home. I did not have the strength to remain in prison even for a few hours longer than necessary, and so I agreed.

Having quickly knocked back a glass of hot coffee – with sugar this time! – at seven o'clock I left our MOK. In keeping with tradition the comrades accompanied me, singing revolutionary songs. My head was reeling, not only from weakness, but also from the complexity of my mixed feelings. The joy of liberation and the feeling of satisfaction at having secured victory was mixed with the pain and sense of grievance for all those who remained, among whom were so many people who had given their whole lives for the cause of the revolution, and who were now firmly in the claws of a Cheka with no conscience. What lay ahead for them?

According to the written conditions Unshlikht had signed, each of us had to report to the secret operations department of the All-Russia Cheka seven days after leaving prison. Since at the time of our release we had not been asked where we wanted to go – to Vyatka, Severodvinsk or abroad – and none of us were obliged to report to the Cheka at any time before those seven days were up, we saw no reason to run ahead of ourselves. We postponed all discussion of finally deciding our fates until we reported to the All-Russia Cheka. Some of the comrades began to disperse to the provinces, with written documents issued by the Cheka stating that they had the right to remain at home for seven full days, however long it took for them to travel there and back.

I remained in Moscow, using the opportunity not only to take part in arranging our party affairs, but also to take a look at the new appearance the communist capital had acquired in the year since I last saw it. My observations gave me little cause for comfort. Trade was now going on in almost every building. But, alas, these were almost entirely 'colonial'-type foodstores, bakers, confectioners, cafés – i.e. shops and establishments catering to very well-off people. The queues at the confectioners' counters were not long at all, and people were paying millions of rubles for a pastry. This new trade was evidently mainly selling luxury items to the 'new rich', who stood out shamelessly against the background of general impoverishment and the monstrous famine. Confused reports of this famine were reaching Moscow in the form of news about mass mortality, appalling cases of cannibalism and so on. But this was all received as if it were news from another planet, and Moscow made merry, treating itself to pastries, fine sweets, fruits and delicacies. The theatres and concert halls were packed, and the ladies began again to flaunt their luxurious dresses, furs and diamonds. Yesterday the 'speculator' ran the risk of being shot, and lurked quietly in corners hoping that nobody would notice him. Today he feels happy, and proudly shows off all his wealth and luxury. This is reflected in all the ways people relate to each other. For the first time in many years I heard carriage drivers, waiters in cafés and porters at the station use the servile expression *barin* ('sir'), which had previously disappeared completely.

In many conversations I heard about colossal salaries ('in gold-backed currency'), about breathtaking 'commissions' on purchases and sales carried out by state agencies, on unprecedented corruption and so on. I was in the office of a good acquaintance, a man of tested honesty, who was now heading one of the state's 'economic' enterprises. While I was there all sorts of employees with reports, suppliers, middlemen and the like were going in and out. I joked to my friend that it felt less like a state enterprise and more like the office of a shady trading company of ill repute, such was the atmosphere of money-grubbing and palm-greasing, without which nothing would happen at all.

Moreover, even the most superficial observation was enough to convince me that, as far as organising and strengthening production were concerned, nothing had been done in that year. Essentially it was just the same redistribution of existing stocks left over from the former times, with just one difference: the number of participants in the carve-up had fallen significantly. As everything consumed now had to be paid for, it was just the 'top ten thousand' – those who had something to pay with – who could take part. The great bulk of the population, workers and employees, had had their direct food allocations replaced by money wages which were insufficient for survival even on starvation rations. Moreover, 'economic accounting' had resulted everywhere in staff cuts. Unemployment appeared, and a mass of young women who had previously filled Soviet offices were thrown out on to the streets without any hope of any kind of wage. And the result could be seen on the streets: Tverskaya was again filled with young women and girls, making use of 'freedom to trade' in order to sell the only thing that remained to them – their own bodies.

The 'gastronomic' nature of Moscow trade was very striking. Very rarely did I find shops with any other kinds of goods, with the exception of women's hats, which were on sale in the shops in pretty good quantities. I went into MUM, the Interdepartmental Universal Store, which occupied a few shops in the Central Trading Rows. I needed the most basic coat lining and some bone buttons, but neither were to be found in the shop – the place where all the central economic institutions of the Muscovite state brought all their riches! The stalls had just small items of haberdashery of the sort of low quality that previously would have been sold only in the most rundown village stores.

I only managed to have a brief look at 'New Economic Policy' Moscow. But what I saw left me with the most depressing impression: not one iota of economic progress, and rapidly developing moral and political disintegration.

My week at liberty passed quickly. On Monday 16 January I went to the Cheka headquarters. I was sent to our investigator Ramishevsky. This utterly phoney man, who could lie to your face without blinking, received me very kindly. I told him I had decided to go abroad, and since the fast trains only went on Mondays and Thursdays, I proposed to travel the next Monday, and therefore asked for all the necessary papers for me and my wife to be prepared. Ramishevsky replied that this would all be done, but there was something he needed to check first. Returning a few minutes later, he told me that the Presidium had decided that all the comrades who had opted to go abroad should travel no later than Thursday 19 January.

The reasons for this speed were fairly transparent. On 20 January fresh elections for the Moscow Soviet would begin, and the powers that be feared Mensheviks like fire. The more simple or frank communists would say this quite openly. However, I protested strongly against this hurry; it was impossible to get all my personal affairs in order in the two days left. Ramishevsky played along, saying that he positively could not understand how I could present such ridiculous demands and so on. Finally he offered to inform the Cheka chairman Unshlikht of my protest. He soon returned with Andreeva, who stated categorically that there could be no question of any delay, and that the Cheka itself would take on the task of preparing all the necessary documents, getting foreign visas, booking space on the train and so on. As for my personal affairs, they were not her concern; I could order them as I pleased. I nonetheless demanded a definite answer from Unshlikht himself. Andreeva went to him and brought back confirmation from him that we had to travel on the 19th. The desire to weaken the Mensheviks at all costs at the time of the elections to the Moscow Soviet was so great that with those comrades who had left the prison later and had therefore reported to the Cheka on 17 and 18 January, for whom the Cheka could not arrange a passport by the 19th, Andreeva insisted that they immediately went away to the provinces somewhere, and they were given some kind of task and free travel permits!

I had to get things together quickly and reported to the Cheka headquarters on the 17th again to fill out the necessary forms. All in all there were eleven of us travelling abroad, two of us with our wives and one with two underage children. Andreeva invited me into her office and found it necessary to explain that, although it was essential that we leave within the allotted time, she for her part was willing to do everything within her power to alleviate our situation. I replied that this had been hard to detect in her behaviour up to this point. Then she responded in hurt tones: 'Do you imagine that we can just forget that we used to be in the same party as the Mensheviks and used to work together? We shall never have the same attitude to the Mensheviks as, say, to the SRs and anarchists.' I must admit I thought it was still difficult to discern where the difference lay, but I was interested to listen to what Andreeva had to say about herself, how she had graduated from two faculties, of medicine and of law, that the party had sent her to work in the Cheka, but had only gone there once 'revolutionary legality' had been declared obligatory, etc. etc. Strangely enough, I got the very strong impression that she was speaking sincerely. But this was presumably one of those far from rare cases of dual sincerity – the hysterical ability to be equally sincere about two diametrically opposite and even mutually exclusive feelings and actions.

Nonetheless, I must admit that over the course of those two days Andreeva showed great concern and attentiveness to all the comforts of our impending journey – of course, insofar as this was possible in that mad rush.

The train was leaving at seven in the evening. Things were somewhat complicated by the fact that 19 January was Epiphany, which even in Soviet practice is regarded as a holiday. Nonetheless, we were told to turn up at midday to get our documents and money. But nothing was ready by that time, and we were asked to come back at four. But at three o'clock Andreeva telephoned me to say that the Latvian consulate had refused to issue a visa in our passports until a German visa had been obtained, and that therefore we could not travel that day. What would happen next, she did not know. We agreed that I would telephone her at eleven that evening. In the evening she told me that the next morning we would all receive a document from the All-Russia Cheka Presidium with definite instructions. I asked whether it was possible to count on travelling on the Monday. She replied that she did not know, but everything possible would be done.

The next day at around midday, two emissaries from the All-Russia Cheka turned up and gave me and Boris Nikolaevsky, who was with me, a piece of paper with the following words: 'In view of the refusal of the Latvian representatives to issue a visa, travelling abroad is not possible. You are therefore requested to indicate on this paper which town you wish to choose to live in, Vyatka or Severodvinsk, and present yourself at two o'clock this afternoon with your baggage to the All-Russia Cheka commandant for dispatch to the place you have indicated.'

On this piece of paper I wrote approximately the following statement: 'The option of travelling abroad was one of the *obligations* that the Soviet government took upon itself when we called an end to our hunger strike. It was *its* job to consider whether it was able to take on such an obligation. I demand that it be fulfilled unconditionally. I regard reneging on it as a breach of trust, and will not voluntarily submit to any new demand from the All-Russia Cheka.' Nikolaevsky wrote a declaration in much the same vein.

Immediately after the Chekists left, I telephoned Andreeva. I expressed my feelings about this latest Cheka stunt in not very carefully-chosen terms, and told her categorically that I would not be turning up at the commandant's office, neither at two o'clock nor later, and that I was not going anywhere. She tried saying something about the hopelessness of the Cheka's position, but since this completely failed to move me, the conversation ended with her saying that if I did not show up, I would be arrested. 'That's up to you!' I retorted and hung up the receiver.

Having telephoned all the comrades I could to inform them of the situation, I awaited further developments, surrounded by all the suitcases and boxes which had been packed up for yesterday.

Around four o'clock a whole company of 'guests' arrived with an order for my arrest. I put my coat on and told them I was ready. 'What about your things? You are going to Vyatka this evening.'

'I am not going anywhere voluntarily, but if you want, you can take me away without my things.' The Chekist tried to convince me, but soon concluded that it was pointless. Leaving a party to await comrade Nikolaevsky's return, he left with me and two Red Army men, and we went to the Cheka headquarters in a waiting car.

Here the commandant affirmed that we would need to leave in three hours, and while we were waiting he put me in a small room. Judging by the sign on the door, it was usually used by the plumbers, who had been sent somewhere else, although they kept coming in to get equipment from the cupboard. Apart from the cupboard the only furniture was a table and two chairs.

An hour later they brought Nikolaevsky in, and a little time after that one of the women comrades, E. I. Gryunval'd. She happened to have some supplies of food with her. A Red Army man went off for some boiling water, and we sat down to drink tea.

At around nine o'clock a young Chekist turned up. We asked him where they were going to take us. Slightly hesitantly, he said, 'I can't tell you anything, but it looks as if things are looking up for you.' We already knew that we were not being taken anywhere today, as the train to Vyatka had already departed. From what the Chekist said we understood that our trip to Vyatka had been cancelled. We started to demand to be taken somewhere where we could lie down. The Chekist replied that he did not want to take us into the infamous 'internal prison', and we would do better to hang on for a while. We agreed, and sat up all night in that little room.

In the morning all three of us were put into one of the three large rooms used for prisoners at the commandant's office and located in the yard. It was quite clean and spacious here. In the afternoon, we unexpectedly acquired a new fellow prisoner. This was Ezhov, my wife's brother. I shall briefly tell the story of his arrest, because it is very typical of the crude and arbitrary way the Cheka works. Ezhov, a member of our CC, had been arrested along with the rest of us in February 1921 and imprisoned with us in Butyrki, but had been released on grounds of ill-health in December, before our hunger strike. He had not been on the list of people sentenced to exile, and in his last conversation with us Unshlikht had mentioned him as one of our comrades who had been released unconditionally. He had ended up in our room in the following way: Andreeva had arranged a meeting with my wife by telephone, in order to discuss our subsequent fate. Because my wife was unwell, her brother had gone along to this meeting in her place. Andreeva had received him, had told him that nothing was known yet, but new efforts were being made to get visas from the Latvian government, so maybe we would be going abroad after all. Thus, twenty-four hours after our energetic protest it turned out that it might be possible to do something which the previous day had been declared to be impossible, which, the Soviet government believed, thereby relieved it of the obligations it had taken on! Andreeva added, however, that in the light of our refusal to submit to the orders of the Cheka, we would be kept under arrest right up to our departure. There was little logic here, since by this new statement the Cheka representative underscored the arbitrariness and bad faith of the order to send us to Vyatka in view of the 'impossibility' of travelling abroad – but there was no point in looking for logic here. It was no secret that the new elections to the Moscow Soviet were at the root of everything.

Ezhov had left the Cheka headquarters, but was arrested by two Chekists on Lubyanka Square, who showed him an order, bearing no name, to arrest 'Mensheviks in hiding from being sent into exile'. His protests did not help. He was put in with us, and spent ten days in prison before being released with an apology that there had been a misunderstanding, in that he could not have been hiding from being sent into exile for the simple reason that he had not been sentenced to be sent into exile. But then he was suddenly told that he too was on the list for two years' exile. Ezhov was seriously ill, and had to spend time in a sanatorium. This compelled the Cheka to postpone his exile, but at the end of April Ezhov was arrested again, and on the third day of a hunger strike, which he had declared in protest, he was sent to Vyatka without his things and under armed guard.

Ezhov told us that all the other comrades who had declared their wish to go abroad, apart from those who had travelled to the provinces, had decided to go into hiding. We later learned that all those who had travelled to the provinces were arrested there on the basis of a telegram from the All-Russia Cheka and brought back to Moscow. Those who had gone into hiding were arrested on discovery. Those provincial comrades who had not managed to use the permission to go into exile abroad before the beginning of April were deprived of that right again by an entirely arbitrary decision of the All-Russia Cheka. The moment of flexibility, when the Bolsheviks had been frightened by the international protest movement, had passed, and all concessions began to be withdrawn as far as possible.

The four of us were held in that room for six days. When it became clear that we were going abroad after all, our relatives brought us our things and food supplies. We started to get visitors. All the arrangements for sending us were dealt with by Andreeva as before, but she carefully avoided meeting with us.

I shall also mention two other characteristic encounters. At one point on the third or fourth day the door of our room opened, and the commandant brought in two elderly 'guests'. They were E. D. Kuskova and S. N. Prokopovich, the most prominent members of the Public Committee to Aid the Starving, which in its time had been inaugurated with such pomp by the Bolshevik government, which had wanted to demonstrate its unity with public forces. As is well known, the committee was soon closed down, its members were publicly accused almost of having links with the Entente; there was even talk of shooting them ... It ended with its 'ringleaders and instigators' spending a considerable period in prison (Kuskova and Prokopovich, incidentally, spent a few days with us in Butyrki) before then being exiled to northern gubernias. Kuskova and Prokopovich ended up in Vologda. But they had hardly managed to get settled in there, when the local Chekists started to harass them. There were two reasons for this. First, the influence that the exiles started to have with the local activists, especially the co-operators, looked dangerous. With the New Economic Policy, the Bolsheviks have been trying to revive the co-operative movement, but only on condition that co-operators behave like obedient bureaucrats. But there was also another reason for the ire of the local Chekists: there is very little accommodation in Vologda, and its buildings, which have not been repaired for many years, are often half-ruined. In order to find somewhere to live, Kuskova and Prokopovich had to repair a derelict house from their own resources. But as soon as they had done this, this little house was espied by one of the influential local Chekists, who started to drive them out in the most blatant fashion. As a result, there was a telegram from the All-Russia Cheka ordering Kuskova and Prokopovich to be sent to Kazan' – a city which is starving and has an epidemic of typhus. It was on their way to Kazan' that they ended up in our hospitable room. Here they were taken off for questioning and were finally told they were to live in Kashin in Tver' gubernia and were allowed to spend three days in Moscow, so long as they did not leave their building and go out on to the street for any reason.

We also had another chance encounter. They emptied a neighbouring room and soon installed a whole group of about fifteen young men and women. These were Left SRs and anarchists who had already served a year in Orel prison. They were all drained and exhausted. Where they were going to be taken, they had no idea. It soon turned out that they were going to be sent on to Yaroslavl' prison, although they had no idea why or for how long. That was my final prison encounter in Russia.

On Thursday 26, we were told in the morning that we would be leaving that day. Towards the evening we were brought to the commandant's office and given thirteen dollars each, which was to cover our expenses in Riga while we waited for a German visa.

Around seven o'clock in the evening a car took us to the station. There was a compartment for us in a carriage of the express train, but it also contained one other passenger in a sailor's uniform. Within five minutes we had identified our travelling companion as a Cheka agent. He would travel with us right up to the Latvian border.

At eight o'clock the train departed, taking us away to that banishment abroad which we had experienced so often in tsarist times. We would not have expected it now, though, in the fifth year of the revolution. I was in a foul mood ...

NOTES

1. This trial took place in the summer of 1922. For a detailed study of it in English, see Marc Jansen, *A Show Trial Under Lenin. The Trial of the Socialist Revolutionaries, Moscow 1922*, Martinus Nijhoff, The Hague, 1982.

APPENDIX I

Socialist-Revolutionary Leader Viktor Chernov's Speech to the Mass Meeting in Moscow in Honour of the British Labour Delegation, May 1920[1]

Comrades!

Allow me to begin my speech by expressing my sincere gratitude to the delegates of the English workers for everything that they have achieved at home, in England, for revolutionary Russia. Only under pressure from the working masses will the ruling circles finally decide to renounce their barbaric system of blockades on Russia, their equivocal policy of half-war, half-peace, and the open and quite unequivocal support that they are giving to our counter-revolutionary adventurers, those would-be Bonapartist military dictators. It is even more opportune to recall that service at the present time, when we have just been reading the alarming telegram announcing that French troops have disembarked at Danzig. We have every right to demand that the proletariat of the Entente countries increase its efforts twofold, threefold, tenfold to prevent their governments returning to the old tactic of armed intervention in Russian affairs. We greet the representatives of the English proletariat here, who were the first to succeed in breaking through the tangle of barbed wire and leaping over the abyss which had been dug out to separate Russia from the rest of the world. But that is not all, not only abroad, but here too, by the mere fact of visiting Russian territory, they are rendering us a further service. It has been a long time since we have seen a meeting like this in Russia – a meeting of this size which has been neither processed nor sifted through dozens of ordinary and extraordinary sieves in advance. This meeting here consists not of the bureaucratic heads of the old trade unions, but of real workers, with free speech from a free platform. We have become unaccustomed to that for a long time, or rather, we have been made unaccustomed to it. But, like the dove on Noah's ark after the flood, with the first green shoot in its beak, so after the catastrophe of

October, which removed the last vestiges of the liberties won in the first revolution, in front of our guests – and along with them – we are seeing the first breath of freedom, and we are inhaling eagerly. Comrades, I propose that we stand and show our unanimous appreciation for the new service rendered us by the representatives of the English proletariat. (The meeting rises and applauds the members of the English delegation present.)

Comrades, our guests, having come to Russia, are witnessing a moment of immeasurable global importance. To find anything like it in the annals of history, we have to go back to the first centuries of Christianity, to the time when it was the religion of the dispossessed, the needy and the oppressed, a religion which would go forward to martyrdom, and which in its first flush of fraternity had even attempted to bring about community of goods.

But then, to everyone's astonishment, that religion underwent a slow, but deadly transformation. It became the dominant religion, it consolidated itself into an ecclesiastical hierarchy, which raised itself from the catacombs to very top of the social pyramid. Men who had not long before taken vows of selflessness and poverty, who despised the riches of this world, became little by little intoxicated by power and its usual attributes – wealth, luxury, flashiness and comfort. They raised themselves way above the crowd, which as before remained starving, shivering and oppressed. These knights of the free spirit, formerly persecuted, in time became despots, oppressors, heresy-hunters, inquisitors of consciences and jailers of bodies and spirits themselves. The ruling party is undergoing the same evolution before our very eyes. At one time the programme of that party constituted the social and revolutionary religion of the oppressed, a religion which was invigorating, audacious and free. Now it has become the frozen, sterile and despotic symbol of the religion of the oppressors. Under the new label of communism, a Soviet bureaucracy and bourgeoisie have appeared, developed and come out in full blossom. Is this what the workers had dreamt about? No, by the very nature of things, they aspired to a free socialism of the working class, one they had created themselves. Could they have anticipated a new absolutism, an absolutism of the party, a socialism of tutelage, an oligarchic and bureaucratic state organisation with barracks and militarised labour as its methods – in a word, Arakcheev-communism?[2]

The best among the Christians, bitterly surprised and disillusioned, then asked the new magnificent prelates of the Church, 'What have you done with our religion, this religion of simple Galilean fishermen and of free workers?' In the same way now, the best among the communists, once they come round from their hypnosis, must ask of their leaders, 'What have you done with our socialism of the working people? Why have you removed its very soul – freedom, the mother of all creativity – from its body? Why have you caused it to degenerate into bureaucracy? Why have you turned it into a living corpse?'

Or perhaps it is not anybody's fault? Maybe the poetry of struggle has to be followed by the mundane language of domination, and after the exaltation of victory comes the heavy hangover of the morning after? No, that cannot and must not be the case. Socialism, this radiant principle of the victory of emancipated labour, has to be different from all the other historical movements which, after their victories, have fallen into darkness and decay. We believe in socialism, we know that the time will come when, in the words of Verhaeren, it will appear, not covered from head to toe in blood and mud, but

> *Que son printemps soit vert ou qu'il soit rouge*
> *N'est-elle point, dans le monde, toujours*
> *Haletante, par à travers les jours*
> *La puissance profonde et fatale qui bouge.*[3]

This is why we believe that socialism as a whole will not have the same fate, must not have the same fate, as the party which is currently in power in Russia. Your presence here is a further guarantee of this. You, representatives of the European workers' movement, have come here, in your own words, to benefit from our experience. Alas, this painful and bitter experience has plenty of instructive material which will enable you to conclude both how socialism should be built and how it *should not* be built. You are people with experience, knowledge and a record of practical work. You will not be deceived by a display along the lines of a Potemkin village, quickly constructed for show, nor by glittering exteriors like a thick layer of foundation on sunken cheeks.

Probe our wounds, not in order to lessen your striving for a better future, but to avoid the fatal errors we have committed, to go towards socialism by correct paths, without getting lost in blind alleys, with a clear conscience and a firm will. If you want to, you will learn, just like we have, that in this country the attractive façades always conceal rot.

All around here there are 'rough-hewn sepulchres' in the most striking colours, from the vivid red of the posters and rosettes to the orange colour that the futurists have been daubing on the trees in Alexander Square. But these sepulchres have the cadaverous stench of corruption, venality, bribery – everything which is inseparable from bureaucratic rule.

If you want to prise open one of these sepulchres, you have all you need – it really is so simple. Rather than letting yourself be guided around by bureaucrats, speak directly to the masses. Take part in general meetings of other trade unionists – of railway workers, textile workers, metal workers – open meetings like this one, where you will not be separated from the masses by a partition wall. Through bitter experience, the working masses have learned to condemn this debased socialism unanimously. We must tip it away, down to the last dregs. Finally, go out into the villages, listen to the voice of the most numerous class in Russia – the workers on the land – and hear what they have to say about this communism which has degenerated into serfdom!

All credit to you, comrade printers. You know, from the your own professional experience, the difference between serving the living cause of a free exchange of opinions which can lead to the truth, and serving a sterile monopoly of the press by one party. This monopoly of official 'truth' has always either ended up as, or has even started out as, a tissue of lies.

You have shown by your example how one must win the right to free exchange of ideas. You will not remain without followers. We say this to all the comrade workers: remember, comrades, freedom of speech, freedom of the press, freedom of assembly and the freedom to decide though universal suffrage on all questions of general significance. All these freedoms belong to you by right. Simply claim them, without asking anyone's permission. Make use of them, just as I have here, using the right to address you from this platform while my fellow members of the Socialist-Revolutionary Party Central Committee have been, are being and again will be arrested and thrown into jail. And, when we are arrested, at least it will become clear that our only sin is to feel the same hatred and the same revulsion at all despotism, whatever it calls itself, the same dedication to the people's rights, whoever is encroaching on them from above. We are inspired by the same feelings as when we were struggling against tsarism.

I will say further, comrades, that even if you wanted to betray the freedom you have won, you would have no right to do so. It does not belong to you alone, and you have not been the only ones to pay for it with your blood. No, it was won with the blood of many fighters, and it is the inalienable possession of all the people, not only of the present generation, but also of generations to come. And if the Russian workers come to forget this, then they will have shown that they are not worthy of freedom. That would mean that while the party in power had been undergoing its tragic evolution from the party of Lenin-Pugachev to that of Lenin-Arakcheev, at the same time the Russian proletariat had been subject to a no less disastrous transformation, from daring falcons to slithering grass snakes. Let that not be true! But we believe, no – we know – that in Russia that will never happen!

NOTES

1. Translated from the French; V. Tchernov, *Mes tribulations en Russie soviétique*, Povolozky, Paris, 1921, pp. 55-60.
2. Count Aleksey Arakcheev (1769-1834), general of artillery under Emperor Alexander I, founded military-agricultural colonies run on strictly hierarchical military lines. They were noted both for their brutality and their economic inefficiency. Many socialist and non-socialist critics of Lenin's regime accused it of *arakcheevshchina*,
3. This is the final stanza of Émile Verhaeren's poem 'La Révolte' from his 1895 anthology *Les Villes tentaculaires*.

APPENDIX II

Letter from the Russian Social-Democratic Workers' Party Central Committee to Members of the British Labour Delegation[1]

4 June 1920

Comrades!

Our open conversation with you, and especially the speeches given in your presence by members of our party at the Moscow Soviet and at the printers' meeting, have resulted in unprecedented attacks on us from the ruling party. We are accused of having given you material denouncing the Bolshevik regime with the aim of weakening the struggle of the British working class against the intervention. In order to poison the dark masses against us, our actions are being linked with explosions at armaments warehouses in Moscow, which have been blamed on Polish military agents. We have been unambiguously threatened with severe repression as 'accomplices of the Polish incendiarists'. On Sunday 30 May the all-Russia Cheka issued an order to all local commissions for merciless retribution against both those guilty/accused of the attacks on the warehouses, and against those who 'snitch to Lloyd George'. This term is now being applied in the Bolshevik press against anyone who had given you unbiased accounts.

Explaining that usage, the Bolshevik press asserts that among the British delegation there are supporters of Lloyd George's foreign policy, even if they are not directly his agents.

The 'theses' of the Moscow committee of the Communist Party, published on 1 June, declare that the Entente governments, in order to weaken the movement of the proletariat in defence of Soviet Russia, sent the delegation of trade unionists to gather incriminating material against the Soviet regime.

On the following day, 2 June, we tried at a session of the Moscow Soviet to expose all this poison and in particular the unworthy slandering of you to the Russian workers. Mr Bukharin, the official representative of the Communist Party, replying to our comrade, declared that among the British delegation there are undoubtedly 'those who side with Lloyd George, and support his policies', and that these people have come to Russia in order to gather materials against Soviet Russia.

At the same time they are explaining to the Russian workers that it is not you, but the delegates of the London factory councils who came here recently who have the right to speak on behalf of the British working class, and that your claim to represent it is false.

We do not need to tell you how the workers in our party react to these sorts of declarations. They are shameless and deliberate lies, obvious to anyone who is at all familiar with the present relations between the British government and the British workers. But, as we have no press at our disposal, we cannot even tell the masses about our own attitude to the dishonourable insinuations of Mr Bukharin, which were repeated by the whole Bolshevik press over the next few days. The broad masses of the Russian people must not remain under the impression that you cannot answer the public accusation that some of you came here with a secret mission from the British counter-revolutionary government, and the others agreed to take part in the same delegation as them. Neither the cause which brought you to Russia nor the general interests of the revolution can permit that, especially since after your departure this same Bukharin will present your silence as confirmation of his accusation.

For our part, we shall of course do everything in our modest powers to protest loudly against this campaign of slander, which so shamefully flouts the most elementary demands of international socialist solidarity. But we consider it absolutely essential that you also reply to this false accusation, made against you in front of the Russian masses, and get the Bolshevik press to publish your clarification of the real relationship between your delegation and the British government. Only then will the slander be killed at the root.

On behalf of all conscious socialist elements of the Russian proletariat we beg, comrades, your pardon for this paradoxical manifestation of our peculiar national hospitality to which you have been subjected in our country. This sort of hospitality finds it quite possible to honour our visitors today with parades, banquets and banners saying 'Welcome', and tomorrow to tell the masses that our visitors deserve the gallows, and are at any rate imposters. We would not want you, on the basis of this example of the culture of the Bolshevik People's Commissars, to draw erroneous conclusions about the cultural level of the people attained by our glorious revolution.

We hardly need to add that we are deeply convinced that this dismal episode, the result of insane party fanaticism, will not weaken at all your sympathy towards the heroic socialist proletariat of Russia. It will not deflect you from your intention to campaign even more energetically than before in Britain against the criminal intervention and for the recognition of Soviet Russia by the Entente countries. No matter how you were received in Russia, your visit here will, we are sure, forge close links between the working class movements of both countries.

The Central Committee of the Russian Social-Democratic Workers' Party.

Chairman: L. Martov.

Members: R. Abramovich, B. Gorev, D. Dalin, F. Dan, O. Ermansky, A. Pleskov, A.Troyanovsky, F. Cherevanin, A. Yugov, and I. Volkov (candidate).

Secretary: B. Skomorovsky.

Chairman of the Bund (S-D) I. Yudin.

NOTES

1. Reproduced in D. Pavlov, compiler, *Men'sheviki v 1919-1920 gg.*, ROSSPEN, Moscow, 2000, pp. 505-507.

APPENDIX III

Menshevik Leaflets and Appeals from the Time of the Kronstadt Revolt, February-March 1921

Proclamation of the Petrograd Committee of the Russian Social-Democratic Workers' Party[1]

February 1921

From the Russian Social-Democratic Workers' Party to the starving and freezing workers of Petrograd

Workers of all countries, unite!
   Comrades! Hunger and cold have once again struck at the population of Petrograd, now only ten times harder. There is no food. There is no fuel. Factories and plants are stopping work, one after the other. They tell us that this is just a short delay, a temporary hitch. Everything will be sorted out. All we need to do is be a bit patient, roll our sleeves up a bit, take a bit of fuel wood to the railways, and all our troubles will be over. What rubbish! Is it really just a matter of fuel wood? Can an enormous country, which not so long ago was consuming millions of puds of coal and oil, live and work on fuel wood alone? Can we be sure that once this has been done, the whole position will not be even worse tomorrow? And are we really so blind as not to see that, for all the Bolsheviks' complacent reassurances, everything is not getting sorted out, but is instead getting worse, year on year, month on month? Can we really not see that neither Baku nor Grozny with their inexhaustible supplies of oil, nor the Don basin and the Urals with their immense coal reserves, nor Siberia, Ukraine and the Kuban' with their stockpiles of grain have been able to help us? Are we such children that we cannot understand that although we have great wealth, we are somehow unable to manage it properly? No comrades, it is a not a matter of individual delays and hitches, but of a general great defect in our state machine, one which cannot just be patched up, but needs fixing properly.

Right now, of course, generalised want has gripped us by the throat and brought us to the very edge of ruin. The authorities are calling on us to exert all our efforts to bring in at least some fuel wood and grain, and not to let the factories and their machinery become ruined and unusable. And right now, of course, we must answer that call, in order to save both our families and our industrial wealth from destruction. And we shall help – but not by trying to extort fuel wood from our brother peasants at bayonet point, as the Bolshevik authorities currently extort grain from them. Instead, we shall again strain every sinew, exert all our strength, all our intelligence, all our organising abilities and direct all our powers of persuasion at the countryside. We shall seek to ensure that in these unbearably hard times all the grain and fuel is shared out equally, and that there are no privileged groups all the time hunger and cold is raging. Let our rulers, who bear responsibility for the current economic system and strictly punish any breach of it, also live on the rations that they are advocating for everyone else! Let them set an example of that patience and spirit of self-sacrifice that they are demanding from every citizen!

But, comrades, will that solve the question? If we bring in a bit of grain and fuel wood today, will that mean that we have escaped the clutches of ruin? No, comrades, once more these are just miserable patches which might just plug the gaps for today, but cannot prevent our economy from falling apart at the seams. If we really want to be rid of our problems, we cannot avoid the great and general questions of our state structure and state policy. We cannot avoid thinking about the roots, the fundamental reasons for the mess we are in.

If we ask the Bolsheviks about the reasons, they will blame the Entente imperialists first and foremost; they are strangling us with their blockade! True enough! While the capitalist robbers of other countries are squeezing us with rings of iron, and until the world proletariat finishes with them, we shall remain in need of many things, we shall be short of many things. But of everything? We do not need to go to the Entente for grain, coal, oil, iron ore, flax, hemp or even cotton! It wants to make concessionary deals to get all that from us. It follows that the Entente cannot be the only reason. By all means, fight the imperialists, expose the Entente, place your hopes in the world proletariat – but do not make blunders yourselves! Can we say that we have not made blunders? Again, if we ask the Bolsheviks, they will say 'No! We have hundreds of millions of puds of grain, but there is no bread because there is a hitch with fuel, we cannot get any in.' And if we ask why there is no fuel, they will say 'Fuel? There is as much as you want in the forests, the coal mines and the oil wells. The problem is just that we have a hitch with grain, and we have nothing with which to feed the woodcutters, miners and oil workers because there is no bread!' So – there is no bread because there is no fuel, and there is no fuel because there is no bread. Is that any kind of answer? It is not an answer, it is a tale of the white bull.[2]

If we ask people of the old school, the servants and slaves of capitalism, they have their answer ready: 'The whole problem is that we no longer have the old master, that the working people have taken their fates into their own hands.' Rubbish! The capitalists have shown – not only in the kingdom of Kolchak, Denikin and Wrangel, but also in all the countries of Europe and America – that they do not think about production so much as about their profits. Giving all power over to people who are concerned above all about their own pockets would not free us from hunger and cold. We would just be putting a noose around our own necks!

Finally, if we ask the anarchists, the people of the black flag, they will say: 'The whole problem is that we have state power at all. We do not need any power or any politics. All we need are individual unions, societies, communes of people, each of which can look to its own interests, so long live the absence of power!' That slogan, too, comrades, is rubbish! The anarchists argue that the efforts of tens or hundreds of thousands of individual communes, turning their backs on politics and following only their own economic interests, can lead to general happiness and harmony. In fact, it could only lead to a general free-for-all and general poverty. If each of these communes, scattered across one-sixth of the earth's surface, were to work without a general plan, without taking account of the needs of other communes, there could only be one outcome: the state power from which the workers had turned away would not disappear. It would just fall completely into the hands of that military, Cheka, civil and economic bureaucracy which already despotically commands almost everything.

No, comrades, we cannot get by, or overcome our devastation, without close links between all individual parts of our country, without a single economic plan, without state organisation and state politics. But the authorities' policy must be a sensible and correct one, run in the interests of the working people. Above all, they should not get diverted into trying to nationalise everything and bring every single handicraft workshop or little store into state ownership. Most of all, they should consider how to interest the peasantry, which comprises the great bulk of the working population, in supporting the revolution and the state; how to make it a friend, rather than an enemy, of the revolutionary town and the revolutionary proletariat; how to make it want to sow more grain and deliver it to the cities.

The Bolsheviks have tried to do this by force, with sticks and bayonets. And we can see the results: the peasants are in revolt, the peasants are reducing their sowings, the peasants prefer to see their grain rot, rather than deliver it to the city which only knows how to address them with its fists. We need a politics not of violence against the peasantry, but of conciliation with it. We need a politics which takes account of the fact that the peasant is not a proletarian, not a worker, but a self-employed property owner who thinks like a property owner and defends his economic interests. But in order for this sensible policy to be implemented, state power needs to be in the hands of the working people, not in words alone, but in reality. We need a state which is not run dictatorially by a communist party which is self-contained, stuffed with bureaucrats and divorced from the working masses. To get this, we need fresh free elections for all soviets everywhere, from top to bottom. In order that these re-elected soviets genuinely represent the will of the working people, not only must the fresh elections be free, putting an end to the shameful machinations and violence which turn any elections into a miserable comedy – the working people themselves must be free. They must have the right to a free press and free speech, they must have the right to organise freely in parties, trade unions and educational associations. The practice of appointing people to leading posts must be ended decisively and for good. The shameful practice of reprisals against all non-Bolshevik parties – through silencing, arrests, exile, and destroying organisations – must come to an end. In other words, workers' democracy must become a reality. A lot is spoken about it, but we can see no sign of it in reality, any more than we can see any sign of implementation of those plans, proclaimed with such fanfare at the Eighth Congress of Soviets, which promised so much.

Comrades – the social democrats appeal to all proletarians, regardless of party or faction, to take this path. We are bound to the working class through decades of struggle. We have been sharing all its hardships. And now the Bolshevik papers, using their monopoly of the printed word, have the gall to accuse us every day of 'playing' on the workers' hunger and cold! ... Only by establishing real workers' power, and pursuing policies which express the interests of working people in town and country, will we be able to triumph over this terrible crisis. Only this can ensure that the small measures we take today will not serve merely as temporary sticking-plasters over the deep wounds in our national economy, but will be the first steps towards really freeing ourselves from the grip of hunger, cold and general devastation. So – long live freedom and real power for the working people!

Petrograd Committee of the RSDRP.

Appeal of the Petrograd Committee of the Russian Social-Democratic Workers' Party[3]

To the workers, sailors, Red Army men and cadets of Petrograd: stop the killing!

The cannons are roaring ... The Communists, who call themselves a workers' party, are shooting the sailors and workers of Kronstadt with cannon.

We do not know the details of what is happening in Kronstadt. But we do know that Kronstadt demanded free elections to the soviets, the freeing of socialist and non-party workers, Red Army men and sailors arrested in connection with the workers' movement, and the convening on 10 March of a non-party conference of workers, Red Army men and sailors to discuss how to get out of Soviet Russia's catastrophic situation.

A workers' government should have established the real reasons for the Kronstadt events. A workers' government should have openly, in front of the whole working class, reached an agreement with the workers and sailors of Kronstadt. But instead, they declared a state of siege, issued ultimatums about surrender and began to shoot at workers and sailors.

Comrades! We cannot and must not calmly listen to the roar of cannon. Each shot can take away dozens of precious lives.

We must intervene and put an end to the bloodshed.

Demand that the government immediately opens negotiations with them, with the participation of delegates from Petrograd's plants and factories.

Immediately elect delegates to take part in these negotiations. Stop the killing!

7 March 1921, Petrograd Committee RSDRP

Leaflet of the Petersburg Committee of the RSDRP[4]
'An answer to the slanderers'
Workers of all countries unite!
The edifice of Bolshevik dictatorship is shaking and collapsing. There are peasant risings in Ukraine, Siberia and South Eastern Russia. There are strikes and workers' unrest in Petersburg, and popular hostility in the rest of Russia ... This is the sad picture of the Soviet Republic three years after the Bolsheviks seized power.

The edifice of Bolshevik dictatorship is shaking and collapsing. The Bolsheviks understand this very well. But instead of admitting that they have made mistakes and changing their policies in order to save the revolution from inevitable rout, the Bolsheviks, foaming at the mouth, are looking for scapegoats for their own failures and are blaming everyone ... except themselves.

The peasants are to blame, for not wanting to surrender their grain for nothing; the workers are to blame, for not having got used to surviving on Soviet soup over the three years of 'their' dictatorship; the socialists are to blame, for daring to have their own opinions and express them publicly.

In their search for a scapegoat, the Bolsheviks have made our party (the Mensheviks) the favourite target for their lying and slanderous agitation.

The Mensheviks are helping the intervention, the Mensheviks are inciting the peasants to revolt, the Mensheviks called for the strikes in Petersburg and the rising in Kronstadt.

This is what the hired scribblers write day in and day out, trying to please their masters and 'honestly' earn their rations.

And in the wake of these thugs with pens come the real thugs from the Cheka, seizing members of our party and workers who sympathise with us from their flats at night, turning the place upside down and arresting anyone they find. Dozens of our comrades have been arrested in recent days, including comrades Dan, Rozhkov, Kamensky, Nazar'ev and Chertkov.

And all this is done in the name of the Petersburg proletariat.

We know that this has nothing to do with the Petersburg workers. We know that in a whole series of factories workers have come out on strike, demanding the release of those who have been arrested. We know that the Bolsheviks are trying to buy them off, offering up to fifty gold rubles apiece. We are pleased to note that the Bolsheviks set a significantly higher price for the workers' conscience than the price once set for Judas' conscience. But we have strong doubts about the success of this undertaking.

The Bolsheviks will not manage to buy the Petersburg workers.

Nor will the Bolsheviks' campaign of slander against our party succeed. It will not succeed because the workers know that the social democrats have always called upon the workers to close ranks and for a united proletarian front, that the social democrats have always opposed war amongst the workers and peasants, and that the social democrats have never called on the workers to rise up against Soviet power. But they have pointed out the fatal consequences of Bolshevik policies, and have called on the workers to wage an organised struggle by democratic means for their class interests.

It is not our fault if the authorities respond to the unanimous demands of the Petersburg and Moscow workers for a change of policy with arrests of workers' delegates, or if they respond to the resolution of the Kronstadt sailors and garrison for new free elections to the soviets with salvoes from artillery.

But every cloud has a silver lining. Now every worker, even the most backward one, will understand that Bolshevik power is not based upon workers' and peasants' soviets, but solely upon naked force. Now every worker will understand that the only way out of this situation is for power to pass into the hands of genuinely freely elected soviets. They will understand, and will fight alongside us for:

> the abolition of states of siege and martial law, freedom of speech, the press, trade unions and assembly for all working people;
> fresh free elections to the soviets and other workers' organisations;
> the release of all socialists and non-party workers and peasants arrested for their political convictions.

Long live genuine workers' power!

Petersburg Committee, RSDRP 8 March 1921

Motions from the RSDRP CC at the Petrograd citywide non-party workers' conference, 10-20 April 1921[5]
(as relayed in G. E. Zinoviev's political report)

Bearing in mind:

1. That the Bolsheviks' gamble on an immediate world socialist revolution, which has cost the republic numerous victims, has failed; that the world socialist revolution, as Marxists have pointed out more than once, has turned out to be a lengthy process full of zigzags; that the sectarian politics of the Bolsheviks, which have tended towards splitting the workers' movement in all countries, have not only not made this process any smoother, but have made it even more difficult;
2. That in the given international situation the idea of immediately realising socialism in Russia is completely utopian and against the interests both of the working class and of the country as a whole;
3. That the Bolshevik slogans of October 'all power to the soviets' and 'dictatorship of the proletariat' have in fact turned out as complete powerlessness for the soviets and a Bolshevik dictatorship over the proletariat with all the consequences which flow from that: bureaucratism, the degeneration of those in power, violence against citizens, police and spies everywhere and shootings;
4. That the forcible nationalisation of the entire economy of the republic, undertaken by the Bolsheviks against the wishes of the great majority of the population, with its attendant violations of the interests of the many millions of peasants, has brought the country to economic catastrophe;
5. That the preservation of the gains of the revolution and the restoration of productive forces are only possible if the utopian idea of immediately turning backward Russia into a socialist society is renounced, and the entire political and economic line of the government is changed accordingly,

This conference demands:

1. The implementation of the Soviet constitution and its further democratisation.

2. The immediate abolition of the death penalty.
3. The lifting of the state of siege and martial law, the destruction of the Chekas and special courts with the latter replaced with an independent unified system of people's courts.
4. The liberation of all political prisoners.
5. Freedom of organisation, assembly, speech and the press, and the inviolability of the person.
6. Immediate fresh elections to the soviets with no interference at all from government, a secret ballot and equal electoral rights for workers, peasants, Red Army soldiers and employees.
7. A consistent policy of rapprochement with the peasants, with the real implementation of the tax in kind etc..
8. Free trade at markets, bazaars and in shops;. the freeing of cooperation from any kind of government tutelage.
9. Denationalisation (excluding the basic branches of industry).
10. Freedom of labour and the emancipation of the working class; independence for the trade unions with fresh elections for all their leading bodies; tariff wage rates should be brought into line with the cost of living; the tariff rates should be regarded as a minimum wage, and private employers should be allowed to set higher rates.

On the Kronstadt events:

1. The Kronstadt events, like all the recent mass disturbances among workers, peasants, Red Army men and sailors, were a natural movement of the broad proletarian and peasant masses against the anti-democratic policies of the Bolsheviks, and against their economic and food policies which have been murderous for the country. They certainly have not had the character of risings against Soviet power itself.
2. Instead of entering into negotiations with the Kronstadters and reaching agreement with them on all questions, the Bolshevik Party distorted the meaning of the events, slandered the Kronstadters with false accusations of counter-revolution and conspiracy, and in its very first address to the sailors threatened to 'shoot them like partridges'.
3. The consequence has been the mass killing of sailors, Red Army men and trainee officers, and brutal executions. The heavy

responsibility for this lies wholly with those in power, who neither would nor could find any language for negotiation with the Kronstadters other than the language of machine guns.

This conference demands an immediate end to the execution of prisoners from Kronstadt. Considering the actions of the authorities to have been criminal, it resolves to elect a commission from those present at the conference to investigate the Kronstadt events, and calls for those in power who are guilty of mass murder to be tried in court.

NOTES

1. *Sotsialisticheskiy vestnik* No. 5, 1921, pp. 6-7; republished in V. P. Naumov, A. A. Kosakovsky, compilers, *Kronshtadt 1921*, Mezhdunarodnyy fond 'Demokratiya', Moscow, 1997, pp. 261-263.
2. 'Tale of the white bull' – a pointless, repetitive and ultimately annoying story.
3. *Sotsialisticheskiy vestnik* No. 5, 1921; republished in V. P. Naumov, A. A. Kosakovsky, compilers, *Kronshtadt 1921*, Mezhdunarodnyy fond 'Demokratiya', Moscow, 1997, p. 264.
4. Central Archive of the FSB RF, f. 114728, t. 16, d. 11; republished in V. P. Naumov, A. A. Kosakovsky, compilers, *Kronshtadt 1921*, Mezhdunarodnyy fond 'Demokratiya', Moscow, 1997, pp. 264-266.
5. *Sotsialisticheskiy vestnik* No. 9, 5 June 1921, pp. 12-13. TsA FSB d. 1123, t. 3, pp. 7-10. Republished in D. Pavlov, compiler, *Men'sheviki v 1921-1922 gg.*, ROSSPEN, Moscow, 2002, pp. 193-195.

APPENDIX IV

Cheka Documents on Dan's Case

Protocol of Dan's interrogation (form and deposition)[1]

Secret Department
Petrograd 19 April 1921
Re: Case No. 902

I, the undersigned, questioned as [ ], affirm

1. Surname: Gurvich (Dan)
2. Name and patronymic: Fedor Il'ich
3. Age: 49 years
4. Origins: Son of Petrograd pharmacist
5. Residence: Moscow, Pokrovka, Vvedensky pereulok 14, flat 14
6. Occupation: party political functionary
7. Family situation: Married, one son at Tashkent University, wife: Lidiya Osipovna Tsederbaum
8. Property status: -
9. Party affiliation: RSDRP unified
10. Political beliefs: [ ]
11. Education: higher, doctor of medicine
12. Activities and service
    a) before 1914 war: party work
    b) before February Revolution 1917: [ ]
    c) before October Revolution 1917: [ ]
    d) from October Revolution until arrest: [ ]
13. Information regarding previous convictions: In 1913 was brought before the court, but the case was stopped in view of the 1913 amnesty. In 1918 was brought before the Moscow Revolutionary Tribunal in connection with the newspaper *Vpered* case, which was de facto stopped.

Statement concerning this case:

On 2 or 3 February 1921 I arrived in Petrograd. I had been sent here to be deployed by the Petrograd Section of the Military Medical Administration (POVSU). POVSU put me in the charge of the territorial brigade doctor, who sent me to work in the Rozhdestvensky Sports Club.

Question: In what did your work in the Petersburg Menshevik organisation consist?

Answer: As a member of the CC of the party, I took the most active part in all areas of the work of the local party. But since this party, despite the resolutions of the All-Russia CEC, is obliged to exist semi-legally in Petersburg, I refuse to give any more concrete details.

For the present moment, I consider it essential for the interests of the working people and particularly the proletariat in Russia that the Soviet system be preserved. However, that system should be, in accordance with its theory and its constitution, a genuinely free form of workers' self-government, rather than a cover for party dictatorship. I believe this system's further evolution towards fully democratic forms to be indispensable for the socialist reorganisation of society. But the tempo and nature of this evolution will depend so much, from the point of view working class interests, on a series of currently unforeseeable international and domestic factors, and so for our party there can be no question of any firm correlation here. As for the Constituent Assembly, on the one hand, I would say that the slogan has lost its relevance. This is because the greatest part of the destructive revolutionary work, for the sake of which our party waged its struggle against tsarism under that slogan, has already been accomplished, albeit in other forms, in the course of the revolution. This was the radical destruction of the monarchy and the purging of the tsarist bureaucratic apparatus, the uprooting of landlordism in agriculture and the transfer of the land to the peasants, the all-round liberation of the working class from the patriarchal cabal, an end to Russia's participation in the imperialist war, etc. On the other hand, the slogan of the Constituent Assembly, as an immediate practical political goal, I consider to be damaging, given the mood of the broad mass of peasants, largely as a result of the

Bolshevik government's policies. A Constituent Assembly elected at the present time would have a majority imbued with anti-revolutionary, anti-socialist and anti-worker attitudes. Consequently, the slogan no longer has the clearly revolutionary significance that it had for our party during the struggle against tsarism (and may apparently still have for the Bolsheviks themselves in the Far Eastern territory), but is, rather, capable of being used as a banner under which all counter-revolutionary forces could rally.

My attitude to the peasant risings: it stands to reason that the only political outcome of these risings could be the triumph of Bonapartism. For this reason our party everywhere and at all times not only did not initiate any such risings or lead them, but spoke out decisively against them. But our party considered and still considers the policy of the government to be a greater crime, in that it refused to take account of the petty-bourgeois social nature of the peasantry. The government thereby automatically pushed the peasants towards continual risings and sowed hatred in the villages towards the towns, socialism and the proletariat. It is only now that the ruling party is starting to implement the same policy towards the peasantry that our party has been advocating for more than three years, and for which the Bolsheviks were denouncing us as lackeys of the bourgeoisie and hirelings of the Entente. Moreover, this belated implementation of our programme, at a time when so much has already been spoiled and can only be put right with such difficulty, can in no way be justified by the exigencies of wartime, as the Bolshevik press now claims. This is shown not only by the whole nature of the polemic with our party, even on the very eve of the replacement of requisitioning by a tax in kind, but also by the fact that the person with the greatest responsibility for the thinking underpinning the war, Trotsky, has admitted that he was demanding this essential reform more than a year back. But replacing requisitioning with a tax and partial permission to trade freely will not change the situation if, when the peasants try to exercise the economic rights they have now been granted, they come up against the barbed wire fence of political arbitrariness, which necessarily comes with a terroristic dictatorial regime. Only by adapting – and quickly – the political superstructure to the new economic base which is now being created can the situation be saved.

The necessity of political reform is even more obvious in relation to the working class. It will come up against questions of politics, the system of free trade and the system of concessions through questions of wages and trade union organisation. While our party has upheld the right of workers to strike in the Soviet state as well, it has always tried to hold the working masses back from using that right, and from strike movements. Our party considers that in a situation of extreme collapse of productive forces, and where the proletariat is atomised, disorganised and in a state of social and political decline, strikes will inevitably be not only useless for the working class, but harmful. They will also inevitably be exploited by the proletariat's class enemies. Therefore, while restraining the workers from striking everywhere, where it is within its power to do so, our party unceasingly tries to direct the discontent of the broad working masses towards peaceful, organised and planned struggle to stand for those rights which exist on paper but in reality have become mere fictions. And if the intensified persecution of our party means that its organisational work is unable to develop – and if the provocative lack of respect towards the masses, atomised and deprived of conscious leadership, nonetheless pushes them to come out actively – then the blame for such a tragic course of events falls entirely on the government.

In my view, the government is entirely to blame for the Kronstadt events, which I consider to be the greatest misfortune for the revolution and the proletariat. When revolutionary strata who can no longer bear the burden of Bolshevik power show dissatisfaction and make demands, and when that power responds with bloody repression rather than agreements and concessions, and when a government resorts to using specially trained and privileged troops like the so-called 'red cadets' in its struggle against the broad masses, then – I am deeply convinced – that government is creating with its own hands all the preconditions for the triumph of Bonapartism.

F. Dan

Decision of the Chief of the Second Special Department of the Secret Department of the All-Russia Cheka regarding cases Nos. 9136, 1074, 9135, 12123, 11248 of members of the RSDRP CC[2]

1) Dan-Gurvich, Fedor Il'ich
2) Tsederbaum-Ezhov, Sergey Iosifivich
3) Ayzenshtadt-Yudin, Isay L'vovich

4) Nikolaevsky, Boris Ivanovich
5) Pleskov, Artur Abramovich
6) Lipkin-Cherevanin, Fedor Andreevich

Charged with leading active agitation to distort the real record of Soviet Power and the RKP(b) with the aim of overturning the existing Proletarian power and replacing it by Bourgeois power.

From examining the materials held in the Second department belonging to the RSDRP CC from 1920 and 1921 (declarations, resolutions, appeals, leaflets, proclamations and articles from the party organ *Sotsialisticheskiy vestnik*) the following conclusions can be drawn:

Without going into the well-known actions of the RSDRP in 1917, 1918 and the first half of 1919, where their deeds were in many cases deemed to be counter-revolutionary, it is necessary to note the line of the RSDRP CC in 1921, which was also directed against the Dictatorship of the proletariat.

Despite the fact that during the war with Poland the RSDRP mobilised its members, thereby appearing to display loyalty towards the Soviet Republic, here too we can discern the insincerity which is always a feature of the RSDRP. The mobilised members of the RSDRP conducted disorganising agitation within the Red Army; many of them were had up by the Special Sections in the front zone and were sent away to other places.

The RSDRP, which for four years of the Revolution had stood in opposition to the RKP and Soviet Power, showed its policy towards them particularly sharply after the end of all the military fronts within the Republic. The RSDRP Cent. Comm., having adopted a stance of unremitting struggle, sent a circular letter to all its local organisations to reactivate themselves and strengthen their local work by word-of-mouth agitation, leaflet distribution, the organisation of circles in factories and plants, the organisation of s-d cells in soviet institutions and Red Army divisions, with the obligation for RSDRP members to enter workers' committees and factory committees. It also indicated that where work could not be carried on completely legally, the party should move to a semi-legal position and work through various cultural and educational organisations. By advancing slogans like 'free Soviets', 'freedom of speech' and 'inviolability of the person' etc., they would generally stir up the masses, leading them to attack the Soviet Government, thereby securing a change in the existing order.

All this is being done when the Republic is in a most difficult position (with famine, a fuel crisis, and hitches in transport). The RSDRP CC has deliberately chosen this moment to try agitation, to stir up the dissatisfaction of the masses in the factories and plants. In order to carry it out its schemes better, it is concentrating its agitation in those major industrial centres of particular importance for the republic, thereby leading to the disorganisation of production. As a result of this work by the Mensheviks, we had a wave of strikes in Petrograd, Tula, Penza, Moscow and other industrial centres. All reports from the localities from gubernia Chekas at the beginning of 1921 tell of the malicious agitation by the Mensheviks and their corrupting influence in the localities, which resulted in stoppages in factories and plants. In places the Mensheviks stirred the workers up to an extreme degree, joining together with the SRs and other anti-Soviet parties. CC members went out to the localities under the guise of travel for work purposes, and made speeches there, predicting that Soviet Power would soon come to an end. Finally, the foul politics of the RSDRP, by exploiting the semi-famine situation and the weariness of the proletarian masses, succeeded and led to the Kronstadt events, in which its members took an active part, with RSDRP members gracing the Kronstadt revkom.

About three weeks before the uprising in Kronstadt the RSDRP Central Committee sent its best-known and most popular member Gurvich-Dan to Petrograd for party work. From Dan's depositions it is clear that he took a most active part in the work of the Petrograd organisation. From a letter to Nazar'ev by the same Dan it is evident that the RSDRP was preparing to form a bloc with the so-called 'opposition' and was counting on being ready to take part in restructuring the Russian state. At the same time the Petrograd RSDRP organisation was putting out a whole series of leaflets and appeals which called for the Petrograd proletariat to struggle actively against the RKP. The literature which was issued maliciously distorted all the undertakings of Soviet power and Soviet Power itself. Playing upon the depressed mood of the working masses resulting from their difficult economic situation, the Mensheviks called on the working masses to disrupt the economic measures of Soviet Power and the implementation of the sowing and other campaigns.

The Delegation Abroad of the RSDRP CC in the persons of Martov and Abramovich has the special task of creating a social-democratic centre in the West. In the foreign press the Mensheviks have not shrunk from any insinuation and shamelessly slander the RKP, trying to win the Western European proletariat over to their side. They send information and secret documents from their members employed in various Soviet institutions, via a CC member specially tasked with contacts with abroad – Nikolaevsky. An illegal underground newspaper was published by the SD Youth League with the knowledge of the CC and Moscow Committee of the RSDRP. A charter was drawn up for it, and they allowed it to be printed in the CC premises, the 'Vpered' club. This league was organised across the whole republic. The CC set up a 'student' fraction and used it to carry out its subversive work among the student youth.

On the basis of the above, all members of the RSDRP CC are implicated in leading covert counter-revolutionary activity, which 1) led to stoppages in a whole series of factories and plants, incurring colossal losses for the republic, and 2) led to the Kronstadt rising in March 1921.

The RSDRP has shown itself for the whole revolutionary period to be a party which is hostile to Soviet power. Mensheviks in various places have taken part in conspiracies and the RSDRP CC elected at the beginning of 1920 has in no way changed its attitude to Soviet power and the RKP. At present it is directing its work towards disrupting Soviet Power, and only distances itself from this when they – Mensheviks – fall into the hands of the Cheka. Therefore, in order to avoid any further subversive influence from the RSDRP in relation to the latest initiatives of Soviet Power on the labour front, and in order to forestall any undesirable events for the republic, the following members of the RSDRP CC are to be exiled to remote gubernias under the open supervision of the local Cheka, each for one year without the right to serve in any elected position or to hold any post which involves contact with the masses: 1) Gurvich-Dan, Fedor Il'ich, 49 years old, descended from citizens of Petrograd, to Mari oblast, Krasnokokshaysk uezd but not Krasnokokshaysk town; 2) Tsederbaum-Ezhov, Sergey Iosifovich, 42 years old, honourable citizen of Odessa, to Tyumen gubernia, Tobol'sk uezd; 3) Ayzenshtadt-Yudin, Isay L'vovich, 54 years old, townsman of Vil'no, to Arkhangel'sk gubernia, Mezen' uezd; 4) Nikolaevsky, Boris Ivanovich, 37 years old, journalist and writer, to Severodvinsk gubernia, Yaremsky uezd; 5) Lipkin-Cherevanin, Fedor Andreevich, 51 years old, citizen of Mogilev gubernia, to Semipalatinsk oblast' excluding gubernia towns; 6) Pleskov, Artur Abramovich, 37 years old, townsman, to Semipalatinsk oblast' except gubernia towns. The file on them is to remain in the Second department of the Cheka Secret Section.

Signed: head of the Second department of the Cheka Secret Section. [Signature indecipherable]

17 December 1921

NOTES

1. TsA FSB RF, d. N 1379, ll. 7-9 ob.; republished in V. P. Naumov, A. A. Kosakovsky, compilers, *Kronshtadt 1921*, Mezhdunarodnyy fond 'Demokratiya', Moscow, 1997, pp. 266-269.
2. TsA FSB RF, d. N-1379, pp. 35-37; republished in V. P. Naumov, A. A. Kosakovsky, compilers, *Kronshtadt 1921*, Mezhdunarodnyy fond 'Demokratiya', Moscow, 1997, pp. 270-272.

APPENDIX V

Review of *Two Years of Wandering* by A. K. Voronsky

As Dan's memoir was never legally distributed in the USSR, Soviet citizens would, in general, only have learned of it by reading reviews, such as this one by the Bolshevik literary critic Aleksandr Konstantinovich Voronsky (1884-1937). It was published in the journal which Voronsky himself edited: Krasnaya nov' *[Red Virgin Soil], issue 5, 1922. It has been included here as a representative example of the tone and register which Bolshevik publicists would almost invariably adopt when discussing their defeated rivals in the Russian socialist movement. In the case of Voronsky, there is a sad irony in his attitude here towards Dan and the Cheka's other socialist victims. By 1927, as a supporter of Trotsky's views and the Left Opposition within the CPSU, it was Voronsky's turn to experience repression, as he was expelled from the party, arrested and sent into internal exile. After recanting in 1929, he was readmitted to the party and allowed to return to Moscow in 1930. His rehabilitation was brief, however: he was expelled from the party again in 1934, arrested in 1935, and executed on 13 August 1937.*

Dan's little book is good in the sense that it clearly shows the depths of the political philistine banality to which the present-day leaders of Menshevism have plunged.

'From his beautiful home in a strange land',[1] Dan tells of his wanderings around Soviet Russia. There is Moscow, and the 'dirty tricks' of Comrade Semashko, and Ekaterinburg, and the labour armies, and the Polish front, and the Congress of Soviets, and Petrograd, and the remand prison, and the Cheka, and Butyrki prison. Almost two-thirds of the book is given over to the Cheka. It tells of all this and much more, with one aim: to show how shamefully the Bolsheviks treat good, genuine socialists.

However, we cannot really say that its aim is met. As far as the Cheka is concerned, the SR version is much better. They tell it with voices quavering, with eyes rolling, with cries and wails and curses (in their book *CheKa*).² They tell of a 'commissar of death' or some such, and you are reminded of Rocambole, of the stories of Dumas, of Sherlock Holmes, and Pinkerton, and Louis Boussenard. They tell it with feeling and a sense of intrigue.

There is no feeling or sense of intrigue with Dan.

'We saw in the New Year in cheerful mood. At first we had an evening of music and literature in the corridor of the isolation block, which we organised ourselves. Then we divided off into our factional groups to see in the New Year, we had a meal, and had even managed to acquire a little wine. Speeches were made, there were readings from a comical paper devoted to prison life, and songs were sung. From one in the morning there was a dancing party for everyone, which continued until the morning.' (p. 176)

We cannot have that. These sorts of admissions and descriptions can only serve to undermine the SRs, who depict the Cheka as something worse than the visions of hell found in those cheap popular prints that publishers used to sell to long-suffering simpletons, Okurovtsy and merchants seeking repentance.³

Of course, it is not easy in Cheka prisons, generally speaking. Dan has not discovered America here. Prison is prison. We should also remember that in 1919-1921 it was enemies of Soviet power who were sitting in Cheka jails, while there was a ferocious civil war at the fronts, and neither the Entente, nor the white generals, nor the SRs, nor the Mensheviks in essence showed any scruples in their choice of means to fight the Soviet republic. And if Dan had even a drop of political decency, he would have remembered the Menshevik and SR prisons on the Volga, in Arkhangel'sk and in Tiflis etc., compared to which the regime he describes in the Cheka prisons would pale. As his little book shows, in Dan's case, this 'regime' was essentially attentive and solicitous, there were 'well-wishers', 'old acquaintances', he was 'recognised', people 'interceded' for him, he was kindly taken about in the cars of the Cheka Presidium, etc. A significant part of his narrative is taken up with this sort of thing. This was at a time when Soviet Russia was stricken with convulsions and exhaustion in the struggle. We cannot object to these privileges and well-wishers, but we must suppose that there would have been far fewer of them if the 'well-wishers' among the Bolsheviks had realised how deeply the leader of Menshevism had sunk into political philistinism.

This book about Dan's 'wanderings' bears ample witness to this. Strike out the word 'Dan' everywhere, and it is no different from the usual stuff that white guard intellectuals write. Their writings may even be better – more engaged, more vivid, more agitational and more condensed.

Dan spent four years in Soviet Russia. He spent time at the front, in the Urals, in Petersburg, in Moscow and in the care of the Cheka – but how miserable and narrow-minded his observations and material are! How philistine his perceptions are! The same old stories and jokes, the same failure to understand and grasp what is going on around him, the same inability to know what to do with himself and pitiful time-wasting during the greatest years of the greatest revolution. We read this time and again in white guard newspapers and books, and hear it time and again in intelligentsia circles.

At one point in his little book, Dan condemns sabotage and saboteurs. But if we flick through the pages we find that Dan was constantly engaged in sabotage and nothing else. His 'work' in Moscow, Ekaterinburg and at the front consisted of skiving in state institutions and using his work position in the interests of the Menshevik CC – that is, sabotage and struggle against Soviet power. It is obvious that this citizen has sent Soviet Russia nothing from abroad other than his ill intent, nor could he send us anything. How far the leader of Menshevism has allowed himself to sink into pitiful nonsense can be seen, for example, in his tale about the Eighth Congress of Soviets, to which he was invited by the Presidium of the CEC.

At the Congress, according to Dan, there was not the slightest trace of enthusiasm, and even Lenin was met with an 'obvious coolness' from the audience. 'So, in order to create the impression of an "ovation", Lenin resorted to a theatrical trick of which, I admit, I would not have thought him capable. He waited behind the scenes, and came out on to the stage at the very moment that the orchestra started to play the Internationale and the whole 4000-strong crowd stood up. It was impossible to tell whether people had stood up and then applauded for the anthem, or for the person of the leader …' (p94) One good admission deserves another, and we must admit that we had not expected this sort of stupidity from Dan. The idea that Lenin would try to get an ovation by means of theatrical tricks – what a pearl! What a picture! This is the sort of 'reliable information' we used to get from the Sukharevka market, of blessed memory!

There is no shortage of 'observations' of that sort in Dan's book. Dan went to the front and brought back the joke that the Red Army is like lice – one million run, one million sit, and one million catch and lead the others.[4] And he says this without his filthy tongue becoming tied, or his shameless eyes bursting, or his face turning crimson with disgrace and shame!

In fact, Dan should have been paying attention to something quite different, but it would have been beyond him to make sense of it. In his story of his imprisonment in Peter-Paul Fortress, Dan tells of how he worked to subvert his guards. According to Dan, this was quite successful. 'Only one of them – a worker by origin, intelligent and politically developed – stood firmly for the line of the Bolsheviks ... He told me he had been living in Crimea, and had been mobilised by Wrangel. Life there was much better and they were better fed than in Soviet Russia. But he could not tolerate the "lordly" attitude of the officers to the workers and soldiers, and for that reason he was prepared to forgive the Bolsheviks everything – there were no "lords" here! I had another opportunity to observe a very sharp expression of this aspect of the people's revolutionary psychology, which many people somehow fail to appreciate fully.

' ... One of the SR prisoners called to his comrades: "Gentlemen! Come over to our cell, we're having a sing-song!" A Red Army man, who had just then been lounging on a bench and cheerfully chatting to one or another of the prisoners, jumped up as if he had been stung, red in the face with his eyes glaring, and bellowed: "Don't you dare say 'gentlemen'! I can't stand that word! If you say it again, I'll lock you all back up in your cells!"' (p. 122)

It seems to Dan that some people have not fully appreciated these aspects of the people's revolutionary psychology. Not fully appreciated ... But the whole essence, sense and content of October lie in these aspects! It is first and foremost Dan who has not fully appreciated them. Otherwise, he would realise the complete vacuity of all the notions about bourgeois democratism as opposed to Soviet 'party' dictatorship, which permeate this book. In the eyes of the workers and Red Army men, only October completely swept away the 'lords'; only October set the real 'demos' in motion. Dan does not understand this, and therefore he mumbles about 'not fully appreciating'.

Dan exploited his connections with the Bolsheviks and exploited his positions at work in order to organise and manage the affairs of the

Menshevik CC, which was masquerading as a legal opposition. But in fact it was and is just as active an enemy of the republic of Soviets as any SR. In *Pravda*, comrade Radek has already noted Dan's remarkable and very characteristic discussion about optimists and pessimists in the Kronstadt days. This discussion shows with complete clarity that Dan stood for the overthrow of Soviet power, but merely considered the moment to be inopportune. (See pp. 104-106.)

Overall, the tone and mood of the book only goes to confirm that Soviet power was not mistaken in offering its author the chance to join the chorus of counter-revolutionary slanderers abroad.

NOTES

1. 'Ah, Russia, Russia, from my beautiful home in a strange land I can still see you!' From Nikolay Gogol', *Dead Souls*, Chapter 11.
2. This refers to a collective volume issued by the SRs in exile denouncing the abuses committed by the Soviet political police: *CheKa. Materialy po deyatel'nosti chrezvychaynykh kommissiy*, Tsentral'noe byuro PSR, Berlin, 1922.
3. Okurovtsy: the inhabitants of Maksim Gorky's fictional 'Little Town of Okurov', a byword for remote, provincial ignorance.
4. The joke works better in Russian: one million run (desert), one million sit (in prison), etc.

APPENDIX VI

Further Reading

There is plenty of information in English on the Menshevik wing of Russian Marxism. Much of it is scattered around the innumerable books and articles published on Russian and Soviet history, the Russian revolutionary movement, and the history of the CPSU, although some of it is ill-informed or tendentious. Most of the scholarly work on Menshevism is available only in Russian. The émigrés themselves generally preferred to write their own history in that language, and since the collapse of CPSU rule in 1991 the centre of gravity for quality research on the political history of the Russian revolutionary movement has naturally returned to Russia. Many of the most recent Russian-language works are referenced in the endnotes to the introduction to this volume.

As for English-language books devoted to the history of the Menshevik movement or its individual leaders, the following titles are all very useful.

Abraham Ascher (ed), *The Mensheviks in the Russian Revolution*, Thames and Hudson, London 1976 – a short collection of primary documents.

Abraham Ascher, *Pavel Axelrod and the Development of Menshevism*, Harvard University Press, Cambridge, MA, 1972.

Samuel H. Baron, *Plekhanov. The Father of Russian Marxism*, Stanford University Press, Stanford, CA, 1963.

John D. Basil, *The Mensheviks in the Revolution of 1917*, Slavica, Columbus, OH, 1983.

Vladimir N. Brovkin, *The Mensheviks after October. Socialist Opposition and the Rise of the Bolshevik Dictatorship*, Cornell University Press, Ithaca, NY, 1987.

Ziva Galili y Garcia, *The Menshevik Leaders in the Russian Revolution: Social Realities and Political Strategies*, Princeton University Press, Princeton, NJ, 1989.

Israel Getzler, *Martov. A Political Biography of a Russian Social Democrat*, Cambridge University Press, Cambridge, 1967.

Israel Getzler, *Nikolai Sukhanov. Chronicler of the Russian Revolution*, Palgrave, Basingstoke, 2002.

Leopold H. Haimson with Ziva Galili y Garcia and Richard Wortman (eds), *The Making of Three Russian Revolutionaries*, Cambridge University Press, Cambridge, 1987 – transcripts of three lengthy series of interviews with Lydia Dan, Boris Nicolaevsky and George Denike.

Leopold H. Haimson (ed), *The Mensheviks. From the Revolution of 1917 to the Second World War*, University of Chicago Press, Chicago, 1974.

Naum Jasny, *Soviet Economists of the Twenties: Names to be Remembered*, Cambridge University Press, Cambridge, 1972 – a study of the intellectual influence of Menshevik ideas on the early development of the Soviet economic planning system, the background to the 'Menshevik Trial' of 1931, and individual biographical studies of Vladimir Groman, Vladimir Bazarov, Abram Ginzburg and others.

Stephen F. Jones, *Socialism in Georgian Colors. The European Road to Social Democracy, 1883-1917*, Harvard University Press, Cambridge MA, 2005.

André Liebich, *From the Other Shore. Russian Social-Democracy after 1921*, Harvard University Press, Cambridge MA, 1997 – a detailed study of the politics of the Menshevik emigration.

W. H. Roobol, *Tsereteli – A Democrat in the Russian Revolution*, Martinus Nijhoff, The Hague, 1976.

N. N. Sukhanov, *The Russian Revolution* (trans. Joel Carmichael), Oxford University Press, Oxford, 1955 – an abridged translation of Sukhanov's classic account of 1917.

Index

Abramovich (Rein), Rafail Abramovich (1880-1963), 20, 35, 48, 200, 216
Adler, Friedrich Wolfgang (1879–1960), 48
administrative exile, Soviet, 18-19, 33, 53, 125, 143, 172n, 174-178, 182, 190-191, 204, 217, 219; tsarist, 4, 7, 163, 174, 176
Agranov, Yakov Saulovich (Sorenson, Yankel' Shmaevich, 1893-1938), 147
Agriculture Commissariat, 60, 66
Aksel'rod, Pavel Borisovich (1850-1928), 5-7, 47
amnesty, of 1905, 5; of 1913, 7, 211; of 1921, 162
anarchists, 37, 129-130, 133-134, 136-137, 143, 160, 162, 164, 168, 187, 192, 203
Andreeva (Andreeva-Gorbunova), Aleksandra Azar'evna (1887-1951), 182, 187-191
anti-Semitism, 88, 105
Arakcheev, Aleksey Andreevich (1769-1834), 194, 197
Arkhangel'sk, 51, 175, 217, 220
Arkhangel'sky (Amosov), Anton Aleksandrovich (1854-1915), 148n
Aronson, Grigoriy Yakovlevich (1887-1968), 21
Artem'ev, Nikolay Ivanovich (1883-?), 160
Ashkhabad, 26

'Assembly of Plenipotentiaries of Petrograd Factories', 135
Austria, 20
Avksent'ev, Nikolay Dmitrievich (1878-1943), 12
Azef, Evno Fishelevich (1869-1918), 35
Azerbaijan Republic, 91, 98n

Baklenkov, Arseniy Adamovich, 140
Baku, 201
Baltic factory, Petrograd, 113
Baty (1209?-1255/1256), 87
Bauer, Otto (1881-1938), 20
Bazarov (Rudnev), Vladimir Aleksandrovich (1874-1939), 32
Bebel, August (1840-1913), 70, 163
Beletsky, Stepan Petrovich (1873-1918), 117
Belorussia, 80-81, 89
Berlin, 1, 4, 19, 20, 28, 30, 135; Conference of 3 Internationals, 119
Berne Conference, 1919, 48, 56n
Binshtok, Grigoriy Osipovich (1884-1954), 155, 182
Blum, Léon (1872-1950), 20, 31
Bogachev, Yakov Terent'evich (1886-1938), 160
Bogdanov, Boris Osipovich (1884-1960), 33
Bogdanova, N. B., 33
Bolshevik Party, Central Committee, 18, 96-97, 147, 183; Moscow Committee, 198;

Politburo, 17-18, 55, 183; Tenth Congress, 1921, 122-123, 142
Bolshoi Theatre, Moscow, 91
Borisov (town), 85-86
Borisov, Chekist, 152
Boussenard, Louis Henri (1847-1911), 220
Branting, Hjalmar (1860-1925), 56n
Britain, British, 29, 82, 193, 200; intervention force, 51; Labour Delegation 1920, 2, 46-50, 56n, 193-197, 198-200; labour movement, 31, 193-194, 199-200
Bukhara, 82
Bukharin, Nikolay Ivanovich (1888-1938), 199
Bund, General Jewish Labour, 48, 56n, 80-81, 84, 91, 200
Butyrki prison, 50, 137, 144-145, 158, 160-172, 183, 190-191, 219
Buxton, Charles Roden (1875–1942), 46-47

Carm, Adolf (1877-1958), 36, 155, 158, 159n
Catherine II (1729-1796), 64
Central Executive Committee, All-Russia Soviet, 2, 10, 12, 15, 56, 89, 91-92, 95, 117, 146, 212; Presidium, 55, 162, 174-175, 178, 180, 221
Cheka, 2-3, 15, 17-18, 28, 31, 36, 38, 78, 86, 98, 113, 116, 126, 203; All-Russia, 154, 162, 168, 174, 176-177, 180, 184, 188, 192; arrests workers, 102, 114, 137-138; campaign against Mensheviks, 52-53, 68, 73-74, 76, 88-89, 107, 135, 137, 139, 173, 176, 190, 198, 206, 211-218; Ekaterinburg, 60, 63, 65; hunts Chernov, 49; interference in economy, 50-52; interrogates Dan, 18, 109-110, 147-148; and Kronstadt rebels, 130-132; perlustrating correspondence, 66, 124; Petrograd, 107, 109, 111, 124, 133, 143; phone tapping, 74; Presidium, 108, 111, 153, 177, 222; prison regimes, 144-145, 149-158, 162-166, 168-170, 179-180, 220-221; transport, 57-58, 152, 154; use of exile, 174-175, 180-183, 187-189, 191; visited by Labour delegation, 47
Chelyabinsk, 57
Cherevanin (Lipkin), Fedor Andreevich (1869-1938), 200, 215, 217
Chernov, Viktor Mikhaylovich (1873-1952), 2, 38, 49, 193-197
Chertkov, David Kusielevich (1885-1957), 115, 118, 206
Chicago, 159n
Chistov, Nikolay Ivanovich (1869-1939), 48
Chistyakov, I. A. (1891-1941), 108-109, 116-117
Chkheidze, Nikolay Semenovich (1864-1926), 8
Christianity, Christians, 46, 49, 56n, 194-195,
Clémenceau, Georges (1841-1929), 108
Columbia University, 35
Commissariat of Labour, 18
Committee to Save the Motherland and Revolution (1917), 13
Committees of the Rural Poor, 95
Communist International, 28, 47, 76, 77n, 83, 86, 91; Third Congress, 155, 158, 159n
Communist Party of Germany, 77n
Congresses of Soviets, 2-3; first,

10-12; second, 12-13, 40n; seventh, 36, 90, 93; eighth 37, 90-98, 204, 219, 221
Constituent Assembly, 1918, 2, 12, 14, 19, 24-25, 41n, 104-105, 136, 147, 212-213
Constitutional Democrat (Kadet) Party, 12
Control Commission, Bolshevik, 164
co-operatives, 6, 18, 191
Council of People's Commissars (Sovnarkom), 13, 75
Council of the Republic (Preparliament, 1917), 12
Crimea, 33, 122, 222
Czechoslovak Legion, 2, 26, 158

Dalin (Dallin, Levin), David Yul'evich (1889-1962), 27, 35, 60-61, 94, 97, 200
Dan (Tsederbaum), Lidiya Osipovna (1878-1963), 5, 10, 18, 21-22, 52, 54, 119-120, 186, 190, 211
Danzig, 193
Darin, assistant prison head, 163
defencists, 7, 11, 14, 23-24
Delegation Abroad, Menshevik, 19-22, 28, 30-31, 33, 216
Democratic Conference, September 1917, 12
Denike, George (Yuriy Petrovich, 1878-1964), 23
Denikin, Anton Ivanovich (1872-1947), 90, 92, 203
Dmitrieva, Praskov'ya Stepanovna (1901-1937), 183
Donbass mines, 120
Donskoy, Dmitriy Dmitrievich (1880-1936), 160, 171
Dorofeev, Dmitriy Petrovich (1882-?), 115

Dorpat (Tartu), 3
Duma, 5, 7-8, 11, 70
Dumas, Alexandre (1802-1870), 220
Dvinov (Gurevich), Boris L'vovich (1886-1968), 5, 18, 28, 31
Dzerzhinsky, Feliks Edmundovich (1877-1926), 62, 163-164, 176

Edinstvo, 24, 104-105
Ekaterinburg, 54-56, 57-77, 78-79, 89, 219, 221
electrification, 95-96
Eloranta, Voitto (1876-1923), 36, 161-162, 171-172n
empiriocriticism, 23
Emshanov, Aleksandr Ivanovich (1891-1937), 93
Entente, 81, 109-110, 122, 191, 193, 198, 200, 202, 213, 220
Enukidze, Avel' Safronovich (1877-1937), 56
Ermansky (Kogan), Osip Arkad'evich (1867-1941), 200
Er'zya (Nefedov), Stepan Dmitrievich (1876-1959), 64
Estonia, Estonians, 3, 114, 158
eurocommunism, 35
Ezhov (Tsederbaum), Sergey Osipovich (1879-1939), 17-19, 160, 190-191, 214

Fabians, 46
famine, 19, 110, 122, 185, 216
Far Eastern territory, 213
fascism, 20
Finland, Finns, 125, 132, 134
Finnish Communist Party (SKP), 36, 161-162, 172n
Forced Labour in Soviet Russia, 35
France, French, 22, 30, 108, 193
Frumkina, Mariya (Ester) Yakovlevna (1880-1943), 81

Ganglez brothers, 161
Garvi (Bronshteyn), Petr Adamovich (1881–1944), 158
Gendel'man, Mikhail Yakovlevich (1881-1938), 160
Geneva, 6
Georgia, 5, 14, 16, 28-29, 31, 42n, 82
Germany, 2, 7, 8, 11, 14, 21-22, 29-30, 52, 76, 82-83, 120, 188, 192
Glavryba, 51
Glozman, Semen Anatol'evich (1888-1949?), 115
Gol'denberg, Iosif Petrovich (1873-1922), 24
Golos sotsial-demokrata, 6
Gorev (Gol'dman), Boris Isaakovich (1874-1938), 200
Gorky, Maksim (Peshkov, Aleksey Maksimovich, 1868-1936), 24, 223n
Gorokhovaya Street, Petrograd, 107, 124, 149, 152
Gosplan, State Planning Commission, 32
Gots, Abram Rafailovich (1882-1940), 12, 160, 171
Groman, Vladimir Gustavovich (1874-1940), 32, 35, 44n
'Group of Struggle for Independence and a Democratic System for Russia', 26
Grozny, 201
Gryunval'd, Evgeniya Ivanovna, 189
Gumilev, Nikolay Stepanovich (1886-1921), 147
Gvozdev, Kuz'ma Antonovich (1882-1956), 14

Haimson, Leopold Henri (1927-2010), 34-35
handicraft production, 51, 80, 204
Haywood, William ('Big Bill', 1869-1928), 36, 155, 159n
Health Commissariat, 3, 17, 50, 53, 55, 78, 91; Surgical Subsection of the Department for Medical Supplies, 50-52, 91
Helsinki, 5
History of the Communist Party of the Soviet Union (Bolsheviks), 34
Hoover Institution, 34-35
hunger strike, 143-144, 156, 160-161, 166, 171, 173-183, 188, 190

Independent Labour Party, Britain, 46
Industrial Workers of the World, 159n
International Institute of Social History, 35
International Socialist Women's Committee, 22
Internationale, 94, 221
internationalists, 7-8, 11-14, 23-24
Ioffe, Kh. I., 25
Ipat'ev, Nikolay Nikolaevich (1868-1938), 64
Irkutsk, 7
Iskra, 4
Ivanov, Chekist, 145
Izvestiya, central Soviet paper, 10, 66, 90; of Kronstadt rebels, 124, 126n, 148n

Jasny, Naum Khaimovich (1883-1967), 35
Jaurès, Jean (1859-1914), 70
Jews, 3, 32, 35, 80-81, 98, 105, 109, 121
Justice Commissariat, 126

Kachinsky, head of hard labour section, 163-164

Kamenev (Rozenfel'd), Lev Borisovich (1883-1936), 27, 178
Kamensky, Vladislav Isaevich (1887-1924), 106, 115, 206
Kamermakher (Kefali), Mark Samuilovich (1881-1943), 48
Kamkov, Boris Davydovich (1885-1938), 160
Kashin, Tver' gubernia, 180, 192
Kautsky, Karl (1854-1938), 4-5, 48
Kazan', 65, 192
Kazukov, Aleksandr Grigor'evich (1888-?), 106, 115
Kerensky, Aleksandr Fedorovich (1881-1970), 12
Khar'kov, 78, 174
Khiva, 82
Khodzhent, 7
Khokhryakov, Pavel Danilovich (1893-1918), 62
Kiental conference, 1916, 7
Kiev, 78, 174
Kisel'nyy pereulok, Moscow, 177, 180
Kitezh, 99
klyoshniki, 111
Knoppe, assistant prison head, 163
Kolchak, Aleksandr Vasil'evich (1874-1920), 2, 63-64, 66, 158, 203
Komarov, Nikolay Pavlovich (Sobinov, Fedor Evgen'evich, 1886-1937), 109-110, 133, 153
Komsomol, 100, 102, 116
Komuch government, 1918, 2
Kornilov, General Lavr Georgievich (1870-1918), 12
Korotoyak, Voronezh gubernia, 180-181
Kotlov, worker, 113
Kozhevnikova, Vera Vasil'evna (1873-1940), 4-5

Kozlovsky, Aleksandr Nikolaevich (1864-1940), 129, 131, 150
Krasnaya gazeta, 130
Krasnaya nov', 219
Krasnokokshaysk, 182, 217
Krestinsky, Nikolay Nikolaevich (1883-1938), 96
Kresty prison, Petrograd, 116
Kronstadt rising, 1921, 17, 29-30, 36, 38, 105, 111, 118-124, 126, 128-132, 134-135, 142, 147, 148n, 150, 205-207, 209-210, 214, 216-218, 223
Krylenko, Nikolay Ivanovich (1885-1938), 15, 142
Krymplan, 33
Krzhizhanovsky, Gleb Maksimilianovich (1872-1959), 96
Kuban', 158, 201
Kurgan, 61
Kurlov, Pavel Grigor'evich (1860-1923), 117
Kursky, Dmitriy Ivanovich (1874-1932), 18
Kuskova, Ekaterina Dmitrievna (1869-1958), 191-192
Kuusinen Club, Petrograd, 172n
Kuz'min, Nikolay Nikolaevich (1883-1938), 130
Kuznetsky Bridge, 145

Labour and Socialist International, 20, 28, 30-31, 56n
labour armies, 60, 62, 66-67, 95, 174, 219
labour desertion, 54, 65
Labour Party, Britain, 31, 46
Lapinsky (Levinson), Pavel Lyudvigovich (1879-1937), 27
Latvia, Latvians, 145, 163, 165, 188, 190, 192
'League of Observers', 32, 44n

INDEX 231

League of Struggle for the Emancipation of the Working Class, 3, 107
Lefortovo prison, 166
Left Opposition, 219
Left Socialist-Revolutionaries, 136-137, 150, 160, 192
Lejta, Chekist, 145
Lenin (Ul'yanov), Vladimir Il'ich (1870-1924), 1-7, 13, 15-16, 24-25, 29, 34, 37, 57, 62, 90, 93-94, 96-97, 107, 122-123, 142-143, 166, 197, 221; cult of, 57, 62, 64, 68, 155
Liber, Mark (Gol'dman, Mikhail Isaakovich, 1880-1937), 14
liberals, 9, 12-13, 22
Liebknecht, Karl (1871-1919), 62
Ligovka, Petrograd, 100
Likhach, Mikhail Aleksandrovich (1887-1931), 160
liquidationism, 6, 23
Liteynyy Bridge, Petrograd, 116
Lithuania, 22
Lloyd George, David (1863–1945), 198-199
London, 5, 26, 47, 199
Longuet, Jean-Laurent-Frederick (1876–1938), 48
Lubyanka Square, Moscow, 154, 190
Luxemburg, Rosa (1871-1919), 62
Lyubim, Yaroslavl' gubernia, 180

MacDonald, James Ramsay (1866–1937), 48
Maisky (Lyakhovetsky), Ivan (Jan) Mikhailovich (1884-1975), 26
makhorka, 59, 61, 76n
Malakhovsky, Evgeniy Efimovich (Khaimovich, 1902-1937), 115, 125
Mari oblast', 175, 182, 217

Mariynsky Theatre, 106-107
Martov (Tsederbaum), Yuliy Osipovich (1873-1923), 3-7, 10, 13-16, 19, 21, 24, 26-27, 32, 34, 37, 39n, 48, 74, 76, 77n, 90, 97, 107, 200, 216
'Martov line', 19-21, 41n
Martynov, Aleksandr Samoylovich (Pikker, Saul Samuilovich. 1865-1935), 6
Marx, Karl (1818-1883), 4, 27, 35, 57, 64, 140
Marx-Engels Institute, 35
Marxism, Marxists, 1, 3, 5, 20, 23, 30, 33, 35, 49, 56n, 140, 208
Maslov, Petr Pavlovich (1867-1946), 35
Mayorov, Il'ya Andreevich (1890-1941), 160
Mel'nichansky, Grigoriy (Gershon) Natanovich (1886-1937), 48-49
Menshevik Party, Central Committee (CC), 12-14, 18, 26-27, 31, 43n, 82, 89-91, 96-97, 109, 160, 177, 190, 208, 214-217; conference, May 1917, 7; Don Committee, 178; Moscow organisation, 73, 76, 183, 217; Organising Committee, 1917, 24; as RSDRP, 9, 18, 22, 24, 34, 44n, 205-207, 211, 217
Menshevik/SR bloc, 1917, 11
'Menshevik Trial', 1931, 32-33
Mezen' uezd, 175, 217
Military Medical Authorities, 54-56, 68, 70, 75, 78, 84-85, 88, 100, 212
Milkić, Ilija (1884-1968), 158
Minsk, 78-80, 82, 84-89, 157
Mogilev, 83, 217
Molière (1622-1673), 134
Molotov-Ribbentrop Pact, 1939, 21

Moscow, 2, 4, 25-26, 31, 33, 36-37, 47, 51, 53-55, 57, 60, 66, 73-75, 78, 80, 89-92, 96-99, 119, 129, 147, 149, 152, 154-155, 157-158, 159n, 166, 170, 175-176, 184-186, 191-192, 219, 221; Arts Theatre, 157; Cheka, 152, 168, 177, 180; gubernia, 52; Menshevik organisation, 73, 76, 183, 217; Military Medical Authority, 54-56; Soviet, 50, 186-187, 190, 198; workers, 48, 50, 75, 207

Moskovskaya Zastava, Petrograd, 116, 138

MUM, 186

Murmansk, 174

Mysl', 32

Naluev, Aleksandr (Aleksey) Anisimovich (1902-?), 183

'Narod' SR group, 91, 98, 137

Nazar'ev, Mikhail Fedorovich (1879-1935), 115, 118, 206, 216

Nazis, 20-21

Nevsky Prospekt, Petrograd, 99-100, 102, 152

New Economic Policy (NEP), 18, 20, 31-32, 36, 96, 147, 152, 154, 186, 191

New York, 21-22

Nicholas II, Tsar, 5, 9, 64, 117, 135

Nikolaevsky (Nicolaevsky), Boris Ivanovich (1887-1966), 35, 160, 177, 183, 188-189, 215, 217

Nikolaevsky Station, Petrograd, 152, 154

Nobel-Dorofeev factory, Petrograd, 114

'non-party' people, 53, 58, 60, 92, 94, 130, 133, 138-141, 205, 207-209

Novaya zhizn', 24

Novyy mir, 21

Novyy put', 21

Obukhov factory, Petrograd, 138

Odessa, 158, 217

okhranka, 107

Okurovtsy, 220, 222

Omsk, 66

Oprodkomzap, 83

Order No. 1042, 93, 95, 98n

Orel, 160, 166, 192

Origins of Bolshevism (1946), 21

Orlov (Vyatka gubernia), 4

OSE, Jewish children's charity, 22

Panyushkin, Vasiliy Lukich (1887-1960), 160-161

Paris, 6-7, 20-22, 30, 64

peasants, 4, 6, 15, 19, 22, 28, 42n, 58-59, 61, 65, 67, 80, 82-84, 94, 106-107, 110, 121-123, 147, 202, 204, 206-209, 212-213

Pechora uezd, 175

Penza, 216

Perepelkin, Petr Mikhaylovich (1891-1921), 36, 130-131

perestroika, 34-35

Peshkova, Ekaterina Pavlovna (1876-1965), 180

Peter-Paul Fortress, 116-126, 222

Petrograd, 2-5, 9-13, 22, 24, 28, 93, 97-98, 99-100, 104-105, 112n, 119, 126, 152, 154, 161, 172n, 212, 219; 'Assembly of Plenipotentiaries', 135; Cheka, 109, 131, 133, 143-144, 149-159, 170, 211; Menshevik organisation, 17, 37, 103, 109, 119-120, 124, 201-207, 212, 216; port, 134, 138; Soviet, 2, 8-10, 14, 33, 45n, 103, 110, 139; workers, 105, 111, 114, 128, 138, 144, 201, 205-208, 216

'Petrozhid', 116, 136, 160
Petrusevich, Kazimir Adamovich (1872-1949), 85-86
planned economy, 31-33, 69-71, 93, 203-204
Plekhanov, Georgiy Valentinovich (1856-1918), 6, 23, 24
Plekhanovists, 104, 136
plenipotentiaries (*upolnomochennye*) movement, 24, 135-136
Pleskov, Artur Abramovich (1884-1937), 160, 200, 215, 218
Poland, 21, 52, 75, 80-84, 89-90, 92, 157, 215
Political Red Cross, 170, 180
'Polygon', Petrograd, 116, 131
Popov, prison head, 162-163, 166-168, 173
Posts and Telegraphs Commissariat, 169
Potemkin villages, 195
Potresov, Aleksandr Ivanovich (1869-1934), 4, 6-7, 34, 39n
POVSU, Petrograd Military Medical Administration, 212
Pravda, 66, 223
printers' union, 48, 50, 196, 198
Profintern, 36, 159n
Progressive Bloc, 8
Prokopovich, Sergey Nikolaevich (1871-1955), 191-192
Protopopov, Aleksandr Dmitrievich (1866-1918), 117
Provisional Government, 1917, 9-13,
Public Committee to Aid the Starving, 191
Pugachev, Emelyan Ivanovich (1742-1775), 197
Putilov works, Petrograd, 112, 138

Rabochaya gazeta, 109
Radek (Sobelsohn), Karl Berngardovich (1185-1939), 119, 223
Rahja, Eino (1885-1936), 172n
Rahja, Jukka (1887-1920), 172n
Ramishevsky, A. Yu., 177, 186-187
Ramishvili, Noy Vissarionovich (1881-1930), 6
Rechkin factory, Petrograd, 138
Red Army, 48, 59, 62, 64-66, 66, 78-79, 98, 100-101, 205, 209, 215, 222; arrests Dan, 107; Chinese troops, 129; desertion from, 63, 83-84; in Polish War, 79, 82-88; as prison guards, 116-118, 120-126, 144, 146, 152, 164-165, 189; as prisoners, 137; rebels in Kronstadt, 130; reliability, 102, 104-105
Red International of Labour Unions, See Profintern,
remand prison, 102, 112-113, 117-119, 124, 127-159, 160, 219
Riga, 137, 163, 192; Treaty of, 1921, 84, 89
Rosenfeld, Oreste (1891-1964), 30-31
Rostov-on-Don, 78
Rozhkov, Nikolay Aleksandrovich (1868-1927), 115, 118, 142-143, 147, 206
Russell, Bertrand Arthur William (1872–1970), 46, 56n
Russian Communist Party (RKP), see Bolshevik Party
Russian Social-Democratic Workers' Party (RSDRP), 3-7, 22-24; congresses, 3, 5, 14, 85, 89; Fifth Conference, 1908, 6-7. See also Menshevik Party.
Ryazan', 155, 160,
Ryazanov (Gol'dendakh), David Borisovich (1870-1938), 11

Rykov, Aleksey Ivanovich (1881-1938), 93

Samara, 2, 26
Samsonov (Babiy), Timofey Petrovich (1888-1955), 18, 177, 182
Sapir, Boris Moiseevich (1902-1989), 42n
Savchenko, Luka Faddeevich (1891-1921), 130-131
Savinov, Ivan Timofeevich (?-1918), 25
Schwarz, Solomon Meerovich (1883-1973), 33, 35
Scribe, Eugène (1791-1861), 134
Selitsky, prison chief, 114-115
Semashko, Nikolay Aleksandrovich, 53-56, 68, 75, 78, 89-91, 96-97
Semenov, B. A. (1890-1940), 133, 143-144, 147
Semenov, Grigoriy Ivanovich (1891-1937), 178
Semipalatinsk, 218
Sennaya Square, Petrograd, 99, 101
Serrati, Giacinto Menotti (1874–1926), 92
Seventh Rozhdestvensky sports club, 100, 212
Severodvinsk, 183-184, 188, 217
SFIO, Section française de l'Internationale ouvrière, 30
Shakhtstroy, 33
Shalyapin, Fedor Ivanovich (1873-1938), 106-107
Shartash, 60
Shaw, Tom (1872–1938), 46
Shmidt, Vasily Vladimirovich (1886-1940), 18
Shpakovsky, Ivan Ivanovich (1881-1938?), 115
Shpalernaya Street, Petrograd, 112

Siberia, 5, 7, 22, 33, 57, 201, 206
Siberian Zimmerwaldists, 8
Simferopol', 33
Skinner, Herbert (1864-1934), 46
Skobelev, Matvey Ivanovich (1885-1938), 14
Skomorovsky, Boris Aleksandrovich (1894-1965), 200
Skorokhod factory, Petrograd, 138
Skvortsov, Menshevik prisoner, 136
Slavic Council, 158
Smolensk, 80-83, 85, 87-90, 97, 183
Snowden, Ethel (1881–1951), 46
Social-Democratic Youth League, 76, 171, 217
Socialist Labor Party, USA, 159n
Socialist-Revolutionary (SR) Party, 2, 9, 12-13, 15, 18, 23, 25-26, 37, 40n, 49, 52, 58, 108, 111-112, 116-117, 122-123, 125-126, 128, 134, 136, 161, 163, 171, 176, 178, 187, 216, 219-220, 222-223; Central Committee, 160, 196; Trial, 1922, 143, 178
Sokolov, assistant prison head, 163, 167
Sol'ts, Aron Aleksandrovich (1872-1945), 164
Sotsial-Demokrat, 7
Sotsialisticheskiy vestnik, 19, 28, 30, 33, 135-136, 165, 180, 215
Soviet Revolution 1917-1939, 35
sowing committees, 95
Spartakusbund, 77n
SPD, Sozialdemokratische Partei Deutschlands, 4, 30
Spiridovich, Aleksandr Ivanovich (1873-1952), 117
St Petersburg, see Petrograd
Stalin, Iosif Vissarionovich (1878-1953), 15, 20-21, 34
Stepanov, Chekist, 109, 126

Stockholm, 5
Stolypin, Petr Arkad'evich, 5
strikes, Petrograd, 101, 104-111, 116, 120-121, 138, 206-207, 216-217
Strumilin (Strumillo-Petrashkevich), Stanislav Gustavovich (1877-1974), 32, 44n
subbotniki, 71, 76n, 95
Sukhanov (Gimmer), Nikolay Nikolaevich (1882-1940), 1, 9-12, 32, 34, 60, 66, 68, 74-75
Sukharevka market, 221
Supreme Council for National Economy (VSNKh), 48, 57

Taganskaya prison, 174
Tagantsev, Vladimir Nikolaevich (1889-1921), 147
Tashkent, 175, 211
tax in kind, 123, 209, 213
Tiflis, 28, 220
Tikhonov, A. N. (1880-1956), 48
Tikhvinsky, Mikhail Mikhaylovich (1868-1921), 147
Tillett, Ben (1860-1943), 31
Timofeev, Evgeniy Mikhaylovich (1885-1941), 160, 171
Tobol'sk uezd, 217
Tomsk, 33
trade unions, 6, 18, 31, 46-48, 65, 91-93, 95, 106, 140, 193, 196, 198, 204, 207, 209, 214; Central Council of, 48
tribunals, revolutionary 142-143, 161-162; Moscow 211
Troitsky Bridge, 116
Trotsky (Bronshteyn), Lev Davidovich (1879-1940), 23-24, 34, 37, 57, 60, 62, 64, 67-68, 88, 90, 93, 94, 98n, 113, 129, 148n, 183, 213, 219
Trotskyism, 35

Troyanovsky, Aleksandr Antonovich (1882-1955), 200
tsarism, 8, 35, 52-53, 84, 107, 113, 130, 142, 163-166, 174, 176, 192, 196, 212-213
Tsereteli, Iraklii Georgievich (1881-1959), 5, 8-10
Tseytlin, Mikhail Solomonovich (1887-1937), 160
Tula, 216
Tunguskov, Andrey Georgievich (?-1930), 63
Turkestan, 7, 174-176
Turkey, 29
Tverskaya Street, Moscow, 186
typhus, 89, 182, 192
Tyumen' gubernia, 217

Ukraine, 201, 206
unemployment, 186
'Union of Struggle for the Liberation of the Peoples of Russia', 33
Unshlikht, Iosif Stanislavovich (1879-1938), 3, 18, 176-177, 180-184, 187, 190
Upovalov, I. G., 43n
Urals, 54, 60, 67, 78, 201, 221
Urals Worker, 64, 66
Uritsky, Moysey Solomonovich (1873-1918), 153-154
USA, Americans, 30, 35-36, 65, 137, 155, 159n, 203
USPD Halle Congress, 76, 77n

Valentinov (Vol'sky), Nikolay Vladislavovich (1879-1964), 32
Vasil'evsky Island, 101-103
Vayner, Leonid Isaakovich (1878-1918), 62
Vaynshteyn (Rakhmiel'), Aron Isakovich (1877-1938), 81
Vedenyapin, Mikhail

Aleksandrovich (1870-1938), 160, 171
Verhaeren, Emile (1855-1916), 195, 197n
Verne, Jules (1828-1905), 165
'Vienna Union', 28, 30
Vikzhel talks, 1917, 13-14
Vil'no, 217
Vissarionov, Sergey, Evlampievich (1867-1918), 117
Vladimir, 158, 160
Vlasov, Andrey Andreevich (1901-1946), 33
Volga region, 2, 26, 220
Vologda, 161, 181-183, 191
Voronsky, Aleksandr Konstantinovich (1884-1937), 2, 29, 219-223
Voskresensk, 52
Votkinsk, Udmurtia, 26, 43n
Vpered, 15, 211, 217
Vyatka, 4, 59, 183-184, 188-190
Vyborg side, Petrograd, 116, 126

Wallhead, Richard Collingham (1869–1934), 46
Warsaw, 79, 83-86, 157
Weekly People, 159n
whites, white guards, 2, 16, 26-27, 62, 66, 110, 112, 121, 136-137, 157-158, 220-221
Wilhelm II, Kaiser, 8, 11
Williams, Robert (1881-1936), 46, 48, 92

Winter Palace, 12-13, 101
Woman and Socialism, 163
women prisoners, 116, 126-127, 134, 144, 146-147, 150-153, 155, 160, 162, 167, 169-170, 179, 192
Workers' International Industrial Union, 159n
Wrangel, Petr Nikolaevich (1878-1928), 82, 84, 89-90, 92, 122, 203, 222

Yaremsky uezd, 217
Yaroslavl', 25-26, 160, 192
Yarotsky, Vasiliy Yakovlevich (1887-1938), 47
Yudin (Ayzenshtadt), Isay L'vovich, 48, 200, 214, 217
Yugov, Aron Aronovich (1876-1954), 200

Zagvozkin, Roman Fedorovich (?-1919), 62
Zapiski o revolyutsii, 34
Zhordania, Noe (Noah, 1869-1953), 29, 42n, 43n
Zimmerwald, Zimmerwaldists, 7-8
Zimnitsky, Mikhail Fedorovich (1884-1950), 140-141
Zinoviev (Radomysl'sky), Grigoriy Evseevich (1883-1936), 64, 77n, 93, 97-98, 119, 126, 140-141, 208
Zvenigorsk, 52

www.ingramcontent.com/pod-product-compliance
Lightning Source LLC
Chambersburg PA
CBHW071710160426
43195CB00012B/1633